The Ethical Attitude in Analytic Practice

The Ethical Attitude
in Analytic Practice

Edited by

Hester McFarland Solomon
and
Mary Twyman

'an association in which the free development of each
is the condition of the free development of all'

FREE ASSOCIATION BOOKS / LONDON / NEW YORK

First published in Great Britain in 2003
by Free Association Books
57 Warren Street
London W1T 5NR

www.fabooks.com

ISBN 1 85343 558 9 pbk

A CIP catalogue record for this book is available from the British Library.

Printed digitally in the European Union by
Antony Rowe Ltd, Eastbourne, England

Contents

Foreword by Lord Alderdice   vii
Preamble   ix
Notes on the Contributors   xi

Section I The Ethical Attitude in Analytic Practice

1   Introduction: the ethical attitude in analytic practice   3
     Hester McFarland Solomon and Mary Twyman

Section II Mostly Theory

2   Ethical Themes in Analytic Practice   15
     Mary Twyman

3   The Ethical Attitude: a bridge between psychoanalysis
     and analytical psychology   21
     Hester McFarland Solomon

4   Ethics: the higher nature and the ego ideal   31
     Philip Hewitt

5   Ethics in Practice   39
     Fiona Palmer Barnes

Section III In the Consulting Room

6   Ethical Pressures on the Analytic Alliance   51
     Christopher MacKenna

7   Birth of the Ethical Attitude in a Clinical Setting   65
     Elizabeth Richardson

8   Don Quixote in the Analyst's Consulting Room   80
     Christian Gaillard

9   On Retiring: some thoughts and questions   87
     Yvette Wiener

Section IV Confidentiality and Publication

10   The Reporting of Clinical Material: ethical issues   99
     Barbara Wharton

11   Finding a Space for Ethical Thinking about Matters
     of Confidentiality   123
     Jan Wiener

Section V Applications:
Thinking Analytically about Ethics in Different Settings

12   Ethical Issues for Psychotherapists Working in Organisations   137
     Mannie Sher

13   Ethical Issues in Working with Children and their Families   152
     Judith Trowell and Gillian Miles

Section VI The Ethics of Supervision

14   The Ethics of Supervision: developmental and archetypal
     perspectives   167
     Hester McFarland Solomon

Index   179

Foreword
Lord Alderdice

In recent years I have taken an interest in the requirements of professional regulation, particularly through the medium of statutory registration. This is not natural territory for a liberal whose instincts are those of freedom and tolerance but I have come to the view that the interests of the freedom of therapists to work analytically, and of patients to be free from abuse, would be best served by creating a protected ethical space designed by practitioners. The alternative is to await state-designed control that is likely to be less healthy and health-giving and while by definition legal, in a deeper sense less professionally ethical.

It seems to me that the notion of ethics is a central one for any profession. It may indeed be that the imbibing and exercise of the ethos of a profession is the most important of the apprentice's tasks, over and above the acquisition of some very fundamental facts and theories. Such a proposition is hardly a very modern (much less a post-modern) one. Today it is widely believed that the necessary facts and skills can be codified, modularised and imparted sufficiently for efficacious and ethical professional training without the need for an apprenticeship. This book gently raises enough pertinent and persistent questions to remove any such easy simplicity in ethics and psychotherapy, and in so doing raises the issues for other professionals too.

Some might imagine that it is a straightforward, albeit not an entirely easy, matter to construct a code of ethics by which a professional might judge their conduct, and indeed be judged by others. The contributors to this book describe many reasons why this is an inadequate view. Let me mention just three.

Firstly, it is entirely possible to remain within an ethical code but behave unethically. It is inevitable from time to time that a therapist and a patient meet and rehearse the outward manifestations of analysis without any real analysis taking place. For an analyst of integrity this will raise questions. For an unethical therapist, so long as the patient attends and pays there may be little to be troubled about. Put in another way, ethics is surely about right relationships, and this bears the same relation to codes of practice as law does to justice – there is a connection, even an important connection, but it is not entirely easy to identify, for on occasion they can actually be in conflict. Ethical practice means something more and quite different from not falling foul of a code of ethics or practice.

In the days when anything not defined as unlawful was legal and legislation was constructed so as not to be in conflict, there was some clarity as to the boundaries of lawful activity. The advent of human rights as a defining instrument has changed this. Human rights are, in principle, conferred on everyone by nature of their being human, rather than being a legal benefit or protection conferred on its citizens by a state. The sacrosanct legal borders of the state have been breached. Some human rights may also conflict with others in any particular case. The requirement to keep detailed notes as a protection for the patient against careless and unprofessional practice may subsequently conflict with the right of privacy of that same patient. In these senses the lack of absolutism in human rights shows some similarity with professional ethics.

Where such a dilemma arises in ethics, however, it may be determined on the basis of the best interests of the individual patient. In the case of the law and of human rights it will be determined on the basis of legal precedent, and this may be a quite different matter.

The dilemma of comparative practice does not just extend to differing codes or laws across national boundaries. Since different faith communities have radically different ethical views, and not only on matters such as abortion and divorce, is it unreasonable to suggest that a psychotherapist from one faith or cultural background might find him/herself acting differently from others in the same country because they have genuinely different ethical principles and understandings? Given that different ethical principles are embodied in state laws it is not surprising that in the past certain kinds of psychosexual therapy were not available even in some western jurisdictions. Is it possible that further legal requirements may make psychoanalytical work as we know it almost impossible for some health care professionals in certain countries? New technologies and new attitudes raise new ethical dilemmas, but the fact that such situations are new does not mean that they are, by definition, progress. As one example: there are suggestions within these pages of a danger that the limits on communicating clinical material to colleagues by way of publication may already be impeding research and real clinical feedback learning.

The variety of human therapeutic experience encompassed in this book ensures that our creative ethical imagination is exercised. The pregnancy of a patient (as that of a therapist), introduces a further person to the triad of patient/therapist/supervisor. The ethical aspects of retirement by choice by a therapist are different from those where the retirement date is one chosen by the therapist's employer. Working within the ethic and regulations of an organisation has challenges and dilemmas on sharing of information, decisions about availability of treatment and much else besides.

Those who are looking for straight simple answers to such complex ethical questions need to read this book, but not because they will find ready answers. Those who are already thinking about ethics in psychotherapy practice will find much to develop their understanding. Those practitioners who just like to get on with their work and leave ethics to the philosophers and the lawyers will come to appreciate through these chapters that an ethical approach is as central to good therapy as it is to good science, good art, and right relations in general.

I commend it to you.

Preamble

Hester McFarland Solomon and Mary Twyman

The theories propounded by Freud and Jung and their followers are marked by a preoccupation with the development of the human personality from infancy to adulthood. Although the men differed widely in many of the ways they conceptualised the structure and dynamics of the mind, a situation made even more complex by their use of different terminology to signify often similar phenomena, their robust engagement throughout their personal and professional lives in depth psychological enquiry, both in their early collaboration and then separately after their tragic estrangement, brought forth from each a richness of ideas that has given their followers much to build upon, including the task of charting the diversity, as well as the similarities, between them.

As we revisit the ground to which both had given such considerable attention, we are charged with the responsibility of continuing our depth psychological explorations in the light of contemporary preoccupations. Our aim in this book is to address society's interest in the provision of right conduct in analytic clinical practice. In particular, the field of ethics has recently caught the attention and the imagination of the lay person and the professional alike, and there is much debate and concern about what factors determine good ethical practice.

This book consists of a series of indepth studies, all of which are written by practising analysts who have a particular interest in professional ethical matters. It has been compiled by the editors in an attempt to respond to the growing interest in ethical questions as these are evidenced in contemporary clinical practice. The book also responds to growing public concern about such issues as professional misconduct, breaches of confidentiality, and duties of care including child protection. Above all, we wish to illustrate through these contributions the everyday nature of the ethical dilemmas faced by analysts, and therefore the ever-present need for ongoing ethical awareness in clinical practice. Furthermore, when analytic understanding is applied to settings outside the consulting room it will nevertheless include similar ethical awareness in ways appropriate to the particular setting.

The editors have taken a stylistic decision to use the terms 'analysis', 'analyst', and 'patient' to cover the treatment situations and the participants in them. This avoids the cumbersome use of the various terms such as 'psychoanalyst', 'analytical psychologist', 'psychoanalytic psychotherapist', 'analytic psychotherapist', as well as 'analysand' and 'client'. We feel justified in doing this because the essential nature of the work being described in these essays is, in the broadest and fullest sense, analytic in its nature.

Contributors

Christian Gaillard holds a doctorate in psychology, is Professor at the Ecole Nationale Superieure des Beaux-Arts (Paris), and lecturer at the Rene Descartes University and at the Jung Institute of Paris. He is a training analyst for the Societe Francaise de Psychologie Analytique, where he has twice served as its President. He is current President Elect of the International Association for Analytical Psychology. He is Chief Editor of the Cahiers Jungiens de Psychanalyse and a member of the editorial boards of the *Journal of Analytical Psychology, Harvest* and *Anima*. He has published numerous articles in analytic journals and in books. His books include *Jung*, published in the Que sais-je? series, *Le Musee imaginaire de Carl Gustav Jung* (Stock), *Les Evidences du corps et la vie symbolique* (ENSBA), *Donne in mutazione* (Moretti e Vitali).

Philip Hewitt is a Member of the British Association of Psychotherapists. He has worked as a psychotherapist in education for a number years. At City University he was Head of the Student Counselling and Advisory Service and now works part time at Westminster School. He is in private practice as an adult psychoanalytic psychotherapist and is also a training supervisor and therapist.

Fiona Palmer Barnes is a training analyst with the Association of Jungian Analysts. She has been involved for twenty years in working with ethical concepts and their consequences. She has written, with others, codes of ethics and practice and has chaired ethics committees, most recently for AJA and UKCP. She has worked as an independent consultant for psychotherapy and analytic organisations, helping them to set up procedures and hear complaints and grievances. Her publications include *Complaints and Grievances in Psychotherapy* (Routledge, 1998) and she has co-edited, with Lesley Murdin, *Values and Ethics in the Practice of Psychotherapy and Counselling* (Oxford University Press, 2001).

Chris MacKenna is an Anglican priest, a Full Member of the Jungian Analytic Section of the British Association of Psychotherapists, and a former member of the BAP's Ethics Committee. He is particularly interested in the ethical dimension of clinical practice, and in the relation between analytical and religious, particularly Christian, understandings. He is currently Director of the St Marylebone Healing and Counselling Centre.

Gillian Miles is a Full Member of the British Association of Psychotherapists and an Adult Psychotherapist in private practice. She was formerly Senior Clinical Lecturer in Social Work (now retired) at the Tavistock Clinic, working in the Child and Family Department, where her responsibilities included assessment and clinical work with families in a multidisciplinary setting, and assessments for the Courts.

She is currently a member of the Ethics Committee of the British Association of Psychotherapists and of the Tavistock Clinic's Research Ethics Committee.

Elizabeth Richardson is a Full Member, training analyst, supervisor and Chair of the Post Graduate Committee of the Jungian Analytic Section of the British Association of Psychotherapist's. She has an MA in analytical psychotherapy. Originally from a medical background, she has a particular interest in working with aspects of birth, separation and death, and with mothers in the ante- and post-natal stages of pregnancy. She is in full-time private practice and also supervises NHS midwives who work with mothers who are coming to terms with expecting a genetically impaired infant, or who are having to decide whether to terminate such a pregnancy after 16 weeks of gestation.

Mannie Sher is a Director of the Tavistock Institute and in this role he consults to senior management of organisations on the role of leadership in effecting strategic change. Mannie has a special interest in what part thinking plays in strategic development and the operations of organisations. A related interest is the role of transference and countertransference in consultancy and how these phenomena are utilised by consultants in acquiring data about and sharing understanding with their client organisations. He is a Fellow of the British Association of Psychotherapists (BAP) and a practising psychoanalytical psychotherapist. He is a former Chair of the Ethics Committee of the BAP and from that role he has extended his interest in ethical issues to the practice of consultancy in different contexts.

Hester McFarland Solomon trained with the Jungian Section of the British Association of Psychotherapists, where she is now a training therapist, teacher and supervisor, and a Fellow of the Association. She is a member of the International Association for Analytical Psychology. She is editor (with Elphis Christopher) of *Jungian Thought in the Modern World* (Free Association Books, 2000).

Judith Trowell is a child and adult analyst and Fellow of the Royal College of Psychiatrists. She was Consultant Child and Adolescent Psychiatrist of the Child and Family Department of the Tavistock and Portman NHS Trust and its Chair Person from 1982 to 1991. She has been Honorary Senior Lecturer at the Royal Free Hospital and at the Institute of Psychiatry's Children's Department. She served as an independent expert to the Orkney Inquiry, Chair of Young Mind, Chair of the Tavistock Clinical Legal Workshop, co-organiser of the MA in Child Protection, and organiser for the MPhil in Psychoanalytical Psychotherapy for Child and Adolescent Psychiatrists.

Mary Twyman trained at the Institute of Psychoanalysis in London. She has served on the Ethics Committee of the British Association of Psychotherapists and is currently Chair of the Ethics Forum of the British Confederation of Psychotherapists.

Barbara Wharton MA (Oxon) is a Training Analyst of the Society of Analytical Psychology and a Training Therapist and Supervisor for the British Association of Psychotherapists. She was an Editor of the *Journal of Analytical Psychology* from 1993 to 2000, and has published a number of papers on analytical psychology. She has experience of serving on the Ethics Committee of the Society of Analytical Psychology.

Jan Wiener, BSc, MSc is a Training Analyst of the Society of Analytical Psychology, where she is Director of Training, and of the British Association of Psychotherapists. She works as Senior Adult Psychotherapist at Thorpe Coombe Hospital (formerly Claybury) and in private practice in London. She is joint co-ordinator and teacher/supervisor to the Developing Group of Analytical Psychology in St Petersburg, Russia. Author of a number of papers on analytical psychology, she is author (with Mannie Sher) of *Counselling and Psychotherapy in Primary Health Care: A Psychodynamic Approach* (1998) and editor (with Richard Mizen and Jenny Duckham) of *Supervised: A Practice in Search of a Theory.*

Yvette Wiener was born in France, where she studied at Aix-en-Provence University. She trained with the Jungian Section of the British Association of Psychotherapists, where she was an Associate Member and worked in private practice until her retirement. She is now involved, as an analyst, in promoting the rebirth of psychotherapy in St Petersburg. She has written on the theme of the perception of time in the analytic situation and the links between literature and psychotherapy.

Lord Alderdice is a Fellow of the Royal College of Psychiatrists, an Honorary Affiliate of the British Psycho-analytical Society and a Consultant Psychiatrist in Psychotherapy working part-time in the NHS in Belfast. He is also Speaker of the Northern Ireland Assembly, and an active Member of the House of Lords. In this latter capacity he has promoted legislation at Westminster in recent years to facilitate the statutory registration of psychotherapy practice in the United Kingdom.

Section I
The Ethical Attitude in Analytic Practice

1
Introduction:
the ethical attitude in analytic practice

Hester McFarland Solomon and Mary Twyman

In the analytic situation, the analyst offers to the patient their reflections, often in the form of interpretations, and based on the total situation between them as the analyst perceives it. These reflections derive from the analyst's ongoing commitment to be in a state of active or open feeling and thinking responsiveness to the patient – the analyst's experience of their own subjective reality, in response to the subjective reality of the patient, reflected upon and then formulated and returned to the patient in the form of an interpretation or other facilitation. The analyst's commitment to the continued exercise of the analytic function includes and is strengthened by their commitment to an ongoing ethical attitude in relation to the patient and to the work between them.

Analysis thus offers a treatment situation which has as its basis the intense and intimate relationship, over an extended period of time, between the analyst and patient. In these conditions of prolonged intensity and intimacy, a major element is the freedom of mind shared by the analytic couple and generated by the analyst's capacity to tolerate and to strive to understand the patient's struggle to communicate diverse aspects of the self. In this process, powerful impulses, both loving and aggressive, are released and become the material of analytic attention. It is in the release of such powerful affects that the potential for creativity and destructiveness is vividly present in the analytic treatment situation. The clash and the conjunction of these opposing creative and destructive forces, and how they are worked through within the analytic relationship, determine the nature of the therapeutic outcome. The ethical attitude as maintained by the analyst can help to ensure that the structure and ballast that the analyst needs to survive the vicissitudes of the powerful affects unleashed by the analytic process are in place, leading to a more likely positive therapeutic outcome.

It is the analyst's task to maintain constant scrutiny of, while at the same time participating in, this complex and profound relationship. The analyst will be aware that the patient's capacity for growth and change will have been mobilised once the working alliance has been established. The analyst will also be aware of the ubiquity of those destructive forces that are constellated in the patient's psyche, especially in the face of the anxieties aroused in the patient by the very potential for transformation. Where strong affects and motivations are present, the ethical attitude of the analyst may be tested vigorously.

Achieving an Analytic Attitude

How does the analyst achieve an analytic attitude capable of interpreting, facilitating psychic change, and sometimes even withstanding negative assaults on the analysis, while remaining available to being affected and influenced by the impact of the vicissitudes of the patient's ever-changing transferential states of mind?

Whatever may have been the analyst's previous experience prior to training, the work of preparation for this endeavour begins with the analyst's own analysis, when they are the patient, during the period of their analytic training. It is through being a patient, within the conditions of a prolonged intimate and intense analytic relationship, that the analyst will have internalised the analytic attitude of their analyst. This will include the trainee analyst's experience and observation of their analyst's capacity consistently to contain and metabolise the effects of the future analyst's, now the analysand's, attempts to dislodge their analyst from the analytic stance, including from their ethical attitude. The analyst in training will therefore have been a patient in every sense and in every way. The analyst in training will also benefit from the experience and observation of their supervisor's analytic attitude in relation to the material they bring to supervision from their training patients, including internalising their supervisor's capacity to maintain an analytic attitude in relation to themselves and the material of the supervision.

Maintaining an Analytic Attitude

Thus the analytic attitude consists of a constant attempt to understand and interpret the unconscious elements present in the relationship between the patient and the analyst. While the patient has consciously chosen to enter analysis and intends to form and maintain a working alliance, inevitably unconscious resistances to the process of understanding emerge that may subvert or block the conscious intention. The analyst's capacity to tolerate the powerful pressures that the patient exerts to sabotage the analytic task is at the core of the analytic attitude. Intrinsic to the analytic attitude is the analyst's respect for the patient as he or she presents themselves, with their own complex pattern of defences, which have been constructed in order to deal with powerful internal psychic forces and sometimes to survive external noxious life experiences. Indeed, the analyst will expect these defences inevitably to emerge during the process of treatment, particularly at times when important affects, memories, and thoughts surface into consciousness. While the analyst's capacity to respect such defensive structures is important in face of the patient's fears of possible re-traumatisation within the intimate analytic situation, nevertheless the analyst will remain aware that these defences also are barriers to integration and can forestall the development of more appropriate, freer internal psychic structures.

The Ethical Core of the Analytic Attitude

In tolerating the sometimes subtle, sometimes extreme pressures that the patient may bring to bear in maintaining previous defensive patterns, the analyst desists from reacting without thought to the patient's attempts at undermining the analytic work. Instead of reacting or retaliating, the analyst keeps a space in mind in which sufficient processing may go on so that the analytic function will be maintained. One of the outcomes of this work may be that the patient eventually may be able to identify with and make use of this capacity to think about, instead of enact, the workings of his internal world. Indeed, such internalisation is necessary when the analysand is in training to become an analyst. This processing, which ensures a stance of non-enactment, and which we call the analytic attitude, is essentially ethical in nature.

The commitment to an ethical standpoint protects the patient from undue impingement by the analyst, such that the patient's freedom of mind, including the capacity for free association, fundamental to the analytic work, is ensured. The analyst's capacity to forgo the gratification that retaliation or other libidinal enactments might bring allows the reality of the subjective otherness of the patient to be recognised and protected. This attitude is in essence ethical.

In creating an intense and intimate relationship in the analytic setting, and ensuring that the freedom necessary for the work of individuation may be available, we create at the same time the conditions in which abuses may also occur. It is the paradoxical nature of the analytic situation that allows for the constellation of the opposites good /bad, which is at the heart of the ethical struggle.

We work for the good of the patient, but how we interpret 'the good' is not easy to define. We know that serious catastrophes in the analytic relationship can happen, despite conscious good intentions. The rapidity and intensity of the unexpected and excessive forces that can emerge from minute to minute in the intimacy of the consulting room hold danger for patient and analyst alike. In order to negotiate these powerful fluctuations, the analyst needs an internal protected space in which to process these psychic events. This space, as we have seen, has as its major component the ethical attitude. In face of the variety of psychic dangers inherent in the analytic work, the analyst finds psychological and professional ballast in cleaving to the analytic attitude, with its ethical core and of which the analyst has had immediate experience through his or her own personal analysis.

Moving Towards an Ethical Attitude

The negotiation from the primal experience of exclusive maternal provision through to the struggle with the Oedipal curtailment of this provision is ubiquitous in human development. What is being asked for is the renunciation of a claim to the exclusive possession of the primary caregiver, usually the mother. We speak of the primary caregiver, the mother, both in her real external role, but also as she is constituted in the infant's inner world, made up of all the infant's experiences of her, both gratifying and frustrating, together with the infant's feeling responses to her and phantasies about her. As a shorthand way of describing these linked outer and inner phenomena, the term 'primary object' is used here.

The claim to the exclusive possession of the primary object (mother or analyst) is a legitimate and also a profoundly privileged claim that was bound to be limited because unconditional. Unlimited support is not realistically possible, nor does it promote the developmental change necessary for psychic growth. However, when it has been experienced sufficiently for the infant to have gathered enough internal capacity and strength, the next stages of development can be robustly negotiated. Equally, in an analysis, the subjective experience of an exclusive claim on the analyst's attentions is guaranteed for the duration of the session, but is experienced acutely as limited in duration and content. The analyst offers their readiness to go on being available to exercise the analytic function with all its demands, including its ethical demands.

Just as the infant will experience the narcissistic wounds that arise from the experience of these inevitable limitations, so too the patient, evoking in both an array of responses including impotence, rage, denial, frustration, and disappointment. The good enough parent seeks to help the infant to overcome the effects of encountering these inevitable limitations. The good enough analyst seeks to respond by the quality of their ongoing presence and responsiveness to the patient, and by interpreting, such that the frustrations of the analytic experience are tolerable. In both cases, it is the figure on whom the infant/patient depends who also frustrates and limits, but who, at the same time, has the capacity to empathise, to identify with imaginatively, and to interpret.

Parent/caregiver and analyst alike are supported in their difficult functions as negotiators through these developmental stages by a sustaining ethical environment. In the case of the parent or caregiver, such ethical support can emanate from the internalisation of good enough parenting from their own parents in the past, their partner in the present, their extended family, the surrounding social groupings, and to some extent from the values of the wider society. These latter have recently been under attack by modern and postmodern tendencies to question and sometimes to denigrate the values of sustained and dedicated effort. The sheer stamina required by parent and analyst alike also places powerful demands on their capacities.

The issue we are addressing here concerns the creation of meaning and value and their relationship to ethical behaviour. The analyst's dedication to finding meaning and value in the analytic relationship provides for and protects the potential for increasing relatedness on the part of the patient. This ongoing and at times relentless work for both parties attests to the primacy that the creation of meaning and value has, both in the parent/child dyad and in the analytic relationship. It is in this dedication that the ethical attitude is manifest.

The analyst draws on the internalised experience of personal analysis, ongoing supervision, either with senior analysts or in peer supervision groups, through the many professional activities that now are thought about under the rubric of continuous professional development, and the ethical provisions of professional organisations, such as the code of ethics and the code of good practice, and the advice and support of the organisation's ethics committee. In recent years there has been a growing awareness in the profession and generally in the public mind of the central importance of an ethical provision for the practice of analysis.

Experiencing Ethical Struggle in the Analytic Relationship

Given the enormity of the analytic task, it is not surprising that the ethical dimension will be continuously activated and at times called into question. We now propose to examine a selection of possible scenarios in which the analytic attitude is put in jeopardy by failures in ethical functioning. We are all too aware of the dramatic loss of ethical functioning in such disastrous experiences as the sexual acting out between analyst and patient, or the breaking of boundaries of confidentiality and other abuses of what has been called the 'right relationship' between analyst and patient.

But there are other, more everyday and to be expected instances in the course of any analysis in which questions of an ethical nature appear and will need to be addressed if foreclosure on the analytic process is to be avoided. The following is a selection of some of the more ordinary instances and issues which may arise.

(i) The enactment of the analyst's unconscious sadism
Given the nature of the analytic task, in which the impulses of aggression and sabotage emerge from the patient's unconscious and impact on the analyst's affective and thinking functions, it is not surprising that the analyst will experience, often vividly and with great urgency, responses that threaten to engage with the patient's unconscious communications in unhelpful ways.

Over a long career – or perhaps because the capacity was undeveloped or because an analyst may under great strain at a particular moment in their lives – an analyst may not have sufficient access to capacities to tolerate the patient's efforts to sabotage or block the progress of the treatment, or indeed the analyst may find themselves unable to withstand the surge of their own unconscious and unanalysed impulses.

For instance, a patient who relentlessly criticised and disparaged the analyst's way of thinking and speaking including threatening to bring a litigious action against the analyst for incompetence, produced in the analyst feelings of helplessness and rage, and the impulse in the analyst to retaliate was strongly activated to make wounding interpretations. The impulse was resisted, because it was possible for the analyst eventually to recognise that the patient's communication was an enactment in which the patient was in the role of a critical and disparaging parental figure and the analyst was cast in the role originally occupied by the patient. This realisation led to the recognition of the painful situation in the analytic relationship and its re-creation of the original parent/child relationship. What must be emphasised is the force, over a long and sustained period of time, of the patient's projection and its impact on the analyst's affective state and thinking function, making it especially difficult to arrive at an understanding that might transform the situation for both patient and analyst.

In the meantime, the analyst was required to tolerate the onslaught without enacting the self-protective impulses that were very much to the fore, without retaliating by interpreting in such a way as to crush the patient or to terminate the treatment. In order to do this, the analyst was aware of cleaving to the internalised analytic attitude, the ethical component of which ensured that the analyst maintained the commitment to go on analysing in the face of the patient's onslaught, despite the power of the internal forces to the contrary.

(ii) The ethical management of the analyst's narcissism

It is an undeniable reality that the analyst's narcissism is engaged in the analytic work at all stages. Having committed themselves to a professional training in terms of time, effort, and money, to a considerable degree, it is not surprising that the analyst seeks sources of satisfaction and self-esteem in carrying out the analytic work over a long career. It is not just a matter of 'doing no harm' as stated in the Hippocratic (non nocere) oath: the analyst needs some form of acknowledgement or evidence that they have done real good. Furthermore, the sustained voluntary inhibition of gratifications of various types over long periods required by the analytic task makes it understandable that the analyst will seek some recompense for these sacrifices. There is an ordinary human need to know that we are effective. It is a factor in the analytic work that this need of the analyst may be thwarted by a patient in the throes of a negative transference. The analyst is then called upon to further tolerate and manage disappointment and the possible loss of self-confidence in the face of the patient's negativity.

For example, after years of working intensively with a depressed patient where there was a recurrent pattern of analytic gains followed by a sabotaging of these gains by a return to the original pathology, the analyst and patient became fused in a state of profound discouragement about the possibility for change. It was not until the analyst was able to discern the patient's triumph at having defeated the analytic process by claiming the intractable success of the illness subverting the success of the work of the analytic couple, linked to similar triumphant attacks in the past on the parental couple, that the analyst was able to find the courage to disentangle herself from the identification with the negative projections of the patient.

(iii) The dual nature of the analyst's capacity for identification

Over the course of training, the analyst will learn to gauge the usefulness of the extent of their capacity to identify with their patients' states of mind. By being open to experiencing the vicissitudes of the patients' affective states, the analyst gains knowledge of the reality of the patient's subjectivity, knowledge that is at the foundation of the ethical and analytic attitude. Without sufficient capacity to enter into such identificatory states, the analyst remains apart from the patient's subjectivity, and the patient's problems remain alien to the analyst. However, over-identification with the patient's affective states risks the abrogation of the analytic function and therein may lie the roots of unethical behaviour.

For example, an analyst was particularly pleased when a patient, who had had a previous abortion while in analysis, became pregnant and carried the baby to term. Having been concerned that the previous abortion was connected with deficiencies in the analytic work, the analyst felt gratified that this time the patient was able to have the baby while at the same time carrying on with a greatly reduced analysis apparently in order to support the pregnancy. The analyst recognised that over-identification with the patient's newly found capacities for mothering had a bearing on the analyst's concerns that insufficient mothering capacity in the analyst had led to the first abortion. Eventually it was possible to recognise and work with the patient's current deficiencies in mothering her baby linked to her ambivalent relationship towards her analyst, once the over-identification was acknowledged.

(iv) The struggle to maintain triangulation
An expected feature of those regressive states characteristic of the intense and intimate analytic relationship is the unconscious pressure that arises from within the analytic couple to maintain fusional, identificatory states. This is in order to avoid the pain of differentiation, separateness and the maintenance of the analytic function. The analytic function in this sense represents the third element which both structures and limits the pre-Oedipal tendency towards fusional states. Attacks on the analyst's thinking, and attacks on the capacity for linking which underpin the associative function of analytic meaning making, arise in order to sabotage development and growth. This is done in the service of those defensive 'benefits' that had previously ensured psychological survival in the face of internal and external trauma, such as catastrophic loss, the use of the self as a narcissistic object by an important and intimate other, and other ego failures.

In such circumstances, the analyst will struggle to maintain the analytic attitude, and in particular to hold on to the symbolic function. It is when there is a loss of the capacity for symbolisation that enactments – often unethical in nature – occur, since meaning is thereby destroyed.

For example, a female analyst treating a female patient whose sexual orientation was at this time in the analysis homosexual, found herself under great pressure from the patient, who was trying to 'recruit' her to a similar homosexual orientation. It was the patient's contention that the analyst remained an incomplete person, and indeed a less than good analyst, for having chosen to remain in a heterosexual mode. The patient had made the assumption of an analyst's heterosexuality without evidence or confirmation, thus making it possible, as well as safe, to explore in the analysis the demands of her internal sexual self. The analyst understood this as the patient's need that the analyst carry the patient's latent heterosexuality while the patient was free to attack and test it in the analysis. The analyst had to cleave to her understanding that the differences between her and her patient were legitimate and indeed essential analytically, and to desist from giving way to the intense pressure, as she saw it, from the patient for identification and her claim that, for psychological survival, sameness was essential. It is as though the patient was implying that the analyst must be the same as her but, at the same time, were the analyst to succumb to that imperative, the analysis would have ceased to function as an agent for psychological change. In the face of the patient's desperate and despairing panic at being unable to seduce the analyst into compromising her sexual identity, and the concomitant fear that she would succeed, the analyst's task was to withstand and tolerate the force of the patient's expressed need. This was accomplished by withstanding the patient's claim to the erosion of differences between the patient and analyst.

The Usefulness of Ethical Safeguards

The essence of the ethical attitude is to protect and promote psychological development. Analytic practice is concerned with allowing the emergence of, exploring, and eventually the dissolving of those impediments to psychic development and their effects in the analytic relationship. The analyst's task is to work to understand the nature of these impediments, including experiencing the force of the defences erected to ensure that the psychic structures are protected against further undue incursion, limitation, or distortion (i.e. against re-traumatisation). Our contention is that in every analysis in depth a pattern emerges, manifestly different in each case, but always involving an apparent paradox: on the one hand allowing for an intensely experienced, ongoing state of dependence, while simultaneously promoting the impulse to psychological growth, separation and individuation. This apparent paradox is of the essence of human development, and has genetic and evolutionary implications. Adaptation is impossible without variation, and variation precludes identification. This essential duality provides at the same time both the foundations and roots of the self and the platform from which the self can safely develop.

To negotiate this paradoxical situation satisfactorily requires the ethical presence of another who is capable of being thoughtful about and responsive to the task inherent in growth without undue identification or impingement. This implies the capacity of the other (parent or analyst) to remain different while remaining related.

What does this mean in day-to-day analytic practice? We are not advocating a doctrine of perfection, characterised by a punishing professional superego, to which analysts should aspire. We are only too aware of the continual struggle posed by the talk of maintaining the ethical attitude in the analyst's mind. Rather, we wish to acknowledge that there is a continuum of ethical functioning, stretching from the everyday provisions (for instance a consistently protected physical environment, reliable timekeeping, proper discussion of arrangements for fees, holiday breaks, etc., the reliability and stability of the analyst's presence) through to the most difficult pressures on the analyst's psychic integrity, such as has been illustrated in the previous examples. Here the analyst must rely on their ongoing ability for self-analysis in face of all attempts to unhitch the analyst from this functioning. The commitment to go on functioning in this way is at the basis of the ethical attitude in analytic practice. This is why we can say that the ethical attitude is an analytic attitude, and that good analytic practice is always ethical in nature.

Structure and Contents of this Volume

The analytic traditions of psychoanalysis and analytical psychology come together in this volume and are represented in the contributions of the authors in the chapters that follow. Although the traditions have in some ways developed along different paths of theoretical formulations, both traditions have a deep commitment to the understanding of psychic growth and development from infancy to adulthood. Both are equally committed to high standards of ethical principles in professional practice. This book is the result of this shared common interest.

Following on from this introductory chapter, which comprises Section I, the book is organised into five further sections. Section II, 'Mostly Theory', offers theoretical formulations underpinning the understanding of the ethical attitude – its development historically and within the individual, and the underlying principles of ethical functioning. In Chapter 2, Mary Twyman explores ethical themes relevant to the development of analysis in western culture. In Chapter 3, Hester Solomon links the development of the ethical attitude in the individual to its emergence in the consulting room, suggesting that the attainment of the ethical attitude is tantamount to the attainment of a developmental stage. Philip Hewitt in Chapter 4 discusses the difference between the ideal ego and the ego ideal in terms of the development of an ethical attitude. Given this developmental background, Fiona Palmer Barnes in Chapter 5 describes some of the desirable structures of professional organisations seeking to promote ethical practice.

Section III, 'In the Consulting Room', begins with Chris MacKenna, who examines the pressures in the analytic relationship that may contribute to unethical enactments. Elizabeth Richardson in Chapter 7 describes a clinical situation in which she participates in the beginnings of her patient's ethical capacity. In Chapter 8 Christian Gaillard uses a detailed clinical vignette as a starting point for a theoretical exploration of the centrality of the Oedipal situation involved in ethical discernment. In the concluding chapter of this section, Yvette Wiener examines numerous ethical implications when the analyst contemplates and negotiates the stages of retirement.

Section IV, 'Confidentiality and Publication', addresses some of the outstanding pragmatic issues regarding the ethics involved in the sensitive area of publication and dissemination of clinical material. Barbara Wharton, in Chapter 10, examines in detail the ethical and legal issues involved in the publication of clinical material. In Chapter 11 Jan Wiener writes of the ethical requirements in different clinical settings – whether private practice, primary health care or psychiatric provision.

In Section V, 'Applications: Thinking Analytically about Ethics in Different Settings', the focus moves from the close one-to-one relationship between the analyst and patient to considerations of the ethical requirements when analysts are working in the wider contexts of society, including mental health provision. For example, in Chapter 12, Mannie Sher deals with ethical issues in organisational consultancy. In the concluding chapter of this section, Judith Trowell and Gillian Miles 13 discuss those ethical questions that are particular to work with children and families.

In the final section, Section VI, 'The Ethics of Supervision', Hester Solomon contributes a chapter that argues for the ongoing provision of supervisory space in professional practice, linking this with developmental and archetypal theory.

Summary

In thinking about how to summarise the contents of this introductory chapter and the general themes emerging from the book overall, several points come to mind.

1. The ethical fault in the treatment situation, from whatever source it may emerge, happens within the analytic relationship. Hence, professional ethics provisions and their internalisation by the analyst seek to foster and maintain what we might call the 'right relationship'.
2. Within the passion of the primary relationship (whether baby/mother or patient/analyst) lies the potential for both creativity and destruction. That both must be known about as fully as possible underlies the possibility of the patient's greatest realisation of their own potential for growth and individuation. The ethical capacity is held actively within the analyst, for eventual internalisation by the patient, in order to protect the possibility for growth and to stand against the forces that seek to deter growth.
3. Codes of ethics and guidelines for good practice are offered by professional analytic organisations in order to support analysts in clinical conditions where undue psychological pressures are unleashed and may take a tremendous toll.
4. These codes and guidelines are also pertinent to analysts working in the wider field of mental health.

Section II
Mostly Theory

2
Ethical Themes in Analytic Practice

Mary Twyman

> The greatest trust between man and man
> is the trust of giving counsel.
>
> Francis Bacon, 'Of Counsel'

To consider the issue of ethics in relation to the activity of psychoanalysis is to encounter at the outset many questions. To most of them there are no complete answers, but the routes which are opened up in considering the questions are full of concerns which lie at the heart of therapeutic practice and which merit our sustained attention. A contemporary writer on ethics, Peter Singer, in starting to write about his subject puts it thus:

> Ethics is about how we ought to live. What makes an action the right rather than the wrong thing to do? What should our goals be? What is ethics anyway? Where does it come from? Can we really hope to find a rational way of deciding how we ought to live? If we can, what would it be like and how are we going to know when we have found it? (Singer, 1994, p. 5)

It is immediately apparent that an ethicist begins with questions, and from the very beginning of the exploration of the field proceeds by the method of questioning, and continues finding that questions lead to further questions. While this is the method of philosophical enquiry, it also has something in common with scientific enquiry. There may be ways in which we can draw parallels here. But perhaps we need a few definitions first.

What is ethics? There are two main senses in which the word is used. The first sense refers to a set of rules, principles or ways of thinking that guide, or claim the authority to guide, actions of a particular group. The Code of Ethics of a professional body of psychoanalysts and psychotherapists would be an example of this meaning of the term. In the second sense the word is used to denote the systematic study of thinking about how we ought to act. This latter activity tends to be the task of professional philosophers in university departments, who study and develop theories which are then offered to the wider world. This tradition has a long history, beginning in the western world from the basis of Greek and Roman philosophy. The terms that we most commonly use in these areas – ethics and morals – come out of these traditions. Both *ethics* and *moral*s have their roots in the word for *customs*: ethics from the Greek *ethos*, and morals from the Latin *mores*, the latter still a word currently in use to denote the customs of a people or a group, a society, a class. Ethos carries perhaps a similar meaning but is generally thought to denote something more diffuse – an atmosphere, recognisable, and characteristic but carrying a meaning more abstract than mores. Morality can, however, in current usage be seen to carry a loading of a stern set of duties that require us to subordinate our natural wishes in obedience to a moral law, and is often seen to carry a religious connotation and to be associated with behaviour regulated by a sense of guilt. These connotations are perhaps most closely linked in our western European culture with a particular conception of ethics based mainly on the Judaeo-Christian traditions but such connotations are not an inherent feature of ethical systems in themselves. Ethics has no necessary connection with a particular religion or religion in general, but ethical issues have been written and spoken about by religious writers in significant ways, ways that have been long-lasting and effective in shaping human societies and human consciousness. The religious traditions of Christianity, Judaism and Islam, as embodied in the texts of the Bible, the Torah and the Koran, remain significant repositories of key ethical systems.

Derek Parfit, commenting on the view that some philosophers express that there cannot be progress in ethics, since everything has already been said, suggests that the opposite is the case. Asking the question, 'How many people have made Non-Religious Ethics their life's work?' he cites some of the Ancient Greeks and Romans, Buddha and Confucius, the nineteenth-century Cambridge philosopher, Sidgwick, and concludes that the systematic non-religious study of ethics began around 1960 (Parfit, in Singer, 1994, p.391). The detachment of the study of ethics from a religious context compels a rigorous examination of what is essential to be considered in human beings' behaviour towards each other. A sense of ethics can still be understood as a natural development arising in the course of evolution of social intelligent individuals who possess the capacity to recognise each other and have the ability to recognise past behaviours of themselves and others, and thus to have a sense of the consequences of their behaviours. It may be that thinking about ethics in relation to psychoanalytic practice represents one of the most advanced and sophisticated areas of ethical enquiry. But such enquiry is also being pursued in a wide range of disciplines, in the social sciences, in the natural sciences, in evolutionary biology as well as in philosophy itself. And there is much that we can learn from this contemporary surge of interest in ethical dilemmas, for it frees us to range more widely and so to equip ourselves with a series of new perspectives on our own dilemmas.

One of the first to contribute to the development of the systematic study of ethics Aristotle wrote this in his *Nicomachean Ethics*:

Virtue then being of two kinds, intellectual and moral, intellectual virtue in the main owes both its birth and its growth to teaching (*for which reason it requires experience and time*) while moral virtue comes as a result of habit. (p. 101)

Applying this to the psychoanalytic enterprise it occurs to me that this might make an appropriate epigraph for the description of a training in psychoanalysis. Clearly both intellectual and moral virtue are desiderata and the emphasis Aristotle places on experience and time resonates with the length and intensity of the trainings undertaken as a preparation for practice. This links also with his idea that moral virtue comes as a result of habit. The habit of good practice is something to be acquired and maintained in the practitioner by constant self-examination such as is internalised from the practitioner's own analysis. It may seem rather prosaic to use the term habit, but in a real way it describes the ongoing, persistent experiencing of unconscious processes in daily sessions, whether as a patient or an analyst. The quotidian nature of the analytic encounter for both patient and analyst creates the setting in which resistances to the psychoanalytic enquiry can be systematically identified and addressed through interpretation.

Iris Murdoch in her book, *The Sovereignty of Good*, explains that she judged Plato to have had a notion of the unconscious mind, holding a view that sexuality led to love and love could extend to an altruistic love of the other; there could be love of learning (epistemophilia) – again this is something which the analytic situation fosters and relies upon. Plato, Murdoch outlines, was also aware that there could be *conflict* between love for the other and the desire to do harm. Much ethical thinking and theorising over the centuries has concerned the behaviour of the ruler and the ruled, the leader and the led, the stronger and the weaker. This can be seen to have relevance in the psychoanalytic setting, for it presents us with further questions about the nature of the analytic dyad. What is the nature of our authority, power and especially responsibility in the analytic situation? How do we exercise all three in the service of the patient? What are the constraints that regulate our behaviour? Hinshelwood's recent work *Therapy or Coercion? Does Psychoanalysis Differ from Brainwashing?* is a contemporary thorough working of these themes and a timely contribution to current thinking in this area of the professional ethics of psychoanalysis. As Hinshelwood ventures in his Preface (p. xi), he

remains unconvinced that we could be so absolutely sure that the pressure we put on our patients is easily and comfortably distinguishable from that of all sorts of other influences . . . we need a criterion for distinguishing benevolent from malevolent influencing. (p. xi)

If we bring psychoanalysis, born in the nineteenth century, more centrally into the picture now we can see that it belongs to the culture of our times. Yet all the issues that psychoanalysis treats, the health and sickness of the will, of the emotions, the responsibilities of private living, the pressures of culture, all these belong in the realm of what could be described as moral life. There is a sense in which Freud can be seen as a pathologist of the ethical sense. Freud said of psychoanalysis that 'it stands in the middle position between medicine and philosophy' (SE vol. V, p.168). In describing how he would guide the education of a physician who would become a psychoanalyst he advises that the candidate was to become a student of history, religion and the arts, and later be referred to the psychoanalyst as 'a secular spiritual guide' (SE V, p.175).

Philip Rieff, in his book *Freud: The Mind of the Moralist*, draws our attention to Freud's reticence as a moralist, citing this as one quality especially that has paradoxically enabled Freud to have been the more influential in the field (p.300). But what Freud certainly did in developing his theories of psychoanalysis was to put ethics under the scrutiny of scientific method. Freud always insisted that psychoanalysis was a science, while noting in *Studies on Hysteria* (p.280) that the case histories were beginning to sound like novellas, and thus seemed to lack the serious aims of science.

The science of psychoanalysis is about plain speaking, about phenomena rather than rhetoric or persuasion; it aims to clarify by analysing, not to obscure or mystify. Necessary to any science's empirical task is its preparedness to discard hypotheses which are not borne out by confirming evidence. Thus hypotheses, pet theories, inadequately controlled observations have to be held as expendable, and with them the analyst's identification with them. Freud set the example here with his abandonment of the seduction theory. Evolving psychoanalytic theory proceeds in this way. Freud discarded elements of theory as he developed more comprehensive ideas and his example enjoins those coming after him to do the same.

What must be noted here and what connects these observations with the theme of ethics in psychoanalysis is that science conceived in this way represents an essentially non-narcissistic enterprise. As such it can be placed alongside the injunction of the Hippocratic oath of two thousand years ago – *non nocere*. The science of psychoanalysis, in that it examines the unconscious processes within the mind of the patient as demonstrated in the patient's relationship to the analyst, manifests itself as dedicated to observation, to the understanding of the phenomena of the transference and with a preparedness, if necessary, to jettison yesterday's ideas as these are superseded by the experience of today's session.

Philip Rieff (op. cit., p.305) conceives of history in three stages when considering systems of morality and how they operate in societies. The first stage comprises the cohesive societies characteristic of primitive man, where repression is exercised by taboo. The second stage achieves cohesion by repression via the theologies of religions. Thirdly, he recognises modern culture where the old repressions are loosened but not yet superseded. Writing in 1959 he saw psychoanalysis as belonging to the culture of the third phase, in which the European Judaeo-Christian societies found themselves in flux with a waning influence of transitional moralities and, as he saw it, the indifference of science to ethics. It is interesting that Rieff was writing in 1959 – as he saw it, at the end of a process. Derek Parfit's view cited above proposed 1960 as the probable date when the serious study of non-religious ethics started. It would be possible to disagree with Rieff in his notion of the indifference of science to ethics. As far as the science of psychoanalysis is concerned, its intrinsic ethical stance – for example, that the examination of the patient's material is in the service of elucidating unconscious conflicts represents something far from indifference.

Levinas and Bauman

Two writers in recent times have offered views of ethical principles and behaviour which appear to me to have particular saliency for the psychoanalytic endeavour, and which address those dilemmas that are crucial to the therapeutic encounter. Emmanuel Levinas (1906-95) centres his philosophical thinking around ethics. Alongside him and further developing his ideas while pursuing his own lines of enquiry is Zygmunt Bauman, a sociologist and writer on the social theory of modernity and postmodernity. Although their theories and the areas they explore are extensive, the central preoccupation of each writer is the nature and scope of the ethical relationship. As such what they propound is of particular relevance to our attempts to study the centrality of the ethical stance and the ethical attitude in psychoanalytic work. Essential to the thinking of both theorists is the concept of responsibility.

Levinas's work emphasises the asymmetry of the ethical relationship, and it will immediately be apparent that this describes precisely the analytic relationship, uniquely expressed in the patient's experience of the transference relationship. The patient feels more deeply, more extensively for the analyst than the analyst does for the patient. Here lies, inherently, the asymmetry of the analytic relationship. Amongst other things Levinas insists that the ethical responsibility towards the other exists before the relationship, that is, as I understand it, it represents a setting in the mind of the subject towards the other. There are recognisable parallels to be found here with the setting of the analyst's mind as the essential preparation for the analytic encounter. We could see the objective of our lengthy training, our own analysis, the supervision we undertake of our training cases and our rigorous study of the theory our science (in our craft) proposes, as the achievement of a setting in the mind that can assume a responsibility towards the patient of a very particular kind. It may be obvious to say that we act with responsibility towards our patients. But the kind of responsibility that Levinas refers to and which I think marks out the psychoanalytic relationship, goes beyond the confines of the ordinary sense of the word. Ethics, for Levinas, is more than a set of rules, however simple or complicated, about how to behave. As he says, 'Responsibility for the other establishes the ego. To be a self is to be responsible beyond what one has oneself done' (quoted in Gordon, *Face to Face*). We could see that perhaps as referring to the analyst's work ego. As we live through a professional life of analysing, this work ego develops and deepens; we gradually become the analyst we are capable of becoming. But I think the meaning of responsibility carries further. Bauman in his *Post-Modern Ethics* (pp. 50-3) elaborates: 'Whatever else "I-for-you" may contain, it does not demand to be repaid, mirrored or "balanced out" in a "you-for-me". My relation to the Other is not reversible. . . .' This most aptly describes the kind of responsibility that lies at the heart of the psychoanalytic relationship. It derives from what I have referred to as the setting in the analyst's mind and carries through to the consistent application of analysing and interpreting that is carried on in the service of the patient. The whole *raison d'être* of the analysis is the understanding of the patient's psychic state, undertaken in the conviction that such understanding is in the best interests of the patient. It is the analyst's responsibility, in the senses that Levinas and Bauman propose, to adhere to that task. Where ethical failures occur in analytic practice it is often in circumstances where the essential non-narcissistic nature of such a sense of responsibility has been subverted. The difficulty of exercising this ultimate responsibility is not to be underestimated. Bauman uses a particularly telling phrase to capture the essence of this difficulty, referring to 'the unbearable silence of responsibility' (1993, p. 78).

It seems to me that Levinas and Bauman offer to the field of psychoanalysis now in the twenty-first century a framework for thinking about ethics in relation to professional practice that is salient. This is especially so in that they lay out in their writings ethical situations similar to those that are faced every day in the consulting room, but they also stand out as thinkers who challenge the analyst to explore more extensively the ramifications of what is involved in their unique relationship. In exploring the nature of the concept of responsibility, there is a widening of the frame which provides a freedom to think beyond the usual confines of ethical codes and guidelines. We are invited to consider more than keeping to the rules and not doing the wrong thing. If Levinas and Bauman, in their writings, are transcending the confines of the study of ethics or moral philosophy, as I think they are, then in the analytic situation we are enjoined similarly to push ourselves to think more extensively about the nature of our ethical commitment in our work. We may then be even more aware of the 'greatest trust' which Francis Bacon refers to in his essay, 'Of Counsel', as that which exists between man and man in the giving of counsel. The sixteenth-century politician and essayist speaks in the same vein as the moral philosophers of the twenty-first century.

References

Aristotle, *The Nicomachean Ethics*, trans. J.A.K. Thomson, London: Penguin Books, 1976.

Bacon, F. (1625), *Essays*, London: Nelson.

Bauman, Z. (1993), *Post-Modern Ethics*, Oxford: Blackwell.

Freud, S. (1953-73), 'The resistances to psychoanalysis', Standard Edition, vol. V, p.168, London: The Hogarth Press.

—— (1953-73), 'Postscript to a discussion on lay analysis', Standard Edition, vol. V, p.210, London: The Hogarth Press.

—— (1895, 1953-73), *Studies on Hysteria*, Standard Edition, vol. II, London: The Hogarth Press.

Gordon, P.(1999), *Face to Face. Therapy as Ethics*, London: Constable.

Hinshelwood, R.D. (1997), *Therapy or Coercion? Does Psychoanalysis Differ from Brainwashing?* London: Karnac Books, 1997.

Murdoch, I. (1970), *The Sovereignty of Good*, London: Routledge & Kegan Paul.

Parfit, D. (1994), 'How both human history and the history of ethics may be just beginning', in P. Singer, *Ethics*, Oxford: Oxford University Press.

Rieff, P. (1959), *Freud: The Mind of the Moralist*, London and Chicago: University of Chicago Press.

Singer, P. (1994), *Ethics*, Oxford: Oxford University Press.

Wright, T., Hughes, P. and Ainley, A. (1988), *The Paradox of Morality: an interview with Emmanuel Levinas. The Provocation of Levinas. Rethinking the Other*, London: Routledge.

3

The Ethical Attitude: a bridge between psychoanalysis and analytical psychology

Hester McFarland Solomon

The expectation that high ethical standards be consistently maintained in clinical practice is common to psychoanalysis and analytical psychology. Both the International Psychoanalytic Association and the International Association for Analytical Psychology have this principle enshrined in their constitutions and codes of ethics. The IPA has recently revised its documents concerning ethics principles and procedures, including updating its code of ethics; similarly, the IAAP is actively engaged in reviewing its ethics provisions. However, with some notable exceptions, ethics in practice does not receive much exposure, if at all, in our training curricula, and even less do theories about the origins and functioning of an ethical capacity or attitude in human beings appear in analytic literature. We insist on 'high ethical standards' but what is our psychodynamic understanding underlying these principles? We require at the institutional level that ethics be taken as a core value, but we seem not to address the bases for this core value within the personality.

It is therefore surprising that, with a few notable exceptions, there is a dearth of theoretical work or published clinical material within psychoanalysis or analytical psychology that seeks directly to address the nature and origins of the ethical attitude, whether in developmental or archetypal terms. Furthermore, there is little attempt to locate it as an intrinsic component of the self and of the analytic attitude which seeks to protect the development of the self and of that so intimate of relationships, that between patient and analyst.

Of course, there are some quick and simple ripostes to my apperception of this state of affairs. Some may point to concepts such as the superego, or the ego ideal, or the feelings of care and concern that characterise the depressive position, and I will address these. Nevertheless, in the literature these concepts are not discussed as constituting the basis of the capacity to form and maintain an ethical attitude. Can we really subsume what we mean by acting in an ethical way or struggling with ethical dilemmas under any of these theoretical concepts, or do we need further understanding of the origins of the ethical attitude?

It seems to me that one of the reasons there has been a dearth of theorising about the origins and dynamics of the ethical attitude in analytical and psychoanalytic literature is that many analysts practise according to the assumption that as long as they have not contravened the code of ethics, essentially they can forget about it and the principles underlying it, and get on with the task of analysing the patient. It is as if they consider that ethical thinking is an unwelcome disruption or intrusion to the analytic task, and that, more or less, as long as they are not sleeping with their patients or otherwise contravening the code of ethics, then they are relieved of the burden of worrying about ethics in their practice. I hope to show that where this attitude about professional ethics occurs, then there is an ethical deficit – that disclaimers, conscious or unconscious, about the place of ethics in analytic practice constitute the tell-tale signs that point to the shadow side of professional ethics.

In the following sections, I will consider such fundamental questions as: From whence derive the ethical principles we are eager to stress as underlying our professional practice? Are the ethical principles that form the professional basis of our clinical practice related to our psychoanalytic and analytical psychology theories? Where does a capacity for ethical thinking and behaviour come from? Is the ethical attitude innate, or do we learn it? Is it an archetypal potential that awaits activation by the right circumstances, or do we learn it through socialising processes and the quality of our object relations? And why is there so little about the origins of the ethical attitude in analytic literature?

The more I have thought about these questions, the more I have realised that ethics is with us professionally all the time in the consulting room, day by day, hour by hour. Even though we are not necessarily made consciously aware of our ethical attitude as we work, we are, as professionals, constantly living within an ethical dimension. Every action that we take in relation to our patients and supervisees (and, I would add, our colleagues) has an ethical aspect which, if ignored, can have serious implications for our capacity to maintain the analytic attitude, the analytic frame, and to do our analytic work in an appropriately professional context.

Historical Perspectives

Freud and Jung shared common ground in viewing the psyche as suffused with the ubiquitous presence of unconscious conflict, of psychological processes and behaviour that are multi-determined and multi-motivated, of unconscious and subversive impulses and desires that can undermine conscious intent, and of the counterbalancing possibility within the psyche of conscious ego choice, moral energy and ethical struggle. To this shared view, Jung added a deep conviction regarding the overriding teleological nature of the self and its continued search to become itself, even in the face of dire internal resistance or malign external forces. All these elements are components of a profound view of the psyche that has a direct bearing on our understanding of the attainment of an ethical attitude.

Freud pointed to the development of two regulating systems relevant to moral behaviour that seem to reflect the operation of the talion law and the principle of agape respectively. They are: (i) the superego, which is related to the internalisation of (usually) the parental figures representing power and authority and capable of evoking in talionic ways such affects as shame, humiliation, the fear of revenge, and the desire for triumph; and (ii) the ego ideal, based on more agapaic emotions such as empathic guilt and the wish to preserve and identify with the internalised good parents. Later, Klein would elaborate the dual system of the paranoid/schizoid and depressive positions. Although she did not specify them in these terms, the paranoid/schizoid position may be thought of as operating according to talionic principles, and these may give way to the more agapaic responses of the depressive position through the capacity for concern and reparation.

Over and over in the Collected Works, Jung stressed the centrality of moral and ethical values as being deeply implicated in psychotherapeutic treatment. He stressed the emotional value of ethical ideas and the fact that ethical issues require that affect and thought struggle together to reach ethical discernment (see, for example, CW 10, paras 855ff).

For Jung, the understanding of the teleological unfolding of the self operating through the transcendent function over the stages of an entire life underpins a view of the self's ethical capacity. In particular, the recognition and integration of the shadow is crucial to the self's capacity to develop and grow, to individuate and thereby to fulfil the self's ethical nature. As Murray Stein (1995) has said, 'for Jung ... ethics is the action of the whole person, the self'.

Jung repeatedly acknowledged (for example, CW 9(ii), paras 14-16) that the shadow is a moral problem that challenges the whole of the personality, requiring considerable moral effort to overcome, and meeting considerable resistance in the process of gaining self-knowledge. The shadow, that portion of the self that the ego designates as bad and projects as unwanted, carries what is treacherous and subversive – what is unethical and immoral – within the self and hides it, relegating its contents to unconscious areas within the psyche where it can then be lived out in projection, using and abusing the other as a vehicle for holding the bad aspects of the self. To withdraw shadow projections can require tremendous struggle of an ethical nature, bringing to consciousness what is unconscious and projected.

To the extent that the other is used as an object of projection, the self remains thereby split and diminished, evoking narcissistic self-care defences that are often perverse in nature. Thus can the knowledge of the true and subjective reality of the other be lost. In accepting the pain of engaging in the struggle to overcome such splits and to integrate the shadow, the ethical capacity will have been activated, and meaning and value thereby generated.

Philosophical Perspectives

It is not possible in this context to review the entire philosophical literature regarding ethics. Instead, I will mention briefly just two figures whose thinking particularly underpins my argument.

The self is not called upon to be ethical in a vacuum. In the struggle to integrate the shadow, the self must recognise the substantive reality and subjectivity of the other. Buber's (1937, 1958) concept of the I-thou relationship as a dialogistic encounter between two subjectivities has relevance here. The teleological project of the self to achieve wholeness requires the withdrawal of projections and the integration of their contents. The self cannot be whole if parts of it are unknown and projected outside itself, in particular its immoral and unethical parts.

It is integral to the notion of the self that it is at once separate and related, divided within itself and instinctively seeking integration and relationship. The contemporary moral philosopher Bauman (1993) has pointed out that the self's ethical capacity is derived not from shared ontological reality – the facts of shared existence – but rather from value and meaning, which are different, higher and unconditional. This is a philosophical position similar in kind to Kant's notion of the categorical imperative. It is the unique and non-reversible nature of my responsibility to another, *regardless* of whether the other sees their duties in the same way towards me, that makes me an ethical being.

Where does this value and meaning, this sense of unconditional responsibility, come from? How do we account for the self's willingness to tolerate the ethical burden, that real struggle involved in the withdrawal of projections and integration of the shadow?

Neuroscientific Perspectives

The internalisation of the experience of non-talionic relating nourishes psychically, mentally and emotionally, as recent neuropsychological research has indicated (Schore, 1994). The young self develops through a good enough holding environment, which can be envisaged as a familial breast, which allows the infant the experience of being held without undue fear of retaliation or undue regard to placating another for its survival. This allows the young self securely to experience the freedom to express him- or herself as an authentic being. This total situation in turn becomes the basis for the potential eventually to develop an ethical capacity. When these conditions are not met, pathologies of the self arise, such as the false self, the 'as if' personality, and the various pathologies relating to the defences of the self and the self care systems.

The new field of psychoneurobiology has shown that the development *post partum* of the neural circuitry and structures of the infant's brain which regulate the development of the higher human capacities (i.e. cognitive and socioaffective) are dependent on the existence and quality of the early interactions between infant and mother or caregiver. Daniel Stern (1985) has made a powerful contribution to this area from the field of developmental psychology, where he has analysed the different modes of fit and attunement between the infant and its mother that create the basic patterns of being and becoming that characterise individuals as their unique selves. The emphasis here is on mutuality, with both infant and mother actively generating exchanges, with direct impact on the development of the infant's neural circuitry.

Thus, since the infant instinctively seeks to participate in activating the type, number and timing of these mutual exchanges, we can infer that the infant, a proactive partner, is thereby participating directly in the development of its own neural circuitry, in its own neural growth. Moreover, it is this particular circuitry that determines the cognitive and socioaffective activity which must eventually have bearing on and underpin the achievement of these higher psychological capacities, including the ethical capacity. This suggests that there are grounds for considering that the ethical capacity is, at least in part, innate, derived from the earliest, instinctually driven exchanges with the primary caregiver, including exchanges initiated by the baby, and, at least in part, influenced by environmental factors, by the impact of that very caregiver's capacity to be responsive to and to initiate appropriate and meaningful interactions with the self (see Solomon, 2000a, for a fuller discussion).

Emergence of an Ethical Capacity

In considering these questions and perspectives, I wish to offer an image to highlight an archetypal potential for ethical capacity. In thinking about the possible origins of the ethical attitude, a primordial image emerges of a combined parental – or perhaps a combined familial – picture. What I am combining is Winnicott's (1964) evocative notions of primary maternal preoccupation leading eventually to the ordinarily devoted mother and the notion of the discerning, discriminating thinking function which is often imaged symbolically in masculine, paternal terms. It is through the combination of these functions – of devotion and thinking – that the ethical attitude is maintained in the parental couple, eventually internalised in the psyche and activated as the self and ego in dynamic relation, eventual parents in the psyche. It is first experienced by the infant as an evoked archetypal potential in the self, with a mixture of unconscious identification and gratitude – also unconscious but experienced bodily as 'not-anxiety'. The idea of the ordinarily devoted mother represents a deeply ethical mode in its instinctual and unconditional devotedness to another, her infant, overcoming her narcissistic needs and frustrated rages, her shadow projections, and resisting by and large the impulse to skew her infant's development through undue acquiescence to her requirements. Of course, later she will leave this state of primary preoccupation and devotedness and will begin the processes of socialisation which are so necessary a part of ethical development – the capacity to say, in different ways, 'no', thereby establishing boundaries and expectations of self regulation, including those in relation to others. To this image of ordinary devotedness to a nascent self I am combining the notion of the discriminating and thinking function of the masculine principle. The activation of an archetypal potential for eventual ethical behaviour will be thus reinforced in ordinary good enough situations by caregivers capable of sharing acts of thoughtful devotedness and of empathic thinking about their infant.

I am conjecturing that the identification with and internalisation of the agapaic function of the parental figures in their empathic holding as well as their thinking and discriminating aspects trigger or catalyse a nascent ethical capacity in a young mind, the first steps of which include those primitive acts of discriminating good and bad which constitute the foundations of splitting and projection. Early (as well as later) splitting and projecting may therefore be instances of primitive moral activity, what Samuels (1989) calls original morality – the expulsion from the self of what is unwanted and felt to be bad onto the other, where it is identified as bad and eschewed. Even in situations where the good is split and projected, it is in the service of maintaining a discriminating, but highly defensive, psychic structure. So we come full circle: the primitive acts of discriminating the bad, and splitting it off from the psyche by projection onto the caretakers, constitute the very preconditions for the creation of the shadow which eventually will require a further ethical action of reintegration – a first, primordial or prototypical moral discernment prior to the state where there is sufficient ego strength for anything resembling proper moral or ethical behaviour to arise.

As we posit, following Fordham (1969,1994), the self as a primary integrate, autonomous but very much in relation to another or others, so we are alone as moral beings while at the same time finding our moral nature in relation to others. To truly find another represents a transcendence of narcissistic ways of relating in which the other is appropriated for use in the internal world, denying the other's subjective reality. To live with the implications of this – a capacity to recognise and relate to the truth of the other – is a step in the development of – and perhaps eventually beyond – the depressive position. The depressive position is usually considered to contain acts of reparation through guilt and fear that the object may have been damaged and therefore may be unable to go on caring for one's self (Hinshelwood, 1989). As such, acts of reparation remain contingent on preserving the other for the benefit of the self. The ethical attitude envisaged here goes beyond this contingency and suggests a non-contingent realm of ethical behaviour. This situation has direct implications for what transpires in the consulting room between the analytic couple (see Solomon, 2000b, for further discussion).

Emergence of an Ethical Capacity in the Consulting Room

Much of the work between patient and analyst concerns the vicissitudes in the modes of and capacity for *coniunctio* between them. Jung emphasised the importance of mutuality in the relationship between patient and doctor, and he was very aware of the psychological dangers and ethical pressures that arise from this, as aspects of what he called unconscious identity, or *participation mystique* (CW 10, para. 852), now usually conceptualised as projective identification, in which primitive levels of communication can lead to states of greatly reduced psychological differentiation between the two individuals within the relating pair. This is now thought of as the counter-transference. However helpful such states may be in providing immediate conduits for unconscious communication, thus enhancing countertransference information, the very real dangers are clear. Unconscious identification without the discriminating function of thinking and reflection can lead to the perversion of the ethical attitude. Boundaries may then be crossed, unhelpful enactments occur, actings out become possibilities, and the safety of the container lost, curtailing thereby the psychological freedom necessary to carry out the analytic work (examples of which are set out in detail by Gabbard and Lester, 1995).

The 'special act of ethical reflection', as Jung called it (CW 10, para. 852), as it appears in the consulting room, itself requires special conditions, in particular the maintenance and protection of boundaried space, the *vas bene clausum*, or in Langs' (1974) terms, the analytic frame. In the unequal analytic relationship, maintaining a boundaried space ensures that the analytic work may proceed safely and with the necessary analytical freedom so that regression and states of powerful deintegration and sometimes dramatic disintegration can occur. Inevitably, the analytic frame may be called into question, and Wiener (2001) has discussed some of the issues that may be involved, requiring the maintenance of what she has called 'ethical space'. This indicates the importance of ongoing supervision or consultation in analytic practice post qualification. One implication of this for training is the need to revise a former primary training aim, which had been to prepare and assess that candidates are ready to work 'independently'. (See chapter 14 in this volume for a fuller discussion of the ethical issues in relation to ongoing supervision post qualification.)

The unbalanced nature of the analytic dyad resembles the situation that I described earlier in which one person takes on unconditional ethical responsibilities towards another who is not obliged to reciprocate in an equal way; so, too, in the consulting room, where the analyst undertakes the maintenance of an ethical attitude which the patient is not called upon to adhere to in the same way. Of course, the patient abides by other rules, such as payment of fees and regular attendance (within certain parameters). In the urgency of the analytic situation, unconscionable pressure may be brought to bear on the analytic relationship, putting both participants at risk. The situation can be experienced in such a drastic way that neither patient nor analyst feels that a solution is possible. Lambert (1981) has discussed the importance for the ongoing treatment that the analyst maintain an agapaic function in the face of the patient's and the analyst's own impulses to behave according to the talion law. If such pressure can be contained in the holding environment of the analyst's capacity for agape, it is then that, as Jung stated, the transcendent function may be activated and a solution found.

For example, a supervisee was seeing a patient three times a week in an analysis that had been established over some time when it was discovered that the patient was paying the analyst with money that was the result of milking the system in which she worked. In her work the patient was responsible for uncovering the fraudulent activities of others, a responsibility in which she took great pride and satisfaction. She was in a relationship where her partner was also sailing close to the wind regarding criminal behaviour, and their marital home had been acquired substantially through ill-begotten gains. Accepting the fraudulent money brought into question whether the analyst was drawn into the patient's perverse system, and the implications of this touched on the supervision which was being paid for in part by the patient's fees. Should the analyst accept the money in the hope that through the analytic work the patient would be able to reach an understanding about her need to behave in a near criminal way, so to increase the possibility of her leading a more ethical life? Should the analyst confront the patient and refuse to accept the money? Does the analyst have responsibilities for reporting the situation to the referring agency, or even to the patient's employers? What were my role and responsibilities as the supervisor?

In this case, the action of the transcendent function as it arose in the patient was provisional and complex, involving both concrete enactments and symbolic representations. The patient became pregnant – after a first abortion – and went through to term, withdrawing from work for a prolonged maternity leave. She continued with her analysis at a less intensive rate, and allowed herself to become an ordinarily devoted mother, not without ambivalence, but with some positive internal psychic changes. The supervisory couple considered that it was in part through actively and empathically discussing together the ethical dimension of the patient's situation, without relaying this overtly to the patient, that it was made possible for the patient to move on psychically.

Beyond the Depressive Position

If the attainment of an ethical attitude is a developmental achievement, then we could venture a view that the ethical attitude is a developmental position. In Hinshelwood's (1989) definition, 'position' is 'the characteristic posture that the ego takes up with respect to its objects'. The emphasis I would make is on the *quality* of the relationship between self and other and the meaning of the relationship for each – an interior and exterior situation.

Jung stressed the teleological view of the self in which the innate capacity for the self to become itself through the process of individuation was a fundamental aspect. An ethically mature attitude is not predicated on the ethical behaviour of the other towards the self, but rather is founded on the earliest experience of the unconditional devotedness of another in relation to the self, regardless of the self's relation to the other. In Klein's view, on the other hand, the capacity for guilt, concern and the wish for reparation seen in the infant results from the self's capacity to imagine the damage it has caused the other and thus how the other's wish or capacity to go on loving and caring for the self may be diminished or disappear. It also represents the concern for and fear of the loss of the self's own internal good objects which are necessary in supporting the ongoing viability of the self and without which psychic dissolution may occur. (See Klein, 1935, 1940.) Here is an internal accounting system at work which remains related in this way to the anxieties evoked by the talion law of the paranoid/schizoid position.

In the teleological perspective in which the self is always becoming more itself, the self is supported in its development through the symbolic capacity of the transcendent function and the creative resources of the unconscious. In speaking about the struggle with an ethical conflict which can leave the person feeling locked in a dilemma from which there seems to be no possible development or recourse, Jung states:

> The deciding factor appears to be something else [than an accepted rule or custom]: it proceeds not from the traditional moral code but from the unconscious foundation of the personality. The decision is drawn from dark

and deep waters. ... If one is sufficiently conscientious the conflict is endured to the end.... The nature of the solution is in accord with the deepest foundations of the personality as well as with its wholeness; it embraces conscious and unconscious and therefore transcends the ego ... a conflict of duty [finds] its solution through the creation of a third standpoint. (CW 10, paras 856-7)

We have seen that it is not always possible to achieve a positive outcome to the struggle to find another in such a way as to relate in an ethical manner. This is as true in the consulting room as outside it, and involves an ethical struggle on the part of patient as well as analyst. Freedom from appropriation for narcissistic use in another's intimate, internal world, may precede the ability to relate ethically to an intimate other. This is the result of the rule of abstinence, whether familial between the generations, or professional between patient and analyst, who are also of two different (analytic) generations. In conditions where such freedom was not available, the self may have had to devise ways of protecting itself from such incursions, erecting defences of the self, and a loss of ethical capacity may have ensued. Much analytic work is then devoted to reinstating this freedom, through facing up to the inevitable forces of sabotage which seek to undermine the ethical, analytical work.

Conclusion

In this chapter, I have explored ways in which the self finds, defines, creates and struggles with ethical value. It seems to me that the concept of the ethical attitude can function as a bridging concept between psychoanalysis and analytical psychology for two reasons:

(i) because it causes us to stretch deeply into the bases of the developing psyche and includes commonly held, collective core values, thus providing an opportunity for the joint study of the sources and conditions for maintaining one of the deepest expressions of our humanness; and

(ii) because how we deal with pragmatic ethical issues in the consulting room, in our analytic organisations, and with our colleagues is a common concern for psychoanalysts and analytical psychologists alike.

The ethical attitude is an essential part of the analytical relationship, and is not just an addendum to the practitioner's work. If it is experienced by the analyst, in projection, simply as the patient's problem, then analytic work may become no more than an intellectual exercise, and the code of ethics a mere checklist that may be forgotten as long as it is not transgressed. Analytic practice and the ethical attitude are intimately bound together; each permeates the other and defines and gives value to the other. This reflects the analytic relationship itself in which, as Jung stressed, both partners make themselves available to, and are liable to be changed by, the encounter with the other. This is the essence both of the analytic work and of the ethical attitude. Thus, we may say that whether psychoanalyst or analytic psychologist, and whatever the diversity of our concepts and our terminology, our shared analytic attitude is in essence an ethical attitude, and therefore that our shared analytic and ethical attitude is embedded deeply within our humanness.

Note

This chapter was originally given as a paper at the conference 'Diversity and its Limits: New Directions in Analytical Psychology and Psychoanalysis', organised by the *Journal of Analytical Psychology* in Prague in May 2001. An earlier version appeared in the *Journal of Analytical Psychology*, vol. 46, no. 3, July 2001. I also discuss the issue in chapter 12 of *Jungian Thought in the Modern World* (Christopher and Solomon, 2000b)

References

Bauman, Z. (1993), *Postmodern Ethics*, Oxford: Blackwell.

Buber, M. (1937, 1958), *I and Thou*, 2nd edn, trans. R. G. Smith, Edinburgh: Clark.

Fordham, M. (1969, 1994), *Children as Individuals*, London: Free Association Books.

Gabbard, G. and Lester, E. (1995), *Boundaries and Boundary Violations in Psychoanalysis*, New York: Basic Books.

Hinshelwood, R. D. (1989), *A Dictionary of Kleinian Thought*, London: Free Association Books.

Jung, C. G. (1959, 1968), *Aion*, Collected Works of C.G.Jung, vol. 9(ii), London: Routledge.

—— (1964), *Civilisation in Transition*, Collected Works of C.G.Jung, vol. 10, London: Routledge.

Klein, M. (1935), 'A contribution to the psychogenesis of manic-depressive states', *International Journal of Psycho-Analysis*, vol.16, pp.145-74.

Klein, M. (1940), 'Mourning and its relation to manic-depressive states', *International Journal of Psycho-Analysis* vol. 21, pp.125-53.

Lambert, K. (1981), *Analysis, Repair and Individuation*, London: Academic Press.

Langs, R. (1974), *The Technique of Psychoanalytic Psychotherapy*, vol. 2, New York: Jason Aronson.

Samuels, A. (1989), *The Plural Psyche*, London: Routledge.

Schore, A. (1994), *Affect Regulation and the Origin of the Self*, Hillsdale, N.J.: Lawrence Earlbaum.

Solomon, H. M. (2000a), 'Recent developments in the neurosciences', in E. Christopher and H. M. Solomon (eds), *Jungian Thought in the Modern World*, London: Free Association Books, ch. 8.

Solomon, H. M. (2000b), 'The ethical self', in E. Christopher and H. M. Solomon (eds) *Jungian Thought in the Modern World*, London: Free Association Books, ch. 12.

Stein, M. (1995), *Jung on Evil*, London: Routledge.

Stern, D. (1985), *The Interpersonal World of the Infant*, New York: Basic Books.

Wiener, J. (2001), 'Confidentiality and paradox: the location of ethical space', *Journal of Analytical Psychology*, vol. 46, 3.

Winnicott, D. W. (1964), 'Further thoughts on babies as persons', in *The Child, the Family and the Outside World*, London: Penguin Books.

4
Ethics: the higher nature
and the ego ideal

Philip Hewitt

> It is easy to show that the ego ideal answers to everything that
> is expected of the higher nature of man... . Social feelings rest
> on identifications with other people, on the basis of having the
> same ego ideal
>
> Sigmund Freud, *The Ego and the Id*, p. 37

Introduction

It is central to this chapter, as much as to the whole book, that psychoanalysis and analytical psychology are characterised by the interdependence of an analyst's emotional disposition and the rules and customs which govern clinical practice. It is how they are affected in a relationship with the patient that becomes an object of much study. Whilst I am writing from a psychoanalytic perspective, it is to be accepted that in analytical psychology as well, the internal world of the therapist is as important as the patient's and is also given a parity of attention. Working analytically with the relationship between the analyst and patient *is the treatment*; it is not just the application of theoretical abstractions to psychological phenomena (Etchegoyan, 1991). In this sense the psychoanalytic model of the therapeutic relationship is ethically uncompromising. Thus the therapeutic professional relationship can have a transforming effect in a particular way, in that it is distinguished by being both professional and emotionally intimate at one and the same time.

Epistemological Considerations

At the level of the individual, the psychoanalytic approach enters into a 'conversation with history' through the process of free association and interpretation, as a patient increasingly discovers inner meanings and experience. The psychoanalytic attitude tries to fathom why we lead our lives in the way that we do. Though fraught with difficulties, the process potentiates new levels of truth and therefore a relationship to the world. For present purposes this chapter is concerned with the way in which Freud converted the positivistic notion of the 'higher nature' into the dynamic concept of ego ideal. According to Freud the ego ideal belongs in a social collective as well as individual aspiration. Psychoanalysis is an historiographic model which relies on a patient's innate capacity to learn from experience. At the heart of the difficulty is ensconced the finely balanced dynamic relationship between ideal and idealisation.

An ideal undergoes some incremental change to idealisation when it is adopted as a kind of 'boundary word'. This can happen without any intrinsic change within the object. Freud referred to the 'thaumaturgic use of words', or the miraculous transforming effect of words, in order to explain this phenomenon: that is to say, the magical way in which our words transform and enable expression of feeling. Yet words are also beguiling and 'words are used to spin meaning'. For example, the combination ego ideal or ideal ego rhetorically throws light on the meaning of the other. The former is an ideal projected on to the ego whilst the latter is the ego taken as an ideal in itself, as in 'self-object'.

In psychoanalysis the interdependence of words and feeling is indispensable to its main activity: interpretation. Without this vital relationship between word and feeling, interpretation may become meaningless and even cruel. Therefore the interdependence of words and feeling is central to the therapeutic intention of psychoanalysis. The assertion that ethics and psychoanalysis are interdependent is even more forcefully stated by Etchegoyan:

> Ethics are integrated into the scientific theory of psychoanalysis not as a simple moral aspiration but as a necessity of its praxis... . A failure of ethics in psychoanalysis leads inexorably to technical failure, as its basic principles, especially those that structure the setting, are founded upon ethical concepts of equality, respect and search for truth. (Etchegoyan, 1991)

Thereby it is possible for psychoanalytic exploration to take up the timeless human preoccupation of what is 'good' and what is 'bad' by constantly examining the psychodynamics of the inner world. Accordingly, in the psychoanalytic attitude there is a constant critique of mental state. It aspires to change through acceptance of pathology, through insight and ultimately through a transformation in the capacity for a better quality of object relations in a process of emotional growth. In this way psychoanalysis is both a depth psychological research method and a psychotherapeutic treatment of illness.

The difficulties inherent in the therapeutic relationship arise from the tension of holding at the same time feelings of togetherness and otherness. It is a constant decoding of inner and outer experience, between self and other, which 'grow and become elaborated in the course of development, a process that results in the progressive socialising of experience' (Stern, 1998, p.123). The difficulties this poses for clinical practice have to do with the analyst's struggle with his own humanity in relation to his patient. It is this which forms the basis of the shared psychoanalytic journey and of the ethical struggle embedded in it. The analyst is able to identify with his patient to the extent that he or she can draw on the universal formative, emotional and physical experiences of human development. The psychoanalytic endeavour is thereby complicated since it is concerned with exploring the unconscious almost exclusively through verbal communication of both psychological and physical phenomena from the very beginning of life.

Development of the Concept of Ego Ideal

Freud first mentioned the concept of ego ideal in his paper 'On Narcissism' (Freud, 1914, SE XIV). At this stage in the development of the concept, the ego ideal was conceived of as the wish to regain lost infantile narcissistic experience. However, it was distinguished from the critical functions equated with conscience. It had no self observing functions but it was very much an idealised relationship, taking the ego as object with its roots in idealised parental figures. Later, in 'Group Psychology and the Analysis of the Ego' (Freud, 1921, SE XIX), Freud used the term to include what is now referred to as superego, but it was not until his paper 'The Ego and the Id (Freud, 1923, SE XIX) that a clearer concept emerged, when he first referred to the superego but at this point denoted it as being synonymous with the ego ideal. In the 'New Introductory Lectures' (Freud, 1932, SE XXII) the superego was referred to as the 'vehicle of the ego ideal'. This usage was foreshadowed in 1924 in 'The Economic Problem of Masochism' (Freud, 1924, SE XIX), where Freud notes that 'the ego reacts with feeling anxiety … to the perception that it has not come up to the demands of its ideal, the superego'. The use of the term 'ideal' here refers to the ideal parents as embodied in the superego (Sandler, 1963). As the concept of the superego – dubbed 'heir to the Oedipus complex' because it is formed through an internalisation of the father figure – became more significant, the ego ideal was taken as being a part of the superego, and linked to primary narcissism.

Later, Melanie Klein's theory, paying greater attention to pre-Oedipal development, reduced the importance of the ego ideal in favour of a superego conceived of as harsh, relating it to the primary defence of the splitting of the good and bad breasts. Projective and introjective mechanisms, sadistic and masochistic processes and the developmental schema of the paranoid- schizoid and depressive positions form the core of Klein's object relations theory. In attempting to clarify the position of the ego ideal, Sandler, Holder and Meers (1963) wrote that it is 'impossible to distinguish sharply between the operation of the "ego ideal" and the superego system, although a number of features which are commonly referred to as constituents of the ego ideal are not fully included within the concept of the superego'. Later Chasseguet-Smirgel (1985) considered the ego ideal in terms of pathological idealisation in both creative arts and the perversions. She referred to the 'malady of the ideal', suggesting that in the relationship between the ego ideal and the perversion there lies 'a nucleus common to certain psychic disturbances, today increasingly widespread. The aim of this seems to be the obliteration of the painful limit imposed by reality on man's boundless wish to extend himself'. In so doing, defences such as denial and splitting are activated in order to deceive the self into perceiving a state of idealisation as a solution to an emotional and psychological difficulty. As theory has developed, the concept of ego ideal fits more easily into an internal object relations model, in so far as the ego ideal has a natural place in the internal world as much as negative objects do. Thus Meltzer distinguishes the ego ideal and superego functions, 'where these two terms need not be used synonymously, but can differentiate functions of the internal in a dialectic relationship'(Meltzer, 1981).

The Analyst as Patient

Much earlier, Sigmund Freud had written of a 'dialectic', of the untidy experience of 'abundant communications' from his internal world in the form of dreams which he construed as having important meaning. In 1895 Freud had a seminal dream which became known in the history of psychoanalysis, as 'The Dream of Irma's Injection', which he identified as the beginning of psycho-analysis. It had such importance for him that he wrote to Wilhelm Fliess in 1900 that there should be a plaque on the house where he had had the dream, recording this fact (Bonaparte, Freud and Kriss, 1954). This is recognised as a significant event in the story of psychoanalysis: Freud had reacted to this dream in a most extraordinary way, in that he made himself the object of his analytic method. By doing so he created the irreducible link between the therapist's own internal life, the way he understands the patient, and the way to understand psychoanalysis. He allowed himself to free associate, and in a daydream-like reverie he analysed his own thoughts and feelings, as well as conducting intense epistolary analysis enhanced by occasional discussions with his inner circle of colleagues.

Within a clinical paradigm, Freud's personal discovery of a symbolic congruity between his own mental life and that of his patient established the ethical core of psychoanalysis. Models for understanding this powerful sense of a dynamic human phenomenology reinforces the link between the patient and therapist. Freud's use of the expression 'abundant communications' (SE XIX, p.39) suggests an extraordinary personal experience. Out of this personal work, two theories of mind form a framework for Freudian theory. Firstly the topographical model of the conscious, pre-conscious and unconscious as specific areas of mental life. Secondly the structural model of the ego, id, superego and ego ideal, which enhanced understanding of the concepts of conscious and unconscious and gave credence to the way in which libidinal drives were more or less contained within these structures. Most dramatically of all, this embraced the importance of the relationship between the child and its mother and father as being an outcome determinant of human development. Following the publication of *The Interpretation of Dreams* (1905), Freud was praised and pilloried for being so willing to reveal himself to even a professional audience, let alone the world. Whatever the motivations for doing this, it also launched a fundamental ethical principle of psychoanalysis, already mentioned: that the personal awareness and the psychic health of the analyst are as much an object of study as those of the patient.

Personal analysis is an integral part of the structure of psychoanalysis and is indispensable to its understanding. Freud first took his own inner world as the object of study in the quest for 'higher nature' and thus set a standard. Nevertheless ideas do change. At the beginning of psychoanalysis, analyses tended to be shorter than they are today so that they may now last, in the formal sense, from a few years to many years, perhaps over a decade. The frequency of sessions, from one to five times per week over a long period of time, has become a crucial determinant of the fullness of an analysis, especially with regard to an analyst in training. When 'frequency of sessions' becomes an idealisation, other aspects, such as the quality of the analytic experience, may be obscured. Thus, in theoretical debates, distinctions are often sought between psychoanalysis and psychoanalytic psychotherapy according to frequency of sessions, usually to very little advantage, except perhaps to expose the dynamic between idealisation and denigration in professional relations.

The acknowledgement of idealisation exposes pervasive tendencies of the therapist/patient to idealise or denigrate experience in the service of self-protective hopefulness or through feelings of inadequacy. So within the psychoanalytic frame there is an in-built self-critical mechanism. The ideal of the psychoanalytic search for meaning and the need to push the limits demand constant vigilance. Thus truth in psychoanalysis is in and of itself a dynamic entity dissected by variables of consciousness and the unconscious. The effect of this is like light changing in a room. As it moves, so the objects in the room take on different colours and shapes, appear in the foreground or fade. In the same way, the ideal is that every thought or analytic interpretation has to be evaluated *in the light of* the patient's response at that time. This in turn is considered within the therapist's countertransference which in modern practice plays a central role in psychoanalysis and indeed is the single most important conceptual link to ethical practice.

The Analyst's Sacrifice of Personal Gratification

One example of the therapist who could not deal with the frustration and non-corporeal nature of the analytic experience is described by Akeret:

> My world is lopsided with prologues, bereft of endings. It is as if someone had ripped the last pages from all the novels in my library. Not simply my curiosity is frustrated, but my aesthetic. Yet my frustration runs far deeper than that. After devoting my entire adult life to helping people examine and change their lives, I don't really know if I have been effective. How can I possibly, if I don't know what becomes of my patients after their therapy comes to an end? In the final analysis I don't know if my life's work has been successful because there is no final analysis. (Akeret, 1995, p.16).

This clinical dissatisfaction led him to seek to trace some of his patients and interview them. The sadness of this journey is one in which the therapist finds how patients have moved on in their lives and essentially have no need of him in person. However, his need of their approbation is obvious. They acknowledge for the most part that he was helpful, but it is unlikely that they would say otherwise in these circumstances. Basically, Akeret has altered the clinical boundaries by satisfying a personal need for reassurance. His attempt at finding 'the final analysis' was as futile as hoping to find someone different upon looking in the mirror, and may have put in jeopardy thereby the experience of analysis that his patients had internalised.

Akeret articulates and acts out the fantasy from the frustration which many therapists have shared at one time or another. It is also interesting that Akeret's commentary on his own work is concerned with a notion of 'people getting better' as a result of therapy. On one level his desire to know whether this has happened is an ethical one of wanting to ascertain the efficacy of the therapy. The assumption that we must all be patients suggests that there is an acceptance that none of us is ideal. Akeret knows something about this from the start, which allows him to seek to realise his desire to follow up his own patients. We can only speculate on what part the original clinical relationships with his patients played in his life. One possibility is that the relationship became idealised, losing its contextual meaning as part of a life and not the whole life.

At the end of his book Akeret reveals his own discovery:

I find myself remembering something Fromm once said to me: 'I see each patient as the hero of an epic poem.' I have always liked that idea, but I don't believe I fully understood it until I took my journey. Until now I did not appreciate the sheer epic proportions of a person's life. The mere fact that in spite of all the obstacles they faced, Naomi and Charles and Seth and Mary and Sasha could make their ways from youth into middle age touches me deeply. I have returned from travels awed by the capacity of Man to survive; that, in itself, strikes me as heroic. And nothing that therapy can or cannot do compares with it. (Akeret, 1995)

Finally, he seems to realise that his contribution to the patient's life is slight in comparison to the patient's own capacity to survive. Movingly he comes to realise that it is the privileged nature of the relationship which allows a therapist to share in another human being's epic and possibly make two lives the more meaningful. Though Akeret's endeavour was an attempt to act out the search for his Ideal Self, he seems to end by realising that this is not bound up in the professional relationships which he had with his former patients but in fact something very personal to him, i.e. his own epic.

The Uses of the Ego Ideal

Earlier, I cited Freud's conception of the ego ideal as being interchangeable with the superego. One response to the superego is the unleashing of ambition as an identification with the superego or a part of it. In a case study, Meltzer draws attention to the emergence and important function of the ego ideal in mitigating the harsh superego. In the course of an analysis with a male patient with a 'highly narcissistic personality', he describes material in which the patient used projective identification in his relationships, which 'transformed the patient's mind into a perforated structure that could hold nothing'. He describes how 'under these circumstances not only do the internal objects lose their ego ideal functions but they also suffer a structural and ethical deterioration' (Meltzer, 1981). In other words, functioning without sufficient ego ideal capacity results in severe impairment in the capacity to relate compassionately to the self and others.

Sometimes it is the harsh superego which dominates a therapeutic session. As part of this and in contrast to collaboration, the patient complains that the therapist is 'too professional'. He says, 'You have always got an answer.' Receiving such a criticism for what I might consider to be 'good thinking' forces me to take stock of what I am doing and what the patient feels. This is a self-critical but ethical manoeuvre in which the patient seeks what he needs and I have to think about what I am giving. Although there is certainly little sense of collaboration but more of frustration or defensiveness, the patient feels free to make a direct critical response. Another familiar retort is that, 'You are always right. I have to be in the wrong. After all you are therapist!' In this way I have often felt the reproach from the other patient/therapist in the room for not providing the longed for 'special words', or because I am ending the session on time but at a difficult point. Being put in touch with these feelings at any time in a session becomes a de-idealising moment, through the revealing blunder, the cruel cut-off. Yet as I work on this experience, the search for another meaning has already begun. The way new knowledge or different meanings often only seep through to consciousness, again like the light changing in a room, constantly challenges our ideals and by doing so requires examination of the beckoning idealisations of the mythical past. Whereas having established the framework of therapeutic rectitude which attracts the patient's sarcasm ('You are always right!'), the therapist's blunders and conceits, when once revealed, may allow for another level of therapy to be activated. At this point the experience of a loss of the ego ideal, if it can be negotiated without too swingeing superego reproaches, may lead to further opening out of the analysis.

Conclusion

The title of this chapter conveys the paradox which lies at the heart of practice: that is, the striving towards some concept of 'higher nature' has more than the whiff of a contradiction in its own terms. Rather, like ideal ego or ego ideal, psychotherapeutic psychoanalysis or psychoanalytic psychotherapy actually have different meanings. Nevertheless each reveals the intention of the other. Ego without superego and id makes no more sense than Winnicott's famous phrase, 'There is no such thing as a baby', i.e. the baby only exists as part of a nursing couple. Thus object inter-relatedness is crucial to our sense of self. In addition to this, Freud posited a theory of social responsibility of which the ego ideal is a product and answers to everything that is expected to the higher nature of man (SE XIX, p. 37)... . The tension between the demands of conscience and the actual performances of the Ego is experienced as a sense of guilt. Social feelings rest on identifications with other people on the basis of having the same ego ideal.

Freud continues that the mastery of the Oedipus complex itself releases projections of religious and moral restraint, overcomes rivalry with the father and is a legacy to the younger generations. Thus the inspirational notion of higher nature, suggesting a higher mentality, has its origins in earliest desire and instinct, which pass through the modifying potentials of a familial and social life. So it is that the wariness with which we approach the ideal is due to its roots in the desire for narcissistic gratification and power over the object. However, even with these roots, and even though idealism may at times compromise sound judgement and disciplined analytic thought, revealing in its wake all too human caprice, nevertheless without it the vast majority who have entered into analysis would be not only the poorer but would have a very strange and atrophied experience of a therapeutic relationship.

References

Akeret, R. (1995), *The Man Who Loved a Polar Bear*, London: Penguin Books.

Bollas, C. and Sundelson, D. (1995), *The New Informants*, London: Karnac Books.

Bonaparte, M., Freud, A. and Kris, E. (1954), *The Origins of Psychoanalysis. Letters to Wilhelm Fliess*, New York: Basic Books.

Chasseguet-Smirgel, J. (1985), *The Ego Ideal*, London: Basic Books.

Etchegoyen, R. H. (1991), *The Fundamentals of Psychoanalytic Technique*, London: Karnac Books.

Freud, S. (1895), 'Project for a scientific psychology', Standard Edition of the Complete Psychological Works of Sigmund Freud, vol. I, London: The Hogarth Press.

—— (1900), *The Interpretation of Dreams*, SE vols IV & V.

—— (1914), 'On narcissism', SE vol. XIV.

—— (1921), 'Group psychology and the analysis of the ego', SE vol. XIX.

—— (1923), 'The ego and the id', SE vol. XIX.

—— (1924), 'The economic problem of masochism', SE vol. XIX.

—— (1932), 'The new introductory lectures', SE vol. XXII.

Meltzer, D. (1981), 'Ego ideal functions and the psychoanalytic process', in *Sincerity and Other Works*, London: Karnac Books, 1994.

Sandler, J., Holder, A. and Meers, D. (1963), ' The ego ideal and ideal self', *Psychoanalytic Study of the Child*, vol. 18.

Stern, D. N. (1998), *The Interpersonal World of the Infant*, London: Karnac Books.

5
Ethics in Practice

Fiona Palmer Barnes

> The individual has a right, indeed it is his duty, to set up and
> apply his own standard of value. In the last resort ethics
> are the concern of the individual ...
> (Jung 1928b, CW 10, para. 912)

In this chapter, I shall suggest that analytic organisations frequently do not distinguish between statements of ethical principles and codes of professional practice. This reflects a presumption within analytic organisations that their members share a common ethos, also a presupposition that the individual practitioner knows and understands the philosophical basis of their work. External pressure for regulation has exposed analysts to ethical scrutiny. It is now necessary for analysts to discuss their philosophical basis and ideals and identify a consensus within their organisations.

In the quote above, Jung is writing about the tension analysts experience between their personal ethical and value systems and the demands and pressures that analytic work places them in.

Jung acknowledged the complexity of contemplating ethical rules, in the Foreword to Neumann's *Depth Psychology and a New Ethic*:

> The formulation of ethical rules is not only difficult but actually impossible because one can hardly think of a single rule that would not have to be reversed under certain conditions. ...The solution, in my experience, is always individual and is only subjectively valid. Despite their subjective nature, they cannot very well be formulated except as collective concepts. But since these reflections constantly recur in practice – for the integration of unconscious contents continually poses such questions – it necessarily follows that, in spite of individual variation, they will exhibit certain regular features which make it seem possible to abstract a limited number of rules. I do not, myself, think that any of these rules are absolutely valid, for on occasion the opposite may be equally true. (Jung 1949, CW 18, para. 1413)

Analysts face a considerable dilemma. How do they define a common ethical attitude, whilst allowing for the individuality of practice? How also do they set out the necessary and sufficient rules to regulate their associations and profession, whilst respecting their differences and the working of the shadow within themselves, their own organisations and society at large? Some professional analytic societies would see their common ethical attitude as coming from their understanding of the analytic attitude of Freud or Jung as reflected in their writings. Other societies would believe that they have moved on from this position. They, too, would assume that there is a collective ethos within their societies. Each might cite the basic ideals of the other as their greatest fault: thus the shadow of the one is reflected in their attitude to the other. Such profound disagreements are the basis of schism. Schism and impasse have been part of the history of a number of analytic associations.

Analytic work involves an assumption of trust and a shared belief in ethical practice existing between analyst and analysand. Beyond that, it involves an assumption of trust and good faith between individual analysts and their organisation, and those organisations and society.

We come to a reflection upon a profound problem. Society, itself, is bound by collective values and reacts to collective concerns. Individuals also believe that society has a role of containing and being trustworthy, but are often disappointed. Society trusts and does not trust. In turn, analysts may believe that their professional organisations should contain and hold them. They, too, may be disappointed. At the level of individual analysis a fundamental experience of containing and holding can be created within the analytic process itself. Initially, however, patients do not trust; eventually they will learn to, through the experience of analysis. Not trusting may be part of their psychopathology and their reason for coming to analysis; much of the work of the analysis may be in exploring the implications of this. Yet it may be right not to trust – for example, if the frame of the analysis is not held by the analyst, resulting in a failure of ethical practice.

This is a position that analysts will do their work ethically without regulation, for the collective unconscious desires but does not trust in any ultimate ethical holding or containing order. The dual nature of these pressures demonstrates how important holding and containing are for the discovery of values, including moral values.

We are living through a time of great social change. In Europe the metaphysical underpinning of Christendom has diminished through a gradual process spread over generations. Jung reflected nineteenth-century philosophical thinking in stating, 'God is dead':

> when somebody hits on the singular idea that god is dead, or does not exist at all, the psychic God-image, which is a dynamic part of the psyche's structure, finds its way back into the subject and produces a condition of 'God-Almightiness', that is to say all those qualities which are peculiar to fools and madmen and therefore lead to catastrophe. (Jung 1945, CW 10, para. 437)

This statement has psychological significance both for analysts and for society. As analysts we need to be concerned not to act omnipotently and to consider the public's expectation for good professional practice. We do this best by considering the ethical principles on which we base our work. As members of wider society, we need to be concerned about 'God-Almightiness', the desire to know all, to regulate and tie down our way of working to a series of definable skills, forgetting the truly ethical and that which is undefinable, and the struggle involved to create something that can be understood and integrated.

In this chapter, I aim to address three things: the personal ethical position which underpins analytical work; the 'ethos' of analytic organisations and their frequent failure to distinguish between statements of ethical principles and codes of practice; and the professional and social pressure exerted upon analysts to practise ethically.

The Personal Ethical Position

When reflecting on an ethical attitude to analytic work, analysts assume that they have a certainty about the nature of their ethical attitude and its logical and philosophical basis. Deeper reflection may reveal uncertainty and confusion about how that attitude was conceived or became established.

Historically, ethics have been informed by universal principles. These often utilitarian principles include such concepts as maximising benefit, minimising harm, achieving the greatest good, acting justly, and respecting the individual and their rights. Misconceptions may have arisen in the very attempt to concretise, to put into language and write down, these ideas and ideals because they are, by their very nature, abstract. As a result these principles may not hold all the concepts necessary for the analyst's ethical thinking because utilitarian logic is not enough.

Jung, quoted above, proposes that an ethical analytic attitude involves both conscious and unconscious processes. The analyst is stretched and tested by personal experience, including the material that each patient brings to the analysis. A differentiation is made between ethics – as reflecting personal values – and morality, as reflecting societal values. Perhaps it is somewhere between personal and societal values that a new possibility lies, arising out of creative struggle.

An individual ethical attitude is formed, and informed, by a number of different elements: reflections of cultural and social views, parents' attitudes, and the effect of education. From 'The Spiritual Problem of Modern Man' (Jung 1928a, CW 10, para. 148-96) and 'The Fight with the Shadow' (Jung 1946, CW 10, para. 444-57) we can note how Jung recognises the role these elements play in the development of conscience. Freud, too, saw moral development as a natural outcome of a successful negotiation the Oedipal stage. This idea runs through his work from 1916 to 1923 and includes his work on the ego ideal. The superego, formed by an internalisation of the demands and prohibitions of the parents, including ideas of castration, is created out of a sense of guilt in relation to Oedipal desires and leads to an identification with the parents and their moral values (Freud, 1923).

Piaget saw child development taking place through play and the processes of assimilation and accommodation leading ultimately towards symbol formulation. There are similarities here to the spiral or oscillating development of Fordham's deintegration and reintegration model. Stern's (1995, p. 93) active observation and research has led him to suggest that the developmental picture is far more complex. He sees psychological development happening through a network of schemas culminating in the schema-of-being-with. This flexible system of psychological growth reminds us that Jung saw the psyche as a dynamic system. Winnicott's (1963) ideas on evolution of conscience also present a dynamic process: the evolution of conscience being fuelled by the child's inner processes as he experiences those around him. A sense of good and bad, right and wrong, develops in relation to the care received.

Solomon emphasises the role of individual experience, pointing out how developmental influences, infantile experience and, particularly, early perception play a part in the growth of an ethical attitude (Christopher and Solomon, 2000, p. 197). Solomon sees an ethical attitude as a developmental achievement.

Further to this argument, the analyst's ethical attitudes will have originally been reflected in their choice of analytic training and the particular ethos of that training. By ethos, here, I am referring to the organisation's 'distinctive character, spirit, and attitudes of a people, culture, era, etc. (*Collins English Dictionary*, p. 502). The internalisation of the analyst's experience of being treated ethically in their analysis will be at the heart of their professional analytic attitude and consequently how they treat their patients ethically.

Within the therapeutic alliance it is vital that there is a 'good enough' therapeutic match between patient and psychotherapist. Coltart understands the implications of this when she states: 'If you are prescribing psychotherapy on a long-term basis you are making a powerful statement: and your respect for the patient should entail that you give him your own insight into his need and his character' (Coltart, p. 134). In other words the analyst uses their ethical base to address the need of the patient. The analyst must be able to provide an adequate container for the patient to feel secure in the analysis, in order to be able to make the commitment, and begin the task of analysis. Counter-indications might include the possibility of not providing adequate analytic time, the analyst feeling unfit for the task because it is beyond their competence, or the psychopathology of the patient indicating that they are without adequate ego, too borderline or psychotic, and therefore not suitable for the rigours of analysis. If analysis has begun and it then transpires that the work is experienced by the analyst as particularly complex, the analyst will need to face their difficulties and seek from colleagues additional supervision and support. Referral to another practitioner may be considered in an extreme case.

One of the tasks of therapy is to explore the tensions within the working alliance. Redfearn refers to the bomb-like nature of the self and its creative and destructive aspects. He says that 'the building up of strength and capacity to the point where the union of the relevant opposites can be creatively contained may take a great deal of work' (Redfearn, 1992, p. 113). Both patient and practitioner can then feel that positive and ambivalent feelings have a place. The creative tension between analyst and patient helps both explore their own ideals and values. The very nature of the relationship between analyst and patient holds at its core the ethical and value foundation of the analyst's analytic attitude, which includes the basic assumption that the analytic work is for the patient's benefit.

Issues of power arise. The importance of the ethical attitude of the analyst is particularly significant in working transferentially with patients, that is, working with the projections of the patient onto the analyst. Working in the transference assumes that analysts understand their own part in the therapeutic dialogue with their patients and as far as possible do not become caught up in their own unconscious processes. It is for these reasons that professional concern is felt about analysts who are involved in working with patients where there seems to be a desire to seek power over the patient, or in cases where there seems to be a need for the analyst to feed their own narcissistic wounds, such that each reference to the analyst rewards their own inner world. It is essential that analysts are well enough analysed so that they may adequately detect the conscious and unconscious processes which come into play between them and their patients.

The individuation process – the key goal of analysis, by which the patient gains a sense of their individuality, distinct from others – by its very nature takes the analyst or analysand to the most primitive places within themselves. They may be drawn into areas which will challenge their moral or ethical viewpoint. These situations need to be understood symbolically in terms of transference if they are to be resolved and worked through. Jung sometimes considered such actions as being teleological, drawing the patient towards a 'new understanding'.

For example, the patient may believe that divorce is inexcusable. During the analysis the patient is drawn into a new sexual relationship, risking his well established family life and marriage. The analytic couple seeks to understand what is happening within the analytic sessions: e.g., Is he enacting an unconscious process arising from the analysis? He is presented with a real challenge to previously held beliefs. But what is its purpose? Here is an opportunity to think on many levels with the patient about his actions, including what arises from the transference.

In turn, analysts in training may be may challenged ethically by difficulties in finding patients who will commit themselves to an intensive therapy. Could it be that at such times the trainee's needs are at variance with those of the patient?

As Jung noted, principles which seem clear and right from the point of ego-consciousness can also serve some aspect of the shadow, in that they

> lose their power of conviction, and hence their applicability, when we consider the compensatory significance of the shadow in the light of ethical responsibility. (Jung 1949, CW 18, para. 1413)

These shadow aspects can be personal or collective. They can influence every aspect of the analysis with patients, as well as the analysts' actions in their analytic societies.

Ethical Principles and Codes of Practice in Analytic Organisations

The dictionary gives a definition of ethics as 'a code of behaviour considered correct, especially that of a particular profession' (Collins English Dictionary, 1979, p. 502). In this definition, behaviour and practice are not distinguished from the ideas or philosophical principles which underlie them. The lack of distinction between philosophical beliefs and behaviour required for professional conduct is also to be found in the Codes of Ethics of many organisations and is true of analytical organisations.

The absence of an agreed underlying set of beliefs is like constructing a house without first having laid foundations. The dictionary definition above presumes the prior existence of ideals which inform a code of behaviour. This sort of conflation of philosophical principles and codes of professional conduct is confusing and evident in many 'Codes of Ethics'. These 'Codes of Ethics' contain no statement of the ideals the organisation believes underlie its shared ethos of practice, which, upon scrutiny, reveal themselves to be practice codes. Codes of professional ethics and practice which began with a statement of principles would carry greater conviction. However, as many Codes do not explicitly state the ethical principles which members of analytic societies have collectively agreed to and assume underpin their code of practice, this may represent a profound gap in the collective thinking.

The same factors which form and inform our personal ethical attitudes also form, in a collective sense, the ethos of our analytic organisations. In other words the collective ethos of the analytic society is formed from the sum of the ethical attitudes of both its past and present members. An analytic society may believe that there is a presumed or assumed common governing 'ethos' informing each individual's practice in their organisation but this may not have been discussed. Indeed it may, in fact, only be an illusion of shared belief. Therefore, as well as each individual analyst needing to decide on the principles which inform their work, there is a collective need to define the ethical principles informing the forms of practice that the organisation feels are acceptable, before relating these principles to practice through practice codes.

Organisations could also usefully draw distinctions between the rules laid down in their practice codes and issues which might challenge the ethical principals of and raise ethical concerns for their members. The general acceptance by members of the rules of the organisation does not remove the necessity for members individually to make judgements about their own particular situations. Acceptance of general ethical principles does not destroy ethical autonomy. It may, however, affect the way that members prioritise the ethical demands or creatively invent ways of giving attention to their concerns.

Organisations also experience conscious and unconscious collusive interactions. This may lead to impasse. If the organisation can move through the processes of 'deintegration' – in Fordham's terms, a loosening of previously held principles and alliances – this may allow a 'reintegration', a reforming, to take place. Problems will then be understood or resolved. A flexible ethos within the organisation may withstand this process. However, the terror arising from the impasse within the organisation may causes it to 'disintegrate' and break apart when division and a schizoid process occurs (Fordham, 1985). This kind of difficulty has arisen in a number of psychotherapy organisations and splits have resulted.

At every level, those responsible within the organisation need to keep in mind the importance of these splitting processes, which can profoundly affect the organisation's ethos and may challenge the belief system of analysts, thus undermining their professional identity.

Institutions can have difficulties in managing their interaction with the external world. They may develop defences in order to deal with the anxiety-provoking content of a perceived threat or the difficulties in collaborating to accomplish a common task. Developing the capacity to recognise how the unconscious mind of the collective group is exhibited in terms of content and dynamics can be containing in this situation.

According to Menzies Lyth (Menzies Lyth, 1989) the solution lies in a knowledge of the past, in the developmental history of the organisation and in the creation of its values. If it is flexible it will have a capacity to grow and create new positions. This parallels Jung's idea of the importance of the individual having a capacity to develop a 'new attitude' if the individual is to progress. Menzies Lyth says that within psychotherapy organisations practitioners need to recognise and honour the loss of that which was, and to acknowledge the possibilities for the future while creating a new 'good enough' position from which to function until the next change is necessary. Therefore, we can say that the value base of analytic and psychotherapy organisations and the strength of the common ethos are reflected in their ability to contain external and internal difficulties. Creatively using these difficulties frees those who may be patients, candidates in training, and analysts, from becoming embroiled in and negatively affected by the processes of the organisation.

Within analytic organisations, thinking about the influence of the organisation's ethos on practitioners will interact in the individual practitioners' thinking about their own principles and values. Making provision for this creative process to take place in organisations may lead to a process of 'deintegration' in order for reintegration to take place (Fordham, 1985). Without the possibility of discussion and formative process, disintegration can be the outcome.

The Profession and Society

A further influence which creates tension is society's emphasis on the importance of the individual. There is also a countervailing desire to erase differences. This can be seen, for example, in the tension arising between human rights legislation and professional regulation. Both poles of this societal concern force professions to be increasingly specific about defining what they offer as a service, while also deciding what constitutes good practice. This creates a pressure for codification, which might determine, in codes of practice and 'good practice' statements, how analysis 'should' be done, or define precisely how analysis is practised, carving external rules in tablets of stone.

We may welcome regulation and codification when it helps to identify poor practice and deals with aberrant practitioners. However, regulation may also lead to an inappropriate externalisation of responsibility, ethical abdication and a fixed, rigid way of practising. The analyst may be drawn to consider external pressures rather than observe their own practice. If so they lose their necessary sense of reverie and working with inner process and therefore their ability to reflect in the analytic session. Analysts may feel that they are compelled to stand outside the 'alchemical bath' containing the analytic work; this may be detrimental to their work as external demands for self-surveillance bring with them understandable anxiety.

Another expression of external pressure on the profession may be found in the increasing number of people wishing to train as counsellors, psychotherapists and analysts. Clearly there is a reflection here of the 'God-Almightiness' of a priesthood, both from the individuals who train and receive the projection of society that they hold the answers, but also from patients who too readily have the desire to be cured and see their therapist as their saviour. Guggenbuhl-Craig reacted to this split, commenting:

A crucial position in the model of the psychotherapist is taken by a figure which we might term the maker of consciousness or the bringer of the light. But professional images always have a dark aspect which represents the opposite of the bright ideal. The analyst's professional shadow contains not only the charlatan and the false prophet, but also the counterpole to the bringer of the light, a figure who lives completely in the unconscious and strives for the opposite of the analyst's conscious goals. We have a paradoxical situation in which the analyst is more threatened by the unconscious that is the non-analyst. (Guggenbuhl-Craig, 1971, p.28)

So we return to the shadow. A shadow aspect of society is that counsellors, therapists and analysts may do the task or carry out the function of holding the shadow for the collective. Those who work in the helping professions, as therapists and analysts, are prized, praised, and berated almost in the same breath.

Conclusion

Our ethical attitudes are multiformed and multi-faceted. They form through the conscious and unconscious influences of culture and society and create an ethos of analytic societies and the analysts within them. As individuals, we may know little about the nature of our own ethical attitude, and may discuss it even less. However, it helps to form and affects the ethos of our professional organisations. It is important to spend time thinking about ethical principles and examining carefully the areas of difference between ourselves and our colleagues within our own organisation and within the profession. It is also important to honour our similarities and establish our common ethos. This could be done, for example, by discussing issues such as race, gender or sexual orientation, where there will be a variety of views and feelings, which will create the 'space' to work out our own ethical attitude as well as helping to form a common ethos with our colleagues. Without our knowing what we believe in, an illusory world exists. Ethical illusions can mask a profound uncertainty that will be reflected in our work with patients, within our analytic organisations and with one another.

References

Christopher, E. and McFarland Solomon, H. (2000) (eds), *Jungian Thought in the Modern World*, London: Free Association Books.

Collins English Dictionary (1979), London and Glasgow: Collins.

Coltart, N. (1987), 'Diagnosis and assessment for suitability for psycho-analytical psychotherapy', *British Journal of Psychotherapy, vol. 4 (2)*.

Fordham, M. (1985), *Explorations into the Self*, London: Academic Press.

Freud, S. (1923), *The Ego and the Id*, Standard Edition, vol. XIX.

Guggenbuhl-Craig, A. (1971), *Power in the Helping Professions*, Zurich: Spring.

Jung, C.G. (1928a), 'The spiritual problem of modern man', Collected Works of C.G. Jung, vol. 10, *Civilization in Transition*, London and Princeton: Routledge and Princeton University Press.

Jung, C.G. (1928b), 'The Swiss line in the European spectrum', Collected Works of C.G. Jung, vol. 10, *Civilization in Transition*, London and Princeton: Routledge and Princeton University Press.

Jung, C.G. (1945), 'After the catastrophe', Collected Works of C.G. Jung, vol. 10, *Civilization in Transition*, London and Princeton: Routledge and Princeton University Press.

Jung, C.G. (1946), 'The fight with the shadow', Collected Works of C.G. Jung, vol. 10, *Civilization in Transition*, London and Princeton: Routledge and Princeton University Press.

Jung, C.G. (1949), 'Foreword to Neumann: *Depth Psychology and a New Ethic*', Collected Works of C.G. Jung, vol. 18, *The Symbolic Life*, London and Princeton: Routledge and Princeton University Press.

Menzies Lyth, I. (1986), 'The dynamics of the social. A psychoanalytic perspective on social institutions', Freud Memorial Lecture. In collected papers, I. Menzies Lyth: *The Dynamics of the Social*. London: Free Association Books.

Redfearn, J. (1992), The Exploding Self, Willmette, IL: Chiron Publications.

Stern, D. (1995), *The Motherhood Constellation*, New York: Basis Books.

Winnicott, D.W. (1963), 'Morals and education', in D.W. Winnicott, collected papers: *The Maturational Processes and the Facilitating Environment*, London: Hogarth.

Section III
In the Consulting Room

6
Ethical Pressures on the Analytic Alliance

Christopher MacKenna

A patient and an analyst decide to work together. Their decision to begin analysis – to form an analytic alliance – will be, at least in part, a highly conscious decision. We might picture the partners in this enterprise as two circles, resting side by side – but this picture is too simple. Although each of the partners in the analytic couple looks discrete, they are open to each other at unconscious levels. As early as 1915, Freud commented that 'It is a very remarkable thing that the *Ucs.* of one human being can react upon that of another, without passing through the *Cs.*' (Freud, 1915, SE XIV, p. 194)

We need to extend the picture of the analytic relationship by adding a 'field' around each circle, so that the two 'fields' overlap. We now have a picture of two centres of ego consciousness existing in two interpenetrating and richly populated psychic worlds. Patient and analyst may consciously aspire to work in an analytic way – in Bion's sense, to form a work group – but myriad less conscious complexes and archetypal forces are involved in, and stirred by, their decision. (There seems to be a near-universal tendency to experience our primary relationships in certain almost stereotypical ways which give rise, for example, to characteristic oedipal fantasies and conflicts. Bion's Basic Assumptions are also examples of the way in which unconscious forces tend to pattern individual and group perceptions. Jung called these tendencies 'archetypal', because they seem to be inborn.)

According to the *Concise Oxford Dictionary* (9th edition, 1995), alliances are not confined to relations between whole objects, like states and persons, but can be affinities of nature or quality. Because unconscious contents have a life of their own there is an automatic tendency for alliances to be struck up between my personal complexes and those of my patient, and archetypal tendencies will also try to structure our relationship along stereotypical lines: for example, mother / baby, victim / aggressor, or the messianic hope of the lost soul seeking a saviour.

Processes of Identification: unconscious identity, projective identification and participation mystique

Such processes are inevitable. The work of analysis could not proceed without them but, as they happen, my autonomous ego consciousness succumbs to heteronomous forces. Jung called this state of unconscious identity (we would now call it a process of unconscious identification), in which there is whole or partial non-differentiation between subject and object, *participation mystique*, a term he borrowed from the anthropologist Lévy-Bruhl. He says:

> When there is no consciousness of difference between subject and object, an unconscious identity prevails. The unconscious is then projected into the object, and the object is introjected into the subject, becoming part of his psychology. (Jung, 1931, CW 13, para. 66)

Jung suggests that 'by understanding the unconscious we free ourselves from its domination' (Jung, 1931, CW 13, para. 64). But it is only as we *emerge* from these unconscious states that we begin to regain a state of mind in which conscious reflection becomes possible. While we are in these unconscious states, all manner of things can happen, hence the importance of analytic technique: it is there to help stop us acting-in to unconscious processes. Odysseus-like, we sometimes need to be lashed to the mast of analytic discipline if we are to avoid shipwreck (Homer, 1970, pp. 190ff).

We might call this process the 'benign cycle' of the analytic alliance (Little, 1986, p.49). Out of the conscious decision to work together come states of unconscious identification. Through unconscious identification the analyst gains knowledge of the patient's inner world; but this knowledge only becomes consciously available as the analyst 'comes to' himself or herself and regains the psychic and emotional autonomy necessary for thought and introspection. Useful interpretations flow from this dark, experiential knowledge.

But what happens if something goes wrong with this process? If, instead of unconscious identification leading to conscious insight, an unconscious complex in me, acting in concert with an equally unconscious complex in my patient, somehow takes charge, forming a new and temporary centre of consciousness? My patient and I are now 'out of our minds'. But because we are of one mind, and this mind now conditions the whole way in which we see and experience our relationship, we are capable of almost any folly – and the problem can be driven by the analyst.

Wynne Godfrey describes such a folie in his article 'Saving Masud Khan'. His painful conclusion was:

> It is now perfectly clear to me that, after seeing Khan daily for several years, and after untold expense and travail, no therapy whatever had taken place. What a trap! He had reproduced and re-enacted every major traumatic component of my childhood and adolescence. The primal union had been ruptured. The confidences which he reposed in me had made me special, just as my mother's had; he had the same need as she to perform and be performed for. And the same destructive gymnastics that I had once had to negotiate, given the deep attachment I had to my deteriorating father, were played out all over again. For the second time I was overcome by a compulsion to attempt the transformation of a drunken, anti-semitic, collapsing wreckage into a living armature on which to build myself. HE COULD NOT JUSTIFY HIMSELF SO I WAS COMPELLED TO SAVE HIM. (Godfrey, 2001)

Had things gone differently, had the benign cycle of the analytic alliance been in operation, Khan and Godfrey might have become conscious of many difficult truths about themselves, for as Jung says:

> the doctor is as much 'in the analysis' as the patient. He is equally a part of the psychic process of transformation. Indeed, to the extent that the doctor shows himself impervious to this influence, he forfeits (therapeutic) influence over the patient... (Jung, 1929, CW 16, para.166)

Situations like this, in which the analytic alliance comes under pressure from unconscious forces, are fertile ground for ethical transgression.

Another type of internal pressure on the analytic alliance occurs when analyst and patient are captivated by an archetypal idea: perhaps the longing either to be, or to find, the Great Mother, the One who can satisfy perfectly our hunger and our need.

In Thrall of the Archetype

Case 1

A patient came to me having had a homosexual relationship with her previous analyst.

My patient had been a premature baby, and the form of the transference suggests that she had suffered an enormous deficit in her early maternal experience. The first years of our work were dominated by her desperate and almost overwhelming feelings of emotional hunger and need. I imagine that this need must have been well to the fore in her previous analysis because her therapist suggested – according to my patient's account – that she should offer my patient her breast. This was the beginning of what became, for several years, a fully-fledged, passionate sexual relationship.

My patient does not believe that the offer of the breast was a deliberate ploy to seduce her – although she had intimated to her analyst that she had once experienced lesbian fantasies about a close friend; and her analyst had said something like, 'We've all done that.' She did feel, though, and with profound resentment, that her analyst had been deeply unconscious of some of her own needs and desires. It seems that her analyst, possibly driven almost to distraction by my patient's overwhelming hunger and need for reassurance, came to believe that she could be a physical substitute for the quality of early mothering my patient believed herself never to have had. Mesmerised by the archetype of the Great Mother (the idea that she could provide what no one else could), she was unconscious of her own longing for adult sexual intimacy with a woman.

The upshot – which began with bliss – ended in total devastation: a nightmare world in which there was no inside or outside; and no meaning, because the symbolic capacity had been collapsed into the literal and the physical.

Intrusion of the Projected Third

Such cases illustrate ways in which the analytic alliance can be subverted by unconscious forces emanating from transference and countertransference. But what happens if a third party comes on the scene?

The intrusion of a third is likely to put pressure on the analytic couple, with the analyst feeling that he or she is caught in a conflict of interest between her ethical responsibility to her patient, and wider ethical responsibilities – perhaps to the profession, or to the general public. This may be the case, but sometimes the appearance of a third person is really an expression of unrecognised elements in the transference.

Case 2

I end a session with a female patient. Two hours later there is an unexpected knock on the door and I open it to find myself confronted by a strange man who announces that he is my patient's husband. His wife has discovered she has lost her scarf and thinks she has left it in my consulting room. She has asked him to fetch it because she is reluctant to call other than at her appointment times.

I am completely dumbfounded and, without thinking – always a dangerous sign – usher him into my room where we both look for the scarf, which isn't there. He apologises and goes away. Only then do I begin to realise that I do not even know if he was my patient's husband. At the very least I have betrayed my patient's confidence: effectively admitting, to a total stranger, that she is my patient.

Fortunately, it turns out that the man was my patient's husband. But what was going on? I had thought, from what my patient had previously told me, that her husband was hostile to her analysis. What I only began to realise, after this incident, was that my patient's husband was carrying *her* negative transference. I think my failure to pick up, and interpret, the negative transference reinforced her tendency to experience herself as caught between two 'dinosaurs' (originally mother and father) who had totally different attitudes to life. Unable to own the opposites within herself (unable, actually, to recognise the part of her which was very frightened by her analysis), she had unconsciously staged a meeting of the 'dinosaurs' in the hope that we would fight it out between us. She could then identify with the winner – without having to acknowledge, and wrestle with, her own ambivalence.

In this case, although the pressure on the analytic alliance appeared to come from without, it actually came from within. By identifying with my patient in her desire to be seen as a good girl, totally in favour of her therapy, I had caused an escalation in her disturbance. It was only when her split-off resistance appeared on my front door step, in the guise of her husband, that I realised my mistake.

Pressure on the analytic alliance which seems to come from outside the consulting room may, in fact, be an externalisation of unconscious forces emanating from within the transference. On the other hand, there are times when genuinely external pressures impinge upon the analytic alliance.

The Changing Social Climate

Considerable pressure comes from the changing climate of opinion in which we live and work. Changes in public opinion may compel us to reconsider some of the fundamental attitudes which have informed our practice. We may not always welcome these impingements, just as we may resist new insights in therapy because they threaten to destabilise the conscious balance of our lives. And yet, with time, we may come to welcome the new insights for the freedom which they bring. In the remainder of this chapter, I will consider three currently vexed questions: consent to treatment, consent to publish case material, and the psychotherapist's duty to protect against harm, all areas in which legal changes are threatening to force change in psychotherapeutic practice.

Consent to Treatment
As a general therapeutic rule we do not do things to our patients without their consent. Respect for our patient's autonomy is one of the factors – in the title of Hinshelwood's book (1997) – which distinguishes therapy from coercion. The Code of Ethics of the British Association of Psychotherapists (BAP) states that:

> Members will act always in the best interests of the patient, such that: the patient or whoever holds legal responsibility understands and agrees to the nature of the treatment, both initially and as it progresses.

Traditionally, there has been a difference between the way consent has been understood in English law, and the doctrine of 'informed consent' developed in the United States. Holmes and Lindley state that, in English law:

> consent is taken to be genuine provided the practitioner has explained in broad terms the nature of the procedure which is intended ... . It is only if the consent is obtained by *fraud* or *misrepresentation* of the *nature* of what is to be done that it can be said that an apparent consent is not true consent.
>
> If a doctor explains in broad terms the nature of a procedure, but fails to spell out adequately the attendant risks and the likely benefits of alternative treatments, in English law she is, at most, guilty of the tort of negligence. (Holmes and Lindley, 1989, p.152)

At first glance, this may appear unexceptional. It seems reasonable that we should explain, at least in broad terms, the nature of the procedure which is intended; and right that it should only be if the consent is obtained by fraud or misrepresentation of the nature of what is to be done that it can be said that an apparent consent is not true consent. However, Holmes and Lindley are dissatisfied with this. They suggest that:

> there is a big difference between what is genuine (consent) in the English (legal) sense, and what an ordinary citizen would call 'genuine informed consent'.

This difference reflects the changed climate of opinion in which we practise. English law recalls the day when people were prepared to take the specialist's word for it. Nowadays people tend to be less accepting of experts and their opinions.
    Holmes and Lindley are influenced by this shift in the climate of public opinion when they say:

If we leave out the practical legal difficulties of enforcement, the American conception (of informed consent) has much to commend it from a moral perspective which takes autonomy seriously. (Holmes and Lindley, 1989, p. 153)

These days the client or customer does not want to be treated like a child: he wants to know what he is buying. We live at a time when power, in the sense of the ability to define expectations, is moving away from professional providers towards the consumer.

American law holds that four ingredients are necessary for informed consent (Holmes and Lindley, 1989, p.154):

1. Understanding the nature of the treatment.
2. Information relevant to making the decision (e.g., fees, holidays, missed sessions, objectives, length of treatment, chances of success, etc.).
3. Risks attendant on the treatment.
4. Alternative treatment possibilities.

Some of these ingredients, such as agreeing fees, present no problem; indeed, they are part and parcel of the analyst's basic 'handling' of the patient, which is important for the development of a benign analytic alliance.

The question of alternative treatment possibilities is a little more compli- cated. When seeing prospective patients we will certainly be asking ourselves whether analysis will be appropriate for them. If we do not think it is, we may well suggest other forms of treatment. But informed consent goes further than this: it asks us to discuss alternative treatment possibilities as a *prelude* to the patient's decision about whether or not to enter therapy with us. Given the number and variety of therapies available this could be difficult and bewildering for the patient.

The other ingredients of informed consent – we are looking at them from an ethical point of view – are even more problematical when applied to analysis. How possible is it to explain the nature of analysis without creating unhelpful expectations? With what precision can we know, prior to starting work, what risks will be attendant on the treatment of this particular patient? Can we predict the outcome of analysis without saddling our patient with the burden of our optimism or pessimism? Indeed, can we predict it at all? Additional complica- tions stem from the fact that, at the time of the assessment interview, the applicant's need and disturbance may well undermine his capacity for rational decision making. There may be resistance to the idea of analysis, or to the thought that analysis has limitations.

Taking these difficulties into account, it begins to appear that informed consent – as applied to analysis – is almost impossible. The ethical dilemma, put in a nutshell, is that every time we take a patient into analysis we are asking them to consent to a process which they cannot adequately comprehend and about which we cannot fully apprehend the outcome.

Of course, we can ignore these problems. We can say that, if the patient has got a general idea of what analysis is about, then they will find out more as they go along. But if we argue like this we are in danger of regressing – in ethical terms – to the principle of paternalism: daddy knows best. Where does this leave our general therapeutic rule, that we do not do things to our patients without their consent? Even Hinshelwood, in his deeply thoughtful discussion of these issues, concludes that: 'Something like a paternalistic act is involved in psychoanalysis', though he qualifies this by maintaining that: 'It is an act of a special kind ... an "act" of learning, rather than doing' (Hinshelwood, 1997, p. 107).

One way round this problem is to deny that psychotherapy is a treatment. If this is true, then it will greatly modify the form of consent appropriate to it. We can simply maintain that consent, as understood in the medico-legal world, is irrelevant to us. For example, Gordon argues that:

While it is reasonable to expect a solicitor to know and understand the basic laws of the land, and a doctor to be able to recognise and offer appropriate treatment for common ailments and illnesses, psychotherapy is nothing of this kind. We are not in the business of diagnosis or treatment and, because the medical or objective model of the person does not apply to what we do, the objective model of recourse does not seem relevant either. *We are engaged in a particular type of conversation with those we see in a mutual attempt to understand their difficulties in living their lives.* (Gordon, 1999, p. 35, my italics)

This line of approach may relieve our ethical anxieties about consent, but it does so at the expense of the idea that we are offering some form of treatment. I remember once hearing an eminent analyst say, 'I thought "curing" was something they did to bacon!' The remark was greeted with considerable warmth and applause in an analytical meeting. But to me it sounded, then, and still sounds, defensive – What was being dismissed? I wonder how many members of the general public would be content with the idea that we are not in the business of treatment and cure? Or, how many of our patients would be prepared to pay for therapy if they did not have the hope that, by engaging in the strange kind of conversation we offer, it will somehow make them 'better'?

If popular opinion is unwilling to let us withdraw from the language of treatment and cure, could it be that popular opinion is more in touch than we are with the medical and religious roots – with their language of healing and transformation – from which analysis sprang? Perhaps – but, if so, what about the problem of consent?

I think there is a circle here which cannot be squared in the terms in which the problem is being put. It is not just that the analyst knows what he or she is offering and the patient does not – and cannot, until they have experienced it. Rather, it is, I believe, that neither patient nor analyst quite knows what they are letting themselves in for when they agree to work together. Consent needs to be as informed as it can be but there are no guarantees. The crucial ingredient is trust. At first, the patient may put their trust in the analyst (and be full of mistrust, too). The analyst, though, is likely to be putting their trust in the process. As Symington says:

> Belief in the psychoanalytical process seems to be the essential ingredient for both parties. However, it seems that it may be the special role of the analyst to carry this belief for the patient as well as for himself, especially early on in the treatment. (Symington, 1986a, p. 268)

In the film *Shakespeare in Love* the harassed theatre manager says, in moments of crisis, when disaster seems to be staring him in the face, 'Something will turn up. It always does.' For me, this bears more than a passing resemblance to the act of faith of a religious believer. We know that nothing may turn up and, if it does not, we cannot make it happen. But the analytic process, once constellated, has a remarkable way of gathering momentum so that even external events – completely outside our and our patient's control – are sometimes drawn into the equation.

So, problematical as the demand for informed consent may be, I am grateful for it. Its practical impossibility exposes the demands of rationalism and the paternalism implicit in the English legal notion of consent and brings out the fact that entry into analysis is – ultimately – an act of faith in a transcendental realm – call it God, or the unconscious, as you please. (1)

Consent to publication
Closely related to the question of consent to treatment is the thorny problem of consent to publication, which is also being influenced by changes in public opinion. Again, I see this as a potentially benign – if unwelcome – pressure on the analytic alliance.

In the preface to the first edition of their *Studies on Hysteria*, Breuer and Freud felt it necessary to write:

> We have appended ... a series of case histories, the selection of which could not unfortunately be determined on purely scientific grounds. Our experience is derived from private practice in an educated and literate social class, and the subject matter with which we deal often touches upon our patients' most intimate lives and histories. It would be a grave breach of confidence to publish material of this kind, with the risk of the patients being recognised and their acquaintances becoming informed of facts which were confided only to the physician. It has therefore been impossible for us to make use of some of the most instructive and convincing of our observations. (Breuer and Freud, 1895, SE II, p. xxix)

Scholarly study has revealed some of the strategies to which Freud, Klein, Jung and most other analysts have resorted in their attempts to circumvent this problem.

Bion introduced a new perspective when he denied not just the possibility but also the value of supposedly factual case reporting. In the introduction to *Second Thoughts*, he says:

I do not regard any narrative purporting to be a reported fact, either of what the patient said or of what I said, as worth consideration as a 'factual account' of what happened. ... The accounts of cases in this book, though sincerely supposed by me at the time to be factually correct (I exclude alterations made and acknowledged on account of discretion), should now be regarded as verbal formulations of sensory images constructed to communicate in one form what is probably communicated in another. (Bion, 1984, pp.1ff)

The problem we face is this. At the time when Breuer and Freud were writing, the felt ethical problem was that of maintaining the anonymity of the patient. Nowadays, I think, the ethical climate has changed, and – in addition to the problem of anonymity – the question which now seems to be forming is: Is it legitimate to 'use' (the word is deliberately ambiguous) a patient's material, in any form, without their explicit knowledge and consent? In other words, who owns the material? Who possesses the right to publish or to veto the publication of the 'verbal formulations of sensory images' which first emerged in the intersubjective field of the analytic alliance?

The question is sharpened by the fact that publication, on which an analyst's professional advancement in some measure depends, almost demands the use of case material. In his paper 'Some Pressures on the Analyst for Physical Contact During the Re-living of an Early Trauma', Casement illustrates the way this pressure can interfere with the analytic alliance. In a Friday session he had agreed, under certain circumstances, to the idea of holding a patient's hand. However, as he says:

My offer had been partly motivated by my fear of losing this patient, which was especially threatening to me just then as I was about to present a paper on this patient to our Society. (Casement, 1982, p. 280)

In the event, Casement decided that it would not be an appropriate action to hold the patient's hand.

The analyst can find herself caught in a conflict of interest between her need for case material and her responsibility, to the patient, not to allow ulterior concerns to contaminate the transference. From the ethical point of view, then, who 'owns' the case material? Whose needs, or feelings, should control its publication? My suggestion is that the material is 'owned' neither by patient nor analyst.

In his book, *The Analytic Experience*, Symington has written about psychoanalysis as a shared quest for truth, a truth which is not possessed by patient or analyst, but exists *in between* the people seeking it: 'Truth in psychoanalysis emerges between the analyst and the patient' (Symington, 1986b, p. 19). The moment of truth, that mysterious revelatory moment when the penny drops and meaning dawns, belongs neither to patient nor to analyst. Rather, it flows from the intersubjective field which lies between them and enfolds them.

In an ideal world, I suggest that we should wait before writing a particular case study, until the patient is ready to read an account of it which includes a reasonably uncensored description of the therapist's or analyst's countertransference reactions.

When I suggest this approach in analytic meetings, the objection is usually made that it would be intolerably disturbing for the patient. I think that this objection can be overstated, although I do fully accept that the analysis would have had to have progressed to the point where anger can be expressed directly and issues such as envy openly discussed. Again, it is Symington who asks the question: 'Is it really necessary to hide oneself so carefully?' (Symington, 1986b, p.328). And he quotes Searles' article, 'The Patient as Therapist to his Analyst', in which Searles maintains that:

> innate among man's most powerful strivings towards his fellow men, beginning in the earliest years and even earliest months of life, is an essentially psychotherapeutic striving ... *the patient is ill because, and to the degree that*, his own psychotherapeutic strivings have been ... frustrated ... . (Symington, 1986b, pp. 329ff)

Symington adds:

> The patient needs to cure the analyst of a character defect so that the analyst can analyse some element that has eluded effective interpretation until that time. (Symington, 1986b, p. 330)

This is true, but it underplays the altruistic element in the patient's desire to contribute something uniquely meaningful to the analyst. On the other hand, the analyst will have to remain mindful of the danger inherent in this view, as it could be an exploitation of the patient's genuine altruistic impulses towards the analyst.

It has been my experience that introducing, at an appropriate moment, the thought of writing about a particular aspect of our shared endeavour, and the discussion and perhaps the modification of my thoughts in the light of my patient's comments, not only produces richer case material but can also be mutually enlightening; a potent means both of realising the shared nature of our work and, also, of correcting some of my own still unconscious assumptions. Of course, it is not always possible to manage things this way. Probably, we will always have to resort to various strategies in publishing patient material. But I believe that where this path is possible, there is the least danger of exploiting the patient for our own ends.

Less benign social pressures on the analytic alliance
Perhaps the most frightening group of pressures on the analytic alliance are those which stem from the 'duty to protect against harm'; and the threat that we may one day find either ourselves, or our case notes, subpoenaed by the court.

The British Association of Psychotherapists' Code of Ethics states that:

Members will act always in the best interests of the patient, such that: all knowledge of the patient is treated confidentially and not passed on without the patient's prior consent, unless the safety of the patient or others is threatened; if the safety of the patient or others is threatened, a professional practitioner or a relative or a significant other person, will be contacted.

By incorporating the duty to protect against harm principle into its Code of Ethics the BAP has followed the example of many American states since the Tarasoff Case, which involved the successful prosecution of an analyst whose patient had carried out a murder threat, originally voiced during analysis. At that time, the Supreme Court of California ruled that 'Protective privilege ends where public peril begins' (Holmes and Lindley, 1989, p. 180). But if we have an equal, sometimes even a greater responsibility towards the public good than to our patient, does this make us the servant of two masters – torn between loyalty to our patient and duty to the state? If it does, it constitutes a huge pressure on the analytic alliance.

Bollas and Sundelson (1995) dispute the inclusion of the 'duty to protect against harm' clause in analysts' codes of ethics, and maintain the principle of absolute confidentiality between patient and analyst. They accept the possibility of a shared code of confidentiality between practitioners – for example, in admitting a suicidal patient to hospital – but are adamant that no one can tell, with confidence, whether a disturbed patient will act upon his fantasies, or not. They remind us that the only known factor which indicates whether a person will cause harm to another is a history of such harming.

Perhaps the most eloquent statement of the case for absolute confidentiality was given by Hayman in her account of her refusal to testify in court, on the grounds that to break confidentiality would be to destroy the very condition which is necessary for therapy to succeed. In the witness box, she refused the judge's suggestion that she might change her mind if her patient was to give permission for her to testify, because that permission might only be the expression of a positive transference. She also made the point that analysis is not seeking 'the "objective reality" the Courts want, and generally we are not in a position to give it' (Hayman, 1965). In the event the judge used his discretion not to sentence her for contempt of court – perhaps swayed by the argument that her evidence would only be of marginal relevance to the case.

From the ethical point of view it is significant that her plea was not based on the duty of confidentiality towards her patient – towards the analytic alliance, as such – but on the principle of loyalty to her profession:

I said that it was essential to my work as a psychoanalyst and psychotherapist that people should feel free to discuss with me everything that concerns them, including matters of great intimacy which they would not be able to reveal if there were any doubt about my trustworthiness. (Hayman, 1965)

Is this an extreme claim to moral autonomy for the analytical profession, akin to the priestly seal of confession? Or is there an argument here that the public interest is best served – as with the Cities of Refuge, in ancient Israel (Numbers, 35, 9-34) – by the creation of privileged spaces in which people may be allowed 'sanctuary', in the hope that this will benefit them, and so serve the common good? Both positions can be argued, but I think there is a third option which privileges the analytic alliance while drawing on advances in therapeutic understanding and technique.

Kernberg distinguishes between classical psychoanalysis, psychoanalytic psychotherapy and supportive psychotherapy. Classical psychoanalysis depends on:

the development of a regressive transference neurosis, and its resolution by interpretation alone, carried out by a psychoanalyst from a position of technical neutrality. (Kernberg, 1999, p. 1,079)

In psychoanalytic psychotherapy, on the other hand, technical neutrality may have repeatedly to be abandoned in order to contain life-threatening or treatment- threatening acting out:

The self-perpetuating nature of acting out in these cases may prove impossible to resolve interpretively without ... structuring or setting limits. In practice this means that, for example, characterologically determined suicidal behaviour ...requires limit-setting. An initial therapeutic contract, in which the patient commits himself either to get himself hospitalised, or else control his suicidal behaviour rather than acting on it, may become a precondition for treatment that clearly represents an abandonment of technical neutrality. ... In short, technical neutrality in psychoanalytic psychotherapy is an ideal working state, again and again preventively abandoned and interpretively restored. (Kernberg, 1999, p. 1,081)

One of the characteristics of Lambert's 'agapaic attitude' is that the analyst does not behave 'a-schematically' (Lambert, 1981, pp. 34ff). Rapid fluctuations between the stance of Kernberg's classical psychoanalyst and that of his psychoanalytical psychotherapist would certainly be experienced as 'a-schematic' by the patient who needs to experience constancy – just as a baby needs constancy from his mother. We are back to the nature of the analytic alliance and the analyst's responsibility to 'handle' the patient in ways appropriate to their need. With one patient, the analyst may rightly contain their anxiety about the patient's murderous fantasies, believing that psychic containment will provide sufficient holding for him. Another patient will need vigorous boundary setting. Such decisions can only be made by attending to the needs of each patient rather than by appeal to a supposedly universal law of confidentiality. Ideally, many of the appropriate parameters will have been decided upon, and discussed with the patient, at the assessment stage.

Life is never quite so simple! It is all too easy for our free-floating autonomy of mind to be captured by a concern in the collective consciousness around us.

Just as we can get caught in unconscious identification with a patient, in which unconscious complexes in both our minds form an alliance, causing us to act in concerted but thoughtless ways, so can we be hooked by collective anxieties about physical violence or legal retribution. I know this is happening when I cease to relate to my patient as *this unique individual*, and begin to ask myself, 'Is he / she one of *those*?' – one of the category of people mentioned in the Code of Ethics. Or, when I begin to look over my shoulder and ask myself, 'How would this look in court?'

Moments like these are charged with anxiety. If we retain some capacity to think, but are unable to process the fear, we may well be driven to espouse an absolutist position: I will *never* break a confidence under *any* circumstances; or, I will *always* inform a relative or GP when my patient is in a suicidal frame of mind. Absolutism is usually a sign that we have lost our autonomous power of thought, that we have been hooked by a social neurosis. Somehow, before taking an action which may breach our patient's ethical rights, we need to regain our professional balance of mind.

Thinking about this, I am reminded of what Jesus did when the woman caught in adultery was dragged before him, and her accusers demanded that he confirm the legal penalty for her offence, which was death by stoning. Jesus said nothing. Instead, he bent down and wrote in the sand. What was he doing? One ingenious early Christian commentator suggested he was listing her accusers' sins. This sounds too concrete. My guess is that – unlike me, when I thoughtlessly admitted my patient's husband into my consulting room – Jesus was creating a space in which to unhook from his identification with the Law, and his instinctive sympathy with the woman and, perhaps, from his anger or fear of her accusers. By his inner act of freedom, Jesus escaped the collusive madness which sought to scapegoat the woman. When finally he lifted his head, he said, simply, 'Let the one without sin cast the first stone.' Then he bent down, and continued his doodling (St John's Gospel, 8, 1-11).

His words broke the malign spell which had bound aggressor and victim, and triggered insight and reflection. The 'benign cycle' was restored and, with it, an ethical basis for relationship.

Note

1. For a most suggestive discussion of the resonances between the concepts of God and the unconscious see Bomford (1999).

References

Bion, W. R. (1984), *Second Thoughts, Selected Papers on Psycho-Analysis* London: Karnac Books.
Bollas, C. and Sundelson, D. (1995), *The New Informants. Betrayal of Confidentiality in Psychoanalysis and Psychotherapy,* London: Karnac Books.
Bomford, R. (1999), *The Symmetry of God,* London: Free Association Books.
Breuer, J. and Freud, S. (1895), *Studies on Hysteria,* The Standard Edition of the Complete Psychological Works of Sigmund Freud, vol. II, London: The Hogarth Press and the Institute of

Psycho-Analysis.

Casement, P. J. (1982), 'Some pressures on the analyst for physical contact during the re-living of an early trauma', *International Revue of Psycho-Analysis* 9, 279-86.

Freud, S. (1915), *The Unconscious* The Standard Edition of the Complete Psychological Works of Sigmund Freud, vol. XIV, London: The Hogarth Press and the Institute of Psycho-Analysis.

Godfrey, W. (2001), 'Saving Masud Khan', *London Review of Books*, 23 (4), 22 February.

Gordon, P. (1999), *Face to Face: Therapy as Ethics*, London: Constable.

Hayman, P. (1965), 'Psychoanalyst subpoenaed', *The Lancet*, October 16, pp. 785-6.

Hinshelwood, R. D. (1997), *Therapy or Coercion?*, London: Karnac Books.

Holmes, J. and Lindley, R. (1989), *The Values of Psychotherapy* Oxford: Oxford University Press.

Homer (1970), *The Odyssey*, trans. by E. V. Rieu, Harmondsworth: Penguin.

Jung, C. G. (1929), *The Problems of Modern Psychotherapy* Collected Works of C. G. Jung, Vol. 16, London: Routledge and Kegan Paul.

—— (1931), 'Commentary on The Secret of the Golden Flower', in Collected Works of C. G. Jung, vol. 13, London: Routledge and Kegan Paul.

Kernberg, O. F. (1999), 'Psychoanalysis, psychoanalytic psychotherapy and supportive psycho-therapy: contemporary controversies', *International Journal of Psychoanalysis* December, 80 (6), p. 1,075.

Lambert, K. (1981), *Analysis, Repair and Individuation* London: Academic Press.

Little, M. (1986), *Toward Basic Unity*, London: Free Association Books.

Symington, N. (1986a), 'The analyst's act of freedom as agent of therapeutic change', in G. Kohun (ed.), *The British School of Psychoanalysis* London: Free Association Books.

Symington, N. (1986b), *The Analytic Experience. Lectures from the Tavistock*, London: Free Association Books.

7

Birth of the Ethical Attitude
in a Clinical Setting

Elizabeth Richardson

Introduction

The mythological story of Odysseus sailing past the sirens tied to the mast of a ship has always held a fascination for me. What could this sound have been like? How could it have been so powerful that it was irresistible? The lone figure of Odysseus, instructing his sailors to lash him to the ship's mast so that he could safely listen to the sirens, and cope with his longing to be closer to their magnetic sound without succumbing to their seductive destruction – what an evocative image this creates. All the other sailors in the ship had their ears plugged in order to defend themselves against hearing the reverberations which would lure them to their deaths, and to avoid heeding Odysseus's pleas to row closer to the sound. Fortunately Odysseus had a reliable, supportive crew who were able to keep Odysseus and the ship stable throughout the crisis.

There are times when analysts working with a patient in the consulting room are drawn to something, like an archetypal finger print, that may almost match our own experience. It is at these times that we are most vulnerable and have to hope that our 'internal sailors', our unconscious voice of reason will be lashing us to our own ethical mast and preventing us from being seduced into acting out with a patient. Hopefully we will hear a warning note within informing us that something is at work in our unconscious that we need to be particularly mindful of. At times like this it is important to consult with a trusted colleague in the hope that they will be able to heighten our awareness of the sirens that may drag us off course, rendering us useless in trying to be alongside a patient in their inner and outer world. It is crucial that the analyst and the analysis remain stable.

From time to time I find myself referring to the Code of Ethics of the organisation with which I trained. Certainly when I first qualified I viewed this code as the rules by which I should practise, and, if I adhered to them, all would be well. However, over the years I have realised that it is the spirit of this code that has meaning for me as I struggle with painful and bewildering clinical situations that sometimes arise. An ethical attitude grows from within, in relationship to another, just as a mother begins to relate to her infant as she feels the first fluttering and stirrings of new life growing within her, and this sense of relatedness continues to grow during the pregnancy. From birth there is the beginning of the actual relationship between mother and baby, a reverie and a closeness that is unique and special. Gradually this closeness develops into a struggle as mother and baby begin to separate and relate to each other as distinct personalities. Dilemmas and perplexities begin to arise between them as new ways of being together, and of tolerating each other's differences, begin to emerge within an attitude of relatedness. No amount of reading and learning the rules of parenthood can prepare a mother for the unique inner relationship that she and her baby will experience with each other, and in the same way no amount of reading and learning the rules of analysis can prepare the analyst for the unique relationship they will experience with a patient. Occasionally predicaments arise between the interpretation of what is written and known, and what is felt about the drama being played out before the analyst and within the analyst in the therapeutic relationship as they experience ethical stirrings, beginnings, struggles and dilemmas. An interpretation of an ethical code may be affected by the level of regression a patient may be enduring, or by a particular external experience they may be going through. A patient may require a specific kind of holding and containing in a very early regressed state, and yet the same holding could be experienced as over-protective, infantalising and as inhibiting psychological growth, in a different phase of the analytic work.

In this chapter, I will describe working with a patient through seven months of her first pregnancy and the first three months after the delivery of her infant son.

The importance of allowing this mother to discover new attitudes towards her infant's sense of self will be discussed, as will how old attitudes and rules about parenting that had been imprinted throughout several generations could be reviewed and changed. According to Stern (1998) during the first two months the infant is actively forming a sense of an emergent self. It is a sense of self that will remain active for the rest of life.

The development of the therapeutic relationship between analyst and patient will be considered, as will the possibility of revisiting and re-learning ethical attitudes. This has been brought about by the unfolding of an indepth sense of relatedness between the analyst and patient which may have allowed fresh neural pathways to form (Solomon, 2000a). I will reflect upon the ethics of beginnings and endings between the patient and the analyst in the consulting room, and link this with attachment and separation issues between a mother and her infant.

Referral

Sally was pregnant for the first time and very anxious. She was afraid that she would not be a good mother to her baby. Her anxiety increased and eventually she saw a psychiatrist who assessed her and felt concerned that she might develop postnatal depression in view of the difficulties she had experienced in her relationship with her own mother. Sally was referred to me for psycho-therapy when she was in the tenth week of her pregnancy.

Her husband was supportive, but found it difficult to understand his wife's excessive fears. He was often away on business, and, because of his concern for Sally during his absences, he encouraged her to seek help.

When I first met Sally she told me she wanted to follow the rules of motherhood. She feared that if she did not mother her baby in the way that her mother would want her to, she would be getting it wrong, yet she feared that if she was like her mother her infant would experience a similar unhappy childhood to her own. Sally's mother had been able to care for her as a baby in a competent concrete way. She had been adept at following the rules about feeding, and keeping the baby clean and warm, but a sense of relatedness between them was missing.

Family History

Sally had been the first baby born to an anxious and obsessional mother who received little support from her distant authoritarian husband. The maternal grandmother had constantly undermined and berated Sally's mother for her poor mothering skills. Mother found she could not cope and lost her confidence, she became very depressed and felt unable to manage her baby girl. During those early months mother and baby were looked after grudgingly by grandmother, who taught mother that her baby was not to be picked up too often, and must learn how to 'wait'. It seems that Sally was often left to cry in her pram in the garden in between being fed and changed. A brother was born three years later, and was described as being hyperactive and needing lots of attention. Throughout her childhood Sally was accused by her parents of being clumsy, thoughtless and ungainly. Emphasis was placed upon her being clean and quiet. Sally was average at school, went on to university and eventually became a teacher. During childhood Sally loved singing, and taught herself how to read music. She continued to develop this interest as an adult and became a successful performer. Despite crushing criticism and denigration from her mother about her musical ability throughout her childhood, Sally managed to protect and to nurture a creative urge that allowed her to find her own voice and to sing out from the depths of her self.

Ethical Stirrings

The need to relate to Sally's inner self was crucial. I worked in the hope that she might feel something 'in the air' between us, not necessarily in what was said or done, but by the development of a sense of trust that would continue to grow, just like the 'rest' in a musical performance when the echo of the silence resonates and enhances what has gone before. I hoped that she might be bathed and nourished in the analytic fluid space between us, in the sealed vessel of the analytic container, in much the same way as her developing fetus would be bathed and nourished in the amniotic fluid in the sealed vessel of his mother's uterus.

From the first meeting I was struck by Sally's open, child-like face, and the intensity of her look. I felt she would scrutinise my face, searching for any change of expression that might give her a clue as to whether I was affirming or criticising her. After a long stare she would smile, this smile would then became frozen and fixed as if she was being photographed. It was a deadening, appeasing smile and I felt held under a spell in which I was paralysed and from which I could not escape until I had smiled back at her. In the transference I felt that Sally believed I would not be able to hold anything other than a smiling appeasing face.

Gradually I learned not to smile back at Sally but instead I held her gaze, and by doing this I was attempting a non-verbal interpretation. Beneath her sickly smile there was a sense of a 'black' look that would not be tolerated and had been banished many years ago. By holding Sally's gaze I was trying to convey a sense of holding her banished self (Wright, 1991). There were no words to describe the many levels of the look that passed between us. I felt I was participating in the eye contact between grandmother and mother, mother and baby, inner world and outer world and between my patient and myself. I felt the eye contact in my gut. I believe this experience was like a non- verbal psychobiological attunement process, mirroring and patterning the subtle transferential and countertransferential visceral somatic responses between patient and analyst as described by Solomon (2000a).

Throughout those early months of working together, Sally needed to tell me in great detail about her visits to the ante-natal clinic, her extreme tiredness and nausea, and her delight which we shared when she told me about the first fluttering movements of the growing fetus she felt within her. During the sessions, she described her bodily changes and her fears of being overwhelmed by this new life developing inside her. As she spoke she would lean forward in her chair, and gaze earnestly into my eyes, searching for a nourishing look from me. Her hunger was quite profound. I felt like a part object nipple that she would fix her famished gaze upon, and suck me in until the look became empty and devoid of sustenance. She would often smile and nod at me and continue to do so until I responded. My physical reaction to Sally concerned me, as I felt unnatural, as if I was mimicking Sally's nodding rather than communicating with an instinctive mirroring response which came from myself. These exchanges were powerful and I felt controlled by them. However, I sensed it was the gaze of an infant desperately trying to communicate with mother in a pre-verbal relationship. She was showing me the hungry eyes and the frozen smiling mouth of a baby that was despairingly anxious to please.

Sally needed me to listen and to be interested as if this was the first pregnancy that had ever happened to anyone anywhere at any time in the past, present or future.

She tearfully told me that she was afraid she would be like her mother and would be unable to mother her baby. She was fearful that she would be compelled to repeat her own childhood, and that her baby might be burdened by her own oppressive past. This theme was to appear again and again, and each time it did I would try to convey to her that she was needing me to know about her fears, and suggest to her that, by remembering, and feeling the pain of her harrowing childhood, it might be possible to come to terms with some of this and to be the kind of mother she was hoping to be and that her baby would help her to become.

In the consulting room, I was aware of the presence of at least four generations. The grandmother, Sally's mother, Sally and her fetus. A pattern was emerging of mothers who had been unable to support daughters during and after the birth of their baby. There were times when I sensed an archetypal presence of mothers and babies.

Sometimes in the transference I felt like a grandmother figure listening to the mother that Sally would have internalised. I sensed that I needed to speak to this internalised mother and reassure her in order to make reparation for the damage caused to her by the actual grandmother. I had a belief that somehow by doing this Sally might be able to feel mothered by her own internalised mother, and gain an experience of mothering which she might then be able to pass on to her own infant.

There was a sense of loss and sadness during these times.

Sally found that her mother was unable to participate in the reverie surrounding the preparations for the arrival of her first baby and her parent's first grandchild. Father was not interested at all. Mother received her daughter's descriptions of her developing pregnancy with a mixture of boredom and derision. This was similar to the way she had dealt with Sally's musical creativity when she was a child. Mother worked within the medical profession and would impart medical knowledge regarding the most recent investigations available to mothers to check for fetal abnormalities. There were comments on how Sally looked fat, and how she was more clumsy than ever. Mother would speak of her own pregnancy, and how ill and anxious Sally had made her. There was little sense of her mother being able to contain and process Sally's anxieties, or to accommodate and process her needs.

Sally was afraid of falling apart when she gave birth to her baby and it seemed to me that at this stage in our work together my main function was that of enabling Sally to experience psychic holding. Hopefully she would be able to internalise this and utilise it in the sense of being able to hold on to her self, and develop a stronger ego which would help her to contain her own and her baby's emotions. Listening to Sally and thinking about the poor relationship she had with her mother I was reminded of Piontelli's observations of fetuses in utero. Using ultrasound scans Piontelli found that there was a continuity of behaviour before and after birth, suggesting that the new-born baby is not 'nature' waiting for 'nurture' to interact with him, but rather that nature and nurture have been interacting for so long in the womb that it is not possible to disentangle them.

During the last trimester of gestation the fetus swallows and excretes amniotic fluid. The content of this fluid is constantly changing as it reflects the mother's hormonal state and her diet, as well as containing the excretions of the fetus. It has long been known that hormonal states are affected by emotional states: an anxious mother may well be conveying the chemistry of anxiety to her unborn child, as he swallows the amniotic fluid in utero. Verney and Kelly (1981) suggests that an unborn child is an already aware, reacting human being who from six months onwards leads an active emotional life. It would appear that patterns of feelings which are deep and persistent have the most effect on the developing fetus.

In an attempt to find the connection between Sally's developing self, and her developing fetus, there was a need to help her to see the repetition of the past in the present. I made links with the time when she was a fetus within her own mother who might well have been experiencing similar feelings of tiredness, nausea and delight when she felt those first fluttering movements which would be made by Sally as an infant in utero. Gradually Sally began to be able to imagine her baby self, and to wonder about her own mother's ambivalent feelings when she was carrying her during her first pregnancy. She began to grieve for the relationship she had never had, and to feel some compassion for her mother. She would also wonder aloud about her grandmother, and the tribulations that she may have experienced, and slowly and steadily a feeling of family relatedness and the difficulties in mothering that had been passed down from generation to generation began to emerge.

In the later months of pregnancy, Sally talked to her developing fetus during the sessions. She would rub her swollen abdomen and say, 'Here we are again little one. What shall we talk about today, then?' There were moments when I was unclear whether she was talking to herself or to her fetus. I believe she was speaking to both. In the transference, I was both the mother and the father that Sally needed to see and to have acknowledge that she was pregnant, and that she was capable of being a woman in her own right. The clumsy, thoughtless and ungainly adolescent was loved and cherished by a husband who wanted to conceive and create a baby with her.

She told me how she would sing to her fetus in the evening before she went to sleep. I commented that Sally was singing a lullaby to her real baby, and to her own baby self and that she had needed her mother to sing to her, and to appreciate her singing many years ago. There was more than one developing self in the consulting room. The failure of a strong ego-formation in her early infancy had resulted in the persistence of a fear-ridden and withdrawn infant self in the depths of her unconscious. Slowly, unrealised potentialities of her personality were being evoked, and she was beginning to trust that she could relate to and affect her actual baby. She was starting to believe in herself, and to be able to feel that she had the capacity to love and to be loved by another.

During a routine home visit by the midwife, Sally asked if the fetal heart rate could be recorded as she sang to the infant inside her abdomen. The monitor registered a decrease in the heart rate. Sally was delighted by this: her baby was responding to her and she began to wonder if, after all, she just might be able to look after her baby. It seemed to Sally that her baby was able to respond and to feel comforted by her singing. This was a very different experience compared with the denigrating criticism of her singing that she had received from her mother as a child. Feijo (1981), in studying fetal conditioning, has noted this kind of reaction as an anticipation of the state of comfort induced by maternal stimulation.

Towards the expected date of delivery we explored the inevitable break from therapy when Sally would be giving birth. Sally expressed ambivalent feelings, saying that she was concerned about the break, yet excited about the pending arrival of her baby. The birth had been carefully planned and talked about throughout the time we had been working together, and she was fortunate to have a midwife who was prepared to listen to Sally's hopes and fears, and her needs during labour.

Ethical Beginnings

Baby D arrived, on time, and with little fuss. A week later I had a phone call from Sally saying she was ready to come back but would need to bring her baby. She explained that she and the baby had not been separate from each other yet. I agreed that for the time being they could both continue to come to the session.

I do not usually see a mother along with an infant during the course of analytic work, as I believe the one-to-one analytic relationship needs to be preserved and protected. Normally I would discourage a mother from bringing a child to her session, and stress the importance of her having time and space for herself, away from her child. However with Sally it was different. From the commencement of therapy Sally and baby D attended the sessions together. For the first six months baby D was inside his mother's abdomen, and after his birth he continued to be in the therapy for a further three months. For me this was a unique therapeutic relationship and I found I was able to make transference interpretations based upon the repetition of the past in the present within the family, within the analysis, and later between mother and her new-born infant. I sensed that Sally needed to show me her eight-day old baby: she wanted me to see the mother and baby couple, and to witness the moments of togetherness and separation they were experiencing. Owing to the unusual situation of being able to work with the mother and her new-born infant, I was able to observe the non-verbal communications that passed between Sally and her baby and I realised that everything that transpired between Sally and her baby was in the therapeutic arena between Sally and me. The dialogue between us moved back and forth between past and present, between this mother and her baby, and between the earlier generations of mothers and babies in the same family, between the archetypal and the real mother and baby dyad and between inner-world and outer-world experiences.

I was aware that it was not usual analytic practice to allow a new-born infant to be present with his mother in the consulting room. However, I felt that to adhere strictly to the 'rules' observing the one-to-one analytic relationship, I would not have been taking into account, and relating to the needs of, Sally and her baby at that time. I felt an innate response to Sally and her new-born infant, which could lead to an enhancement of the sense of relatedness between mother and baby, and patient and analyst in the analytic relationship. I was able to be present with a mother who was struggling to establish a deeper connection with her new-born infant. She was striving to throw off old sets of rules she had inherited from her mother and generations before that, and I was striving to throw off old sets of rules that I had learned from venerable text books and codes of practice. Ethical thinking is enhanced and developed in the early infant-mother relationship by the caregiving, responses and interactions that take place between mother and infant. There is potential for this kind of relating in the consulting room between patient and analyst, where ethical thinking may be unfolded and enhanced through the processes of identification, internalisation and projection. In the mother-infant, patient-analyst dyad, the innate ethical response – the voice of reason – forms a third in the relationship, a vital ingredient, which protects the couple from idealisation and losing touch with reality. There were times when I was working with Sally and her infant that I felt like a father observing, and being excluded from, the mother-baby couple, yet I was aware that I needed to hold them both within the safety of the relationship. Sometimes I felt resentful towards baby D, who seemed to be taking all Sally's attention and intruding into our creative work together. This was fertile ground for the dawning of ethical thinking in the consulting room.

Sally had been afraid that I would not allow her to bring her baby into the session. We talked about what having the baby with her might mean, and that whilst we both acknowledged that in fact her baby had been coming to the sessions for the past six months, albeit in utero, Sally might feel impinged upon by her baby's external physical presence in the consulting room. She was tearful and told me that she really needed the sessions for herself but at the moment her baby was still part of her. It was also important that the focus to remain on Sally, and to avoid being lured into idealising the wonder of the new-born infant. I felt that Sally's psyche was still in the process of catching up with her soma, mother and baby were still in a psychic uterine attachment. To reject the real baby from the session at that stage would have been like rejecting Sally's infant self, and would have been tantamount to dealing with Sally according to the punitive rules that her mother had used to deal with her.

As I sat like a grandma with Sally and she sat holding her baby in the first session after baby D's birth, there was a sense of affirming and relatedness. I was aware of being in a place where mother and baby were meeting each other in so many different levels of being and understanding. There were silences where only the breathing of each of the three of us was audible and yet it was as if the breath of many babies and many mothers from the past, present and future was in the air.

At the next session Sally looked tired and anxious and she told me that, 'Baby D was squealing like a piglet throughout the night, and wanted to hang on to her nipple for hours at a time.' She was exhausted and so was her husband.

I was mindful of the link between Sally's description of Baby D wanting to hang on to her nipple for hours at a time, and the hungry look that I had experienced from Sally when I felt like a part object nipple that she fixed her famished gaze upon. When Sally spoke of what she called baby D's greediness, I would speak of Sally's hungry feelings of needing love and encouragement from her mother and her grandmother, and how difficult it was for her when grown-ups did not understand what she was missing. Sally would give me one of her long hungry gazes and then smile with tears rolling down her cheeks.

During the next few sessions with Sally and her new baby I was aware of her growing anxiety, and her need to feel contained and assured as a mother. I felt Sally was struggling to hold baby D comfortably. She seemed to have difficulty in putting her arms around him. Instead her arms were underneath him as if she was carrying a wooden box. I struggled with my own wish to take hold of the baby and murmur soothing words to him. However, I knew that this might confirm Sally's fears that she was not holding her baby in a comforting way, and she might experience me as being like her mother accusing her of being clumsy and ungainly. It was Sally who needed the soothing words, and I would often speak about how important it was for her to feel held and supported during these difficult early weeks when she felt anxious and tired. I would wonder aloud about how it would have been for her as a tiny baby who was sad and frightened of being left alone in the long dark night and how much she had needed to be held and comforted by a motherly person.

There were times during a session when she would stare at her baby and then ask, 'Am I doing it right'?' She looked at me beseechingly, longing for a response. I asked her if she could imagine what her baby might be feeling. She would gaze at him and say, 'It is all right, isn't it?' She seemed to search his sleeping face for reassurance, and then look back at me and smile. I gave an acknowledging nod to her smile and she settled again. The interplay of attunement between mother and baby and analyst and patient was almost tangible at these times. My sense of mimicking her movements which I described earlier was lessening, and my mirroring responses were spontaneous. Sally's awkwardness began to diminish over the next few weeks and I observed a growing enjoyment in her moments of physical intimacy with baby D.

Sally had found the ending of sessions difficult from the outset of our work together, and I sensed she had needed a few moments to collect her thoughts together and adjust her mind to the outside world again. In the third week that baby D was present he began to stir and pass copious amounts of wind about five minutes before the session was due to end. I felt there were two young selves in the room, both fearful of separation, and I tried to put the feelings of the infant Sally into words by saying how much she had needed her mother and how she had no one to turn to when she was left in her pram at the bottom of the garden. Sally laid her tiny sleeping baby son on the couch as she put her coat on. He awakened, uncurled his fingers and stretched an arm out above his head. I spoke to him saying that he knew his mummy would pick him up and hold him safely, just like his mummy knew she would be held safely in mind here with me until the next session. As I said this to the mother and baby in the room, I experienced a kind of resonance with many analysts who might say this to their patients in their consulting rooms and the significance of belonging and being held in mind felt almost tangible. At that moment there was a feeling of a coming together of many mothers and many babies. Although these actual words may never be spoken during the course of an analysis, they are conveyed to the patient through the containing rituals of analysis and the consistent holding of time and space.

In reviewing recent neuroscientific studies regarding fetal and neonatal cortical development, Solomon (2000a) suggests that the formation of the attachment bond between the infant and caregiver gives rise to experiences which shape 'the maturation of structural connections within the cortical and subcortical limbic areas. The quality of attunement between mother and infant, in which both members of the dyad play an active role in creating, is crucial to the infant's ongoing neural development'. The infant directly participates in the formation of its own neural structures. As a trusting relationship develops and deepens between a mother and her infant the mother learns from her infant how to intuit her infant's needs, and the infant leans how to communicate its needs to its mother. In the same way in the analytic relationship the analyst learns from the patient what it is that the patient is trying to communicate and the patient learns how to communicate in such as way as to be understood.

In describing the system of reciprocal mutual influences within the infant and mother dyad, Allan Schore (1996) suggests that these newly formed neural structures are responsible for the capacity to take care of one's self, and underpin social affective and cognitive development, and the identity of the self. The relationship and interaction between mother and infant can directly affect the formation of these neural structures which enable the capacity to show care and concern for self and others.

Jung stressed the importance of the need for the analyst to be aware of, and responsive to, the impact of the therapeutic relationship. I believe there are times during this relationship, for example during a deep regression, when the quality of attunement between the patient and the analyst is such that both members of the analytic dyad can play an active role in the formation of fresh neural pathways. As this new experience of a trusting sense of relatedness develops and deepens, so, too, does the potential for the formation of an ethical attitude to grow from within in relationship to another.

Separations and Ethical Struggles

Baby D was ten weeks old. He was asleep in his pram in the entrance to the consulting room. Sally and I were exploring the possibility of a time when she would feel that she could leave her baby with a sitter so that she could have her sessions all to herself. Baby D awoke and for a few minutes lay gurgling and kicking his legs in the air. He began to whimper and then to cry loudly. It became impossible to hear what each other was saying and baby D's face was becoming red with rage, his back was arching and his fists flailing, his cries turned into screams. Sally began to cry angry, helpless tears. I spoke of how angry she was feeling because she was being deprived of the time and space she was needing with me, and that baby D was upset because he wanted his mother and here we were talking about a time when he would be separated from her. I expressed how difficult and frightening separations can be and how upsetting this must have been for Sally as a baby when she was left to cry. There was no one there to respond to her and to know that she was needing to be held and comforted. Sally went over to the pram and picked up baby D. She rocked him in her arms and murmured to him through her tears. Slowly his cries abated. I spoke of how Sally had been able to understand what her baby had needed, even though she was feeling deprived and distressed herself. I said that it was important that she had time for herself here with me, and although it was distressing for her baby when he was left, if he was not left for too long, gradually he would get to know and to trust that she would be coming back. We looked further at the possibility of Sally making arrangements for baby D to be looked after during her session. This would enable her to have some time and space for herself in her therapy.

I linked baby D's screams with how Sally might feel angry towards me when I have breaks, and that just as baby D was learning how to trust her, she would learn that she could trust me and that I intended to return when I went away. Sally was able to tell me how angry and neglected she felt when I end the session on time, and when I have a break. She said that she felt as if she had been left to hold the baby all by herself. As she was speaking Sally and baby D had been gazing into each other's eyes. Sally smiled at baby D and he smiled back at her, his right arm flailed out towards her and Sally took hold of his hand and curled his fingers around her thumb. She looked at me and our eye contact held for a moment or two, we smiled at each other and then she looked back at her baby. I felt that baby D had taught Sally how to receive a smile, and how to reciprocate. The frozen famished smile that I had experienced at the beginning of therapy was becoming more natural and engaging.

Here was an example of the reciprocal mutual influence in the infant-mother dyad as described by Allan Schore (1996). At the same time as baby D was developing neural structures that would underpin his social development, and his identity, he was also teaching his mother how to do the same. Just as there was a reciprocal mutual influence happening between mother and baby, so, too, between Sally and me.

Sally was able to leave baby D at home with father. This was her first separation from her baby and she was agitated and tearful. She wondered how baby D would be managing without her and if her husband would be able to cope. As the session progressed she was able to talk about the feeling of something missing, and her guilt at having me all to herself. Working with Sally's remembrances of her own suffering and desolation, enabled her to use these feelings as a form of protection for her baby. Unconscious destructive feelings were becoming conscious, and it became possible to talk about her negative feelings towards her mother, and her fears of being like her mother towards her baby and the compulsion to repeat her own oppressive past.

This is a small vignette of the analytic task that Sally and I have undertaken together. There is much to do as Sally explores and discovers her developing self. I sense that as baby D grows and develops in his own identity, more of Sally's fears will become apparent, and that in order to contain her fears from her childhood, her identification with her mother will become more discernible. Equally, her negative feelings towards me will become more accessible. The understanding of her childhood pain will become a powerful deterrent against repetition in her parenting of baby D.

During the time I have been working with Sally, I have become increasingly aware of how analysis can open up the possibility to the formation of fresh neural pathways, not necessarily by what is actually spoken, or even by what is consciously understood. It is as if something is in the air, a growing assurance of being believed in can generate a feeling of being held psychically in the rhythm and rituals of the therapeutic container, and in the analyst's mind. The ego's capacity to contain grows out of experiences of being contained. These experiences begin in utero and continue through infancy, childhood and into adult life.

My understanding of this is that during analysis the patient experiences being held in mind by the analyst, who is able to respond, and to interpret that the patient is experiencing being held in mind. The patient internalises both the experience and the interpretation. Schore (1996) describes this as an affect-regulating symbolic interactive representation. He goes on to state that a secure emotional attachment facilitates the transfer of regulatory capacities from caregiver to infant. The experience of being with a self-regulating other is then internalised into an interactive representation. It may then be possible for different neural pathways to form when there is a secure emotional attachment to another, and old ways of responding to early separations can be transformed.

Are we born with a capacity for ethical thinking and behaviour, or do we learn it through the socialisation processes of identification, internalisation and introjection?

Solomon (2000b) states that the development post partum of the neural circuitry and structures of the infant's brain which regulate the development of the higher cognitive and socioaffective human capacities, including ethical capacity, are dependent on the existence and quality of the earliest interactions between infant and mother or caregiver. In those early months of working with Sally and baby D, I was able to observe the interactions between a mother and her first child. There were moments when it was quite evident that baby D was learning how to elicit a positive response from his mother which enabled him to feel comforted. When his mother realised that she could give comfort to her infant she became more confident as a mother, and within herself. Her baby was then able to internalise his experience and his mother's response to that experience. I believe an unconscious learning process was also happening. Sally was learning from her infant how to elicit positive responses from me. She could internalise what she was experiencing together with my response to her. This led to a greater spontaneity in the way she began to relate to me, enhanced her social, affective and cognitive development, and increased her sense of her own identity.

Ethical Dilemmas

A new-born infant can be quite ruthless in his demands, but with good enough circumstances this ruthlessness can gradually change into a state of awareness and concern and consideration for the self and for the caregiver. Sally has a tendency to be quite ruthless and it is a necessary part of our work together to help her to elicit some concern for herself, and for others. If she can realise some concern for her internalised ruthless mother, she will be able to assist her infant son towards his own states of concern. Melanie Klein's way of describing this developmental place is the transition from the paranoid-schizoid stage of emotional development into what she called the depressive position.

Several months have passed since the early work with Sally and baby D. What is much more apparent now is Sally's difficulty in accepting her own internalised ruthless parents, particularly her mother. She is unmerciful when speaking of their lack of consideration for her. She has returned to work and complains that her manager lacks interest in her and her husband is unhelpful. I experience much of what she is telling me as projections of her own internalised state. Attempts to interpret these cruel vindictive withholding figures as aspects of herself leave me feeling judgemental. There are times when Sally expects me to collude with her in a battle against her externalised bad object parents. She resists my attempts to try to understand her bad objects and to perceive them as parts of herself. Negative feelings are projected out into authority figures. Withdrawal of these negative projections and working towards integration of them and being able to accept them as hidden aspects of herself is likely to take many months of analytic work.

There are times when I make a transference interpretation, linking her relationship with me to that of the relationship she had with her mother and the one she has with her baby son. I suggest that she is needing me to have concern for her without colluding with her against authority figures in her life. This was met with defensive hostility, and she commented that I just did not understand, I was like all the others and she felt completely alone. During a recent session I wondered aloud about the importance of my being honest and relating to her in such a way as we could both know that we were being as truthful as we possibly could be with each other. I queried with her if she sensed my truth as coming from a place of compassion or if she felt it was coming from a place of hostility. This comment was met with a long penetrating stare, followed by silent tears. We had reached the end of the session, Sally left my query reverberating around the room and departed.

Sally had internalised a narcissistic mother who was unable to relate to her daughter as a separate person. In my countertransference I experienced great difficulty in collecting my own thoughts and expressing myself in certain situations, particularly when Sally was berating her mother for her lack of interest. I felt I was expected to see things Sally's way and had to agree with her at all costs. I was split between my internal sense of wanting to protest, and struggling to maintain an analytic attitude that was appropriate to Sally's stage of development. I was wrestling with a need to be congruent. It was only when I was able to extricate myself from the siren sound of Sally's internalised mother and to hear my own inner voice warning me not to collude with what she was saying that I was able speak from my countertransference feelings and my own voice of reason. This was difficult and took several attempts. I felt guilty, unsupportive and even ruthless. The change came when I spoke of the need for truth and honesty, and when I queried with Sally where she thought I was speaking from. This seemed to enable her to recognise her own inner voice of truth, and to ignore the little Sally within, who mimicked the sound of her own mother. Sally is discovering her own compassionate voice, the voice that baby D will hear. Hopefully Sally will be able to relate to baby D as a separate person and enable him to develop and to listen to his own inner truths, all part of his painful but essential journey from the place of ruthlessness to the place of concern, a move from the paranoid-schizoid position to the depressive position, the transitional place where the genesis of ethical thinking takes root.

Sally tells me that baby D continues to respond well to her, although irritations are beginning to arise when her infant makes demands that she is not expecting. As baby D becomes more separate and self-assured, conflicts with his mother become more apparent. Sally tells me about her naughty child and asks me about suitable punishments. She is now more able to accept linking interpretations, and to wonder with me where she is speaking from when she asks me about chastisement. We are both able to recognise the voice of Sally's internalised punishing mother.

Conclusion

The analyst's desire to be a good mother and to support and sympathise with the patient against uncompromising parents is ill-founded, as it prevents the patient from looking at their inner self and their own contribution to their suffering. Sally seemed to be imploring me to be kind to her and would wreath me in smiles which I felt obliged to return. I was like Odysseus being lured by the sirens, meeting a hidden inner need to be a good mother. Fortunately my discomfort and sense of unease made me question what was happening in the room between us.

There are times I have had to be like the sailors in the Odysseus story and block my ears to Sally's pleas to join in her overtures about external ruthless parents. There were times that I was uncertain if I was being the ruthless unfeeling parent, or if I was receiving a projection of hers, or if there was an archetypal presence of many ruthless parents in the room. I could not discern where the parental 'voices' were coming from. At these times I found all I could do was to put the anchor down and ride the storm. The experiences were so powerful and so irresistible that it was crucial to have a stable ship and a reliable crew to be able to withstand the internal and external sirens that had the potential to destroy the analytic container. I had to trust the analysis to remain safe and run its own course whilst I held on to my own analytic attitude, lashed to the mast of training, experience, and inner truth that we learn so painfully in our own analysis.

Sally entered analysis to get help with her fears of becoming like her mother with her new baby, but now she is searching for something more than that. Sally wants to become a person in her own right, to believe in herself and to discover who she is and where she is coming from within herself. As she started to trust in my presence and allowed me to participate, she began to experience her analysis as a container with a space for relatedness, a non-judgemental place where it is safe enough to be honest, and where inner truths can be searched for, discovered and communicated.

An ethical attitude grows from within, in relationship to another. No amount of reading and learning the rules of parenthood can prepare a mother for the unique inner relationship that she and her baby will experience with each other, and no amount of reading and learning of ethical codes can prepare for the unique relationship which may develop between the analyst and the patient, or the ethical conflicts and dilemmas that may arise. The analytic encounter has the potential to change each of us, it can create a change of heart, it may even engender a change of soul.

References

Feijo, J. (1981), 'Le fetus, Pierre et le Loup', in E. Herbinet and M. C. Busnel (eds), Cahiers du Nouveau – Ne N.5. 192-209, Paris: Stock.

Kay, D.L. (1984), 'Foetal psychology and the analytic process', *Journal of Analytical Psychology,* 29, 317-36.

Peerbolte, L. (1975), *Psychic Energy,* Wassenaar: Serviere Publishers.

Schore, A.N. (1996), 'The experience-dependent maturation of a regulatory system in the orbital prefrontal cortex and the origin of developmental psychopathology', *Development and Psychopathology,* 8, pp. 59-87.

Stern, D. (1998), *The Interpersonal World Of The Infant,* London: Karnac Books.

Solomon, H. M. (2000a), 'Recent developments in the neurosciences', in E. Christopher and H. M. Solomon (eds), *Jungian Thought in the Modern World,* London: Free Association Books.

Solomon, H. M. (2000b), 'The ethical self', in E. Christopher and H. M. Solomon (eds), Jungian Thought in the Modern World, London: Free Association Books.

Verney, T. and Kelly, J. (1981), *The Secret Life of the Unborn Child,* London: Sphere Books.

Wright, K. (1991), *Vision and Separation,* ch. 15: 'Self and symbol', p.206.

8

Don Quixote in the Analyst's Consulting Room

Christian Gaillard

In this chapter, I have chosen to remain close to my experience as a clinician. Such a choice is not at all a simple one. The difficulty lies, on the one hand, with thought's quick demand for a free rein and its loathing to be confined to the particular, seeking to generalise. I have therefore firmly set limits to flights of fancy without, I hope, curtailing fruitful exploration.

Furthermore, conveying what transpires in our clinical practice is not self-evident. To keep and guarantee confidentiality about what presents itself and is at play in the consulting room is a clinician's basic ground rule, particularly when it comes to the possibility of disclosing the identity of those who have confided in him. I will therefore tell a story about a patient but the facts that I will narrate will be an alteration and substitution of the details of the actual story with which I dealt.

My argument is threefold. Taking this transposed account as my starting point, I shall, firstly, attempt to describe those qualities which seem to me necessary and those rules which are essential for the analyst's hearing to be most unbiased. Secondly, I will consider whether the privilege we experience within the confines of our consulting rooms in entering the intimate inner worlds of our patients does not come with a price, and whether we are really prepared to pay such a price. Finally, the brief clinical account here evoked will lead me to sketch out some thoughts about the responsibility which is ours at the current juncture in our collective history.

The Analyst's Receptivity

As a clinician and an analyst, I am used to spending a large part of my time in listening to and eliciting from my patients' experiences (or re-experiences), and in experiencing myself, all kinds of events, and the appearance of all sorts of stories which sometimes come from far away, from a very far past, from a past already meant to be dealt with and surmounted, but which are at play in the present along the road that life follows, in good times and bad, during an analysis, and which are still especially active in the present of that so strangely familiar and so astonishingly intimate story which we call the 'transference relationship'.

The narrative I wish to evoke here is a curious occurrence that appeared during a particular analytic session. It concerns a woman, in her sixties, at the time already in analysis with me for some considerable time. Before starting her work with me, she had been in a long-term analysis with someone who died suddenly and unexpectedly, during the course of the analysis. After the death of her analyst, the woman approached me in order to continue her work.

The woman had worked for a long time with her husband in a fairly successful business, but had separated from him and, after numerous legal debates, the divorce was pronounced shortly before the session I want to evoke. She has also had, during her life, strong religious leanings that led her to assume a teaching function and other responsibilities in several parishes. She appeared a very determined person, intellectually able, with a tendency to rationalise everything, rather harsh, and little aware of her own emotions or those of the people around her. She was quite small, rounded, most often with messy hair and not well dressed.

The analysis takes place face to face, which is not my usual way of working, at the rhythm of one session per week, which is not usual for me either. She mentioned few dreams, the sessions being mostly occupied with her current struggles, and with references to her past which I try to render as emotional as possible, focusing especially on the most marked episodes of her childhood. Just before the separation from her husband, she had undertaken the study of psychology while continuing to earn a salary, and after many years of very hard work at university she acquired all the qualifications required in France to become a clinician. Having obtained her final university diploma, and so the status of a professional, she presented herself to an association of psychothera- pists for admission into their training program, but she was refused. She showed few emotional reactions to the refusal apart from, of course, some waves of bad temper and caustic criticism of the rigidity of our institutions and the inhumanity of my psychotherapist colleagues.

After her divorce, and so during her analysis with me, she was diagnosed with cancer. She underwent surgery, took time to rest, followed a course of chemotherapy, and had subsequent plastic surgery to correct the resulting physical disfigurement. She reported that the operation had been a success.

Since the separation from her husband, again in the course of her analysis with me, she has had a few amorous crushes, notably on certain of her university professors, but none of these often secret infatuations blossomed to a concrete relationship.

In my responses to her, I found that she rather annoyed me, but I was open and sensitive to her life story and touched by her undertakings and struggles. I began to find her a little more feminine, and no doubt this perception corresponds to a transformation on her part in relation to me.

In the session I want to narrate, she said to me, a bit embarrassed, 'I have to say that I dreamt of you.' 'Which is very rare', she added. 'I saw you as Don Quixote', she told me. And she explained that the scene was not really very clear but more like a sketch or the vague memory of an engraving by an artist she did not recall, where Don Quixote is represented on his old mare Rosinante. 'Sorry, it's not very flattering', she added, more and more embarrassed.

At that time in my own professional life, I was engrossed in how I was going to compose a statement I had to write, announcing my standing for a position of responsibility in an association of analysts to which I belong. Well tucked into my analyst's chair, I surprised myself thinking, 'Which windmills am I fighting against, then?' At the same time, in another of the professional societies to which I belong, we were struggling with a lively, even tempestuous dispute regarding some decisions recently taken by the leading members, of whom I am one. This was greatly occupying and preoccupying me. 'What are the windmills of our association?', I asked myself.

But these personal and institutional considerations were interrupted by the slightly dreamy reflection on her part: 'My previous therapist [whom she greatly appreciated] was more of a Sancho Panza.'

While listening to her, my own interior thoughts followed their course. I remembered that quite young – I must have been less than ten years old – I had received as a gift from my godmother a French translation of Cervantes' *Don Quixote*. At that time I had only a partial knowledge of world literature, and I remember that my most powerful feeling while reading this book was compassion for the cruel adventures lived by the poor Don Quixote, and as much again for the misfortunes of Sancho Panza, especially when he was made governor of I can't remember which little topsy-turvy state at his own cost.

'Poor Don Quixote is ridiculous, of course', I heard myself telling her, 'but do you not find him rather sad and endearing because of his misfortunes?' She looked at me with a strange expression and, after a long silence, she explained a train of thought, quite meditative, a little depressed, which she had never yet allowed herself to experience. She began to express how she held men in low esteem, starting with her ex-husband, how she constantly tended to belittle men, even to deplore them, without any attention or empathy for what they might live or suffer.

This curious occurrence, quite unexpected, marked a turning point in her analysis, that is in her relationship both to others and to herself, as explored in our sessions, and notably in the transference and its analysis. There are some lessons to be drawn from this in what concerns the ethical attitude of an analyst in his/her practice.

This little story gives in effect the opportunity to show and underline that the first and most essential dimension of our ethics as analysts consists in accepting the manifestations of the work of the unconscious – here the figure of Don Quixote – and to be open to the consequent emotions that can be felt and recognised (Humbert, 1992). To open ourselves, the analyst as much as the analysand., this is for me the first ethical requirement that imposes itself on an analyst.

It is this which can permit us to work effectively face to face, not necessarily using the couch. When the analyst and the analysand are both sitting, a space of emergence is created between them where the most unexpected parts of themselves can take form. Don Quixote, and behind him Sancho Panza, placed themselves as the *third party* between us, mobilising in both of us that which occupied each of us, largely without our knowing.

But on condition, and this condition too is ethical, that that which occupies the analyst should be at the service of that which occupies the analysand, helping him or her to take on board and gauge the importance of what arises in their own life, so as to confront it. Here, through me, the figure of Don Quixote mobilised in my analysand feelings of compassion which are unusual for her. Then she could bear me her mind for the first time the progressive and slightly depressed recognition of the low esteem in which she held men, including her ex-husband, followed by the feeling of sadness and mourning that she never felt after the death of her previous analyst, nor after her divorce, which finally led her to the edges of a sadness which she had never yet expressed but which was nevertheless there when she had had cancer, when she had been refused by the association of psychotherapists to which she had applied for admission, and when her all too fanciful love stories failed to take shape.

My Don Quixote, the one I carry in me, could serve the work of my analysand. I could even speak to her about him because he is between us, using the Jungian technique of amplification. The use of my internal Don Quixote was legitimate on condition that *her* Don Quixote, and her work on herself at this time in her life and in her analysis, were facilitated and fed, not encumbered. The usefulness of this depends on the fact that I was not too offended when she saw me as Don Quixote, and that I saw her as a pitiful suffering young girl, not as an annoying woman or an impossible Dulcinea. In the event, that which emerged from my own depths was able to contribute both to her seeing herself, and acting, a bit differently.

Mourning

At this point, another question emerges: Who is this Don Quixote who unexpectedly arrived between us and gave rise to a different relationship of my analysand with herself, with the protagonists of her own life, including myself, and so to a different relationship with her unconscious?

Don Quixote shows himself to be an excellent personification of the power of the imaginary. He is a typical representation of what we are, and what others can be, when we do not manage to detach ourselves from our ideals, despite all that can happen to us, despite all reality testing. He is a figure of the misfortunes that can befall us when we are too absorbed in the imaginary and in fantasy.

Jungians are well trained, in accepting and cultivating the symbolic life and emotion. But perhaps they are not always as proficient when it comes to separation, loss, mourning, and acceptance of pain and rage. Speaking of the imagery and its power leads to a vocabulary which is not traditionally ours, because it is more Freudian, or post-Freudian. Is this to say that today Jungians must, for the needs of their clinical practice, have recourse to the advances of a different psychoanalytical theory from their own? Let's leave this question open. But to be sure, to throw oneself without reserve onto the other traditions of the psychoanalytical movement – here, being French, my vocabulary suggests the theory developed by Jacques Lacan and our Lacanian colleagues – would be to show oneself rather ignorant of Jung's own theory, from his first writings and all through his work.

Indeed, Jung dedicated his first major, truly Jungian work, the one which marked his rupture with Freud, entitled *Wandlungen und Symbole der Libido* (in English *Psychology of the Unconscious*, and then, for the edition of 1952, *Symbols of Transformation*, CW 5), to the fantasies, mythological poems, dream associations and misfortunes of a young woman who was overcome by her fantasies and therefore unable to face the realities of her age, especially the possible amorous encounters that could in fact create themselves in her life.

At the heart of his work is the question of the role and function of the hero (or pseudo-hero), of sacrifice of a childhood already behind her, and of the attachment to her mother – in sum, therefore, the sacrifice of the bygone pleasures of childhood incest fantasies. Jung will never cease, throughout his life and work, to develop, deepen and renew his theory of sacrifice and incest, showing that it is here that resides the difficulty of our attachments to and detachments from the power of a Mother-unconscious where we are always tempted to find refuge. Jung's strength is to have shown that at the heart of the analytic relationship there is this attraction, which can go as far as fixation and engulfing, to an unconscious matrix, so rich and full as to tempt us to lose ourselves there. This is even the most distinctive characteristic of Jung's theory of transference.

In fact, every day in our consulting rooms we live the intimacy, the disturbing proximity that is played out from one session to another, between analyst and analysand, strangely brought together by their respective journeys into the unconscious. This is at the same time extremely human and inhumane, because of the conditions and rules of the analytic relationship. I say inhumane because the forbidden is at the heart of this strangely privileged relationship that one can be tempted to prefer to any other. For the analyst, this situation can be hazardous. These are analysts for whom practically nothing is more important, nothing makes them feel more fulfilled than their professional life.

My patient who, in her dream, had seen me as Don Quixote, is asking me to remain potent enough to be in control of the unconscious life that is in me and animates me, and at the same time to contain her depressed self, because she needs that herself at this moment in her life and her analysis. She needs to yield to the experience of her solitude, her disillusionment, including that which she felt in relation to the happiness she had found in her analysis so far, with her first analyst and then with me.

The second ethical requirement of analysis is to mourn our essentially incestuous impulses to withdraw into the lively, enchanting joys of an interior animation that would love to ignore both time and history. This ethical requirement is the experience of a test of differentiation and individuation, from out of a backdrop of incest, that is of the incestuous attraction to and fascination with being included in the regressive riches and fantasised safety of the Mother-unconscious.

Evidently we have a lot to learn from our colleagues of other psychoanalytical traditions (Didier-Weil, 1995; Guyomard, 1998). But the work on loss, sacrifice, separation, mourning, and the solitude of the processes of individuation, constitute an essential, axial dimension of Jung's life and work as well.

The Unrealised. The Not-Yet Thought

We are 'circumambulating' Don Quixote. We have seen that he is a fairly typical representation of our symbolic life in so far as we can call such a life collective. But this is not quite right. For Don Quixote is above all else a book, written between 1605 and 1616, and in Spain. That is to say, at a certain time, in a certain place. And this book has changed our relationship to the past, to the present, to the future, and to the unconscious.

Jung took it as his fundamental task in the years 1935-6 to recast collective history into a new perspective. He realised this task through his works on alchemy, on Christianity, in *Answer to Job* and especially *The Psychology of Transference.* Jungian theory can be thought of as *transgenerational* at least since 1916, when in *Septem Sermones ad Mortuos* Jung addressed the dead 'who had not found at Jerusalem what they were looking for'. Jung 'teaches them', as the text says, meaning that he gave them what he had learnt from his own experiences of the unconscious, which constituted the advances of his thinking, which was still seeking its path but already distinctive as his own (Maillard, 1993). The question that is posed by this text and more firmly in the works of the later Jung, is that of our heritage, and at the same time that of our tasks today.

The third ethical requirement, in my view, is to take a stance as to our way of life, our way of being clinicians, and as to our own thought in a world which changes, progresses, feeling its way, inventing what it will become. It is to create that which has not been, and to think, with our contemporaries, that which asks to be realised. The third ethical requirement of the analyst is to find the best possible expression and realisation for that which has not been recognised and lived thus far (Solomon, 2000; Ricoeur, 2000; Gaillard, 2000, 2001). In this creative relationship to history there is a particular, and particularly exigent, dimension of Jungian ethics.

Conclusion

In relation to the surprising emergence of Don Quixote in my consulting room, we have been led to take our attention to the acceptance of the unconscious life in its most spontaneous and unexpected expressions. Then we went on to examine the role of separation and mourning. Now arises the question of *the position and action we have to assume, individually and together, at the point where we are today in the course of our collective history* – a position and action which will not be, one can hope, too Don Quixotesque.

References

Didier-Weil A. (1995), *Les trois temps de la loi*, Paris: du Seuil.
Gaillard, C. (2000), 'Otherness in the present', *Harvest*, vol. 46, no. 2.
—— (2001), 'For a measure of left-handed thinking', Journal of Jungian Theory and Practice, Fall 2001, vol. 3.

Guyomard P. (1998), *Le désir d'éthique*, Paris: du Seuil.

Humbert, E. G. (1992), *L'homme aux prises avec l'inconscient*, Paris: Retz.

Maillard C. (1993), *Les sept sermons aux morts de C. G. Jung*, Nancy: Presses Universitaires de Nancy.

Ricoeur, P. (2000), *La mémoire, l'histoire, l'oubli*, Paris: du Seuil.

Solomon, H. (2000), 'The ethical self', in E. Christopher and H. Solomon (eds), *Jungian Thought in the Modern World*, London & New York: Free Association Books.

9

On Retiring: some thoughts and questions

Yvette Wiener

In 'Analysis Terminable and Interminable' Freud (1937, p. 219) says: 'If one is prevented by external factors from reaching this goal [the goal of analysis], it is better to speak of an incomplete analysis than of an unfinished one.' Fordham (1978) and Zinkin (1998) differentiate between 'ending' and 'stopping' in analysis, while Robert Samuels after Lacan (1993) stresses the opposition between separation and alienation which, he says, 'is crucial in any theory of the end of analysis (p. 140).

When I made the decision to retire, I became fully aware that I was depriving my patients of the opportunity of ending their analysis. Ending implies a mutual decision, negotiations and shared mourning, and it requires, as both Zinkin (1998) and Shirly Williams (1997) suggest, some rite of passage which recognises and contains both the pain of parting and the hope of a fulfilled future. What I was offering was a unilateral decision, a date of my own choosing, and a kind of ultimatum for my patients to grow up, what Freud, speaking of his treatment of the Wolf Man, refers to as 'blackmail'.

Lesley Murdin (1994) has written about the clinical difficulties surrounding therapist-induced endings. She writes of the difficulties of managing the unconscious play of love and hate and stresses the importance of assessing her patients' position in the transference at the time of parting, not only to decide whether to refer them on but also to use this awareness to make sense of the ending and, perhaps, look forward to a new beginning. I was also aware of these problems. What preoccupied me in particular were the moral implications of my decision. The questions I found myself asking more and more pressingly, were: is there an ethical way to retire? Is it ethical to retire? I also realised, when I looked for guidance and the comfort of other therapists' experiences, that nothing had been written on retirement and that, in fact, few analysts retire.

In what follows I shall attempt to describe my own experience and my patients' reactions and to formulate the questions which confronted me. Most of these remain unanswered. 'Whatever one's theoretical attitude to the question may be,' says Freud (1937, p. 249), 'the termination of an analysis is, I think, a practical matter.' I shall therefore write of the practicalities of ending, the when and how, and examine more specially the status of the retired analyst *vis à vis* his or her professional association and in the context of post-termination meetings. I shall pay special attention to the dimension of time in the pre-termination period and ponder the difference between a retired analyst and a dead analyst in patients' fantasies. In a second part I shall try to define the terms of the ethical tension I experienced and record the loss of self as suffered by the analyst.

A Pre-Retirement Episode

I shall begin with a pre-retirement clinical episode. The work with my second training patient was not very successful. He was a very damaged young man who had already exhausted a number of therapists and the progress we had achieved was very limited. He had remained in treatment six months beyond the eighteen required by the training organisation before we ended. But nearly two years later he telephoned me to say that he had cancer of the testes. 'I wanted you to know', he kept repeating, and later: 'I wanted you to know because you know both sides of me. My mother and my girlfriend only know my positive side. You know how destructive I can be.' At that point we did not meet in person but, for nearly two years, we would speak from time to time on the telephone; on a few occasions he wrote to me. Our conversations were in no way analytical: he would just let me know the ups and downs of his condition, his hopes and the increasingly frequent relapses. These were little chats. Only once, a few weeks before his death, did he ask, 'You know me so well, do you think I am doing this to myself?' My answer was vague but partly truthful: 'I think you have had a lot of bad luck.'

This story has little to do with retirement; yet it was then that I began to ponder the meaning of ending and the extent of our responsibility. I began to realise the artificiality of the boundaries in time and space we insist on and without which the work would not be possible and the cruelty of the paradox we live daily with our patients. Like Joshua and his trumpets we work on their defences, but at a given hour we throw them out: *fuori porte*, outside the walls, vulnerable and alone. This is a constant aspect of analytic work, which is highlighted when an analyst decides to retire. The patient has trusted us with the whole of his or her self, 'both sides of me', as my young patient said. He seemed to imply that that 'total he' lodged in me for ever. What should my professional attitude have been with him? Should I have offered him an appointment, given him his fifty minutes, charged him my usual fee? Should I have answered his last desperate question analytically? Did I behave unprofessionally, maybe even unethically? I do not, even now, have answers to those questions but they became relevant when I decided to retire, in my chosen time and for my convenience.

When and How

Hester Solomon (2000) writes that 'ethics implies an attitude achieved through judgement, discernment and conscious struggle, often between conflicting rights or duties' (p. 191). In the light of that definition, I found that the process of retiring, including the decision-making process and up to the last 'It is time... .' of my last session, was an ethical process.

The tension between the demands of my private life and my profound wish to stay with my patients until they were ready to leave became difficult to bear. A small drama was being played within me between three protagonists or groups of protagonists: on the one hand, the significant others of my personal life, on the other, my patients and in the middle I myself, divided between the certitude that my professional life was the way to wholeness and individuation and the realisation that my health required slowing down and rest.

I became aware that all ethical choices demand a measure of sacrifice. Like the pruning of a tree, some branches, however fruitful, must go so that the whole may prosper. It also felt a challenge to my fantasy of omnipotence, of being able to do everything. I was reminded of the sadness of the rich young man in the gospel (Mark, 10:17; Matthew, 19:16) who could not follow Jesus. The Scriptures speak of riches and possessions but these also involve responsibilities and duties. The story finishes: 'so he went away sorrowful'.

I had planned the time of my departure, I thought, carefully and responsibly. I had stopped taking new patients well ahead of the date I had chosen, so that my retiring, I hoped, would not interfere with the progress of those of my patients who were therapists in training, and when, as far as I could foresee, nobody would be in such a deep state of regression that my leaving would be an intolerable trauma. As far as I know, they and I were fortunate and this was so. I had also to decide about when to tell them about the timing of my retirement and thought it both wise and kind to announce my leaving a year ahead. I felt that I had done 'the right thing'. I soon realised that it was not so simple. One of my patients immediately accused me of selfishness and thoughtlessness: 'You probably feel very smug and that you have acted professionally but, in fact, you are robbing me of a year.' Somebody else sarcastically said: 'Imagine Gordon Brown saying that he would devalue the pound next week! Surely it would be devalued on that day!'

These remarks alerted me to the fact that announcing my decision had opened a new chapter in our shared story and that we were entering a transitional and uncharted space. Soon it became evident that, in spite of much painful working through, some patients experienced the year as devalued and defensively, but perhaps prudently, withdrew from further engagement. In Lacan's words they did not feel separated but alienated. They felt angry and I felt guilty.

The time scale also diffused the anger which, in the case of one patient in particular, could only be expressed in the last moments of our very last session, allowing no time for working through and leaving us both with a heavy heart. In some ways we were all in mourning and the knowledge that I was leaving inevitably coloured all aspects of the work. There was no longer space for illusion. Thus my own experience seemed to reflect the conclusion of Gillman's research on analyst-induced termination reported by Schachter (1992, p. 140): 'Sadness, mourning and feelings of loss were described in 75 percent of the patients. Rage, anger and hostility were expressed in more than half of the patients.'

I did not share with my patients the reason for my retirement. Talking of my health would have begged sympathy, of family pressure provoked envy, and mentioning my age seemed irrelevant. To say nothing, however, felt withholding and remains unsatisfactory.

Yet in spite of and through the anger and mourning, I began to realise that there was in my patients' minds a wish and a need to keep me alive and that a retired therapist was not a dead therapist. Not only did they want to know whether I would remain available should they need me in a crisis, they also wanted the reassurance that I should stay the same: creative and potentially receptive to their creativity. A patient to whom (in response to his questions) I had said that I had no plans for the future became very agitated and anxious: 'How can I go on and plan my career if you are not creative... you must write... do something!' Another young patient inquired timidly: 'Do people send you photographs of babies and things?' The internalised analyst thus was to remain witness and mirror, model and guide.

Schachter writes (1992, p.139):

> If the patient has incorporated the analysing function of the... analyst and identified with the analyst's self analysis, he/she will have internalised an observing ego, and he/she will then be in a better position to deal with the residues of transferences that are known to exist, as well as with the challenges and stresses that lie ahead.

In the last few weeks of our work together a patient had two dreams:

> She is in a garden where there is an old apple tree: it is on fire and falls down as she comes near. She then realises that a new sapling is growing inside the trunk.

> In the second dream she is walking along the ridge of a mountain. Again she is walking away from a burning village. She is aware of being safe and that somebody is walking with her, slightly behind and on her left.

As she tells me the dream and points with her hand to where she feels that person to be, she realises that it is where I am sitting. This is appropriate and how it should be: the presence of the analyst sufficiently internalised to make separation possible and the way ahead manageable and exciting. But what happens when an unforeseen catastrophe occurs, when, as in the case of my young patient, darkness falls? Must we remain silent or can we allow ourselves to reappear, not as a fairy godmother but as a mirror where our patients might, once more, become aware of their wholeness and their strength?

Post-Termination Contacts and the Special Situation of the Retired Therapist

In the article I referred to above Schachter quotes Loewald:

> During therapy we say: everything is grist for the mill; but what if the mill is to be dismantled? ... to what extent is termination analysable? (Schachter, 1992, p.146)

He asks whether the patient's expectation that no future contact with the analyst is likely, facilitates the work on mourning in the post-termination phase, as many analysts believe, or whether it impairs such work? I personally believe, as indeed does Schachter, that the answer to this question is a matter of clinical judgement. I therefore felt comfortable in telling my patients that I would remain available should they need to see me, as a sign of my ongoing concern.

I thought that, in most cases, the work would have been good enough and that there would be no need for further meetings. I have, however, seen three patients since my retirement. One waited a year before contacting me and wondered whether we could meet yearly or twice yearly so that we could discuss her development in both her professional (she is a therapist) and private life. Another (also a therapist) wanted to share with me the difficulties of one of her children and I felt that she contacted me not as a transference object but as a real object. The third one was going through a crisis similar to the one she had experienced several years before and which had precipitated a psychotic breakdown and required her hospitalisation. She was coping well and, as she left, she said, 'I wanted to see you but I also wanted you to see me.'

As Goldberg (1988) points out, that patient's need for mirroring from the analyst had blossomed into internal pride (as quoted in Schachter, 1992, p. 142).

Whilst I was happy to see these patients and think that these meetings have been beneficial and a natural continuation to, and not a devaluation of, the analytical work done before, I am much more confused about my professional status as a retired analyst.

Ours is a lonely profession, where membership of our professional association offers both the opportunity to share problems with colleagues and the containment and safety necessary to our functioning as analysts. I was not, and am not yet, quite sure whether it is right for me to take this for granted now that I have retired. Neither am I certain what my professional insurance requirements are. The absence of guidelines on these issues has made me feel insecure, in a no-man's land, without a professional code of conduct. (1) Again I experienced a tension between a wish to provide my ex-patients with the support and continuity I felt they were entitled to and an unsettling feeling that, having retired, I no longer had the right to exercise my profession. I have, since then, thought about this situation in terms of consultancy and of using my skills, but I remain troubled and wish I had found some clearer support in, for example, my professional association's Code of Ethics.

Time in the Pre-Termination Period

As I was suggesting to a patient that, perhaps, it was difficult to bring something new in the session since I was going to leave, he said, 'Oh, it has been like this since you told me, since you started the clock ticking!' What that patient was reminding me of, was that my introducing clock time into the session had rendered impossible the timelessness of the analytical hour without which unconscious processes cannot take place.

As soon as we let go our consciousness of measured time, we are in touch with other, very different, temporal experiences where part of a session becomes "all time", or where a second is an eternity of pain. (Yariv, 1999, p. 37)

Thus I became aware of what my patient's remark about robbing him of a year meant. He could no longer reach that depth of being where time stands still, where there is no need for order or causality. From then on we were ordering, labelling, drawing conclusions, finding patterns, all of it necessary and important work but exclusive of new revelations, surprises and wonder. Like a sick man putting his affairs in order and making his last goodbye we were preparing for a kind of death. We no longer believed in eternity.

Gail Yariv again:

When a person becomes absorbed in an activity, or reflection, he enters a deep silent time and has no sense of the clock; an hour or a minute might have passed. This type of concentration implies trust that there will be no invasion or sudden disruption. Patients who are able to trust the therapist are able to sink into reverie within the frame of the session and associate more freely, calling up a larger range of their inner life, experiencing eternity in the hour. (Yariv, 1999, p.46)

I am aware that this re-entering the world of temporality was an important part of mourning and necessary to the separation process. Patients had to take out into the world the work done in the *vas bene clausum* of the consulting room and take charge of their own history. As Rodney Bomford writes:

The processes of the unconscious system are timeless; i.e. they are not ordered temporally, are not altered by the passage of time, they have no reference to time at all. Reference to time is bound up, once again, with the work of the conscious system. (Bomford, 1999, p. 13)

On the one hand, this travelling back from the depth to the surface seemed right; life unfolds 'in consciousness'. Yet I felt that at a profound level my retirement was a betrayal, not necessarily of the initial contract with my patients but of the most essential (i.e. having to do with Essences) aspects of the therapeutic alliance. I became aware that, though I was acting 'professionally', as my patient had said with irony, at another level I was betraying certain values, values which had more to do with the concept of agapé, which underpins and motivates our work, than with professional contracts or even Codes of Ethics. Like the prisoners in the simile of the cave in Plato (*Republic*, ch. 7, paras 514, 515) I could only see the shadows but intuited that the reality lay elsewhere, and that my patients and I had had glimpses of it in some privileged moments in the analytic encounter. Bomford draws a parallel between the experience of the mystics and numinous moments in the consulting room:

it reflects something of those experiences which may be called transcendent. Such experiences are generally fleeting. While the heavens may open and eternity be glimpsed, yet the disclosure is only for a few moments. The impact of it may, nevertheless, last a life-time and through it, a whole world of meaning may be bestowed. (Bomford, 1999, p. 11)

Nunc movens and Nunc stans

The notion of transcendence which I introduce in the Bomford quotation made me reflect on the nature of the conflict within my self. The tension I felt mirrored, in a minor way, the fundamental philosophical paradox of the two orders of reality (Plato) and the distinction between time and eternity in Christian thought, between 'nunc movens with its beginning and end, and nunc stans, the perfect possession of endless life' (Kermode, 1966, p. 71). This paradox is also found in Kant's concept of noumena or things-in-themselves which he distinguishes as different categorically from ordinary reality. In another context (Wiener, 1996), I have written of the difference between Chronos (measured time, the time of past-present-future) and Kairos (endless and cyclical time). I realise that all analyses are contained between these two categories: on the one hand we constantly deal with our patients' chronology, their history, try to reconcile them to their past and envisage their future; on the other, in 'the moments of the soul's attentiveness' as St Augustine puts it (quoted in Kermode, 1966, p. 720), we have an experience of timelessness without a before or an after. This dichotomy is exacerbated at the time of ending. The date fixed for the termination keeps analyst and patient firmly 'in time', nevertheless there is in both protagonists the realisation that something of 'the other' and of their common experience is internalised and will dwell in them for ever.

In the same way, it was right for me to move on and pursue my own history, but the price I was paying was not only a challenge to my omnipotence, but also a loss of illusion. There was a category of 'things-in-themselves', of goodness and truth, loyalty and love, an idealised image, an *idea* in the Platonic sense, of the analysis and of the analyst, which had been sacrificed for my convenience, and somehow, they would not quite leave me in peace!

I believe that this is what Hester Solomon has in mind when she writes:

> The ethical capacity cannot be derived from shared ontological reality, the facts of existence; rather it is derived from value and meaning, which are different, 'higher' and unconditional. (Solomon, 2000, p. 203)

The challenge, the ethical tension, resides in our attempt to reconcile these unconditional imperatives with the existential limits imposed by the human condition.

The Analyst's Loss

As I have implied above, ending is not only a time of losses for the patient but also for the analyst. These losses are listed by Viorst:

> Termination (for the analyst) involves many different kinds of loss - the loss of the whole real object; the loss of a healing symbiotic relatedness; the loss of some specially pleasing role; the loss of a host of professional and therapeutic ambitions; and the loss of the analyst's dream of his or her own

perfection. (Viorst, 1982, quoted in Schachter, 1992, p. 141)

These losses apply to any analyst facing an ending but I believe that there is a specific loss for the retiring analyst, and that is in terms of the self.

'*Ars totum requirit hominem*' quotes Jung (1944, CW 12, p. 6). The opus requires the whole man. In our search for wholeness in our patients, we engage the whole of ourselves.

In a play about Melanie Klein (Nicholas Wright, *Mrs Klein*, National Theatre, 1988) she is portrayed as behaving most of the time as a selfish, irresponsible and foolish human being, but in the last few minutes we watch her preparing herself for her analysis of Paula Hayman. She sits on her chair, becomes quite still, both relaxed and focused in her attentiveness and availability: a state of grace. I believe that we all experience something similar in the few minutes before our patients come in. Alone with ourselves, we meet ourselves: we become aware of what is most essential, most true in ourselves, and this includes our ethical base. We need that *prise de conscience*, that descent within ourselves, the moment of touching down to the core of our being to face the assaults to come, be they rage or seduction, or more subtly, unconscious projections and the moment of confusion when we do not know what belongs to whom. I do not believe that, in what I call 'civilian' life, this happens naturally. Not only does domesticity reclaim one, but all kinds of *divertissements* in the Pascalian sense distract one from oneself and, as in a present day *Pilgrim's Progress*, all manner of dangers lurk ahead. They include, among others, futility and the ghost of depression. I do not say they cannot be overcome, but I am aware that one must be vigilant.

My ex-patient needed me to see her so that she could see herself. I, too, needed my patients for me to see me.

Conclusion

In this chapter, I have attempted to describe a very personal experience of ending, ending not only a particular analysis but ending analysing altogether, that is retiring. I have tried to place this experience, as indeed I have lived it, in the context of an ethical struggle, and stressed the autocratic and arbitrary character of my one-sided decision and its repercussions on the work and the 'coming to terms' of the transitional period. I referred to the two levels of reality in which the analysis takes place, both in terms of time and of values, and stressed the difference between the acceptable pragmatism of our everyday conduct and the exacting demands of other innate, 'in-being-for-ever' values which, as Solomon says, are 'embedded in the human psyche'. Finally I assessed the therapist's loss in terms of the self.

In conclusion I should like to ask Freud's question once again: Is analysis terminable? Looking at analysis as a semantic exercise (language being, in his view, both raw material and sole instrument of all Freudian psychoanalysis), George Steiner reminds us of Wittgenstein's irritation that Freud never shows when to stop the process of free association, and he concludes that:

the process of psychoanalytical decoding and reading in depth can have no intrinsic or verifiable end...there are always further layers to be excavated, deeper shafts to be sunk into the manifold strata of subconscious inception. (Steiner, 1989, p. 46)

This is so on the level of discourse. But I also believe that, more importantly, the unconscious processes go on. I have written elsewhere (Wiener, 1996) of the two levels of time evoked here and stressed the importance of what I have called instances of Kairos which I believe are mutative and everlasting. Zinkin (1998, p. 247) also recognises one aspect of analytic time as 'circular or cyclical, never begun and never ending'.

The only answer to Freud, therefore, has to be a paradoxical one, one which takes into account the two levels of reality: whilst it is inevitable that analyses be terminated (and it might be said that all decisions to end are arbitrary), it is also true that the internal process goes on for ever.

Note

1. Whether a practitioner should continue to hold professional indemnity insurance after retirement remains a matter for discussion in the Ethics Committees of pyschotherapy organisations.

Bibliography

Bomford, R. (1999), *The Symmetry of God*, London/New York: Free Association Books.

Fordham, M. (1978), *Jungian Psychotherapy*, London: Maresfield Library, Karnac Books.

Freud, S. (1937), 'Analysis terminable and interminable', Standard Edition, vol. XXIII, London: The Hogarth Press.

Jung, C. (1944), *Psychology and Alchemy*, Collected Works of C.G. Jung, vol. 12, London and Princeton: Routledge and Princeton University Press.

Kermode, F. (1966), *The Sense of an Ending*, Oxford University Press.

Murdin, L. (1994), 'Time to go: therapist-induced ending in psychotherapy', *British Journal of Psychotherapy*, vol. 10, no.3.

Plato, *The Republic*, Penguin Classics, 1974.

Samuels, R. (1993), *Between Philosophy and Psychoanalysis*, New York and London: Routledge.

Schachter, J. (1992), 'Concepts of termination and post-termination patient-analyst contact', *International Journal of Psychoanalysis*, vol. 73.

Solomon, H. (2000), 'The ethical self', in E. Christopher and H. M. Solomon, *Jungian Thought in the Modern World*, London: Free Association Books.

Steiner, G. (1989), *Real Presences*, London and Boston: Faber & Faber.

Wiener, Y. (1996), 'Chronos and Kairos: two dimensions of time in the psychotherapeutic process', *Journal of the British Association of Psychotherapists* vol. 1, no. 30, Part 1.

Williams, S. (1997), 'Psychotherapeutic ends and endings', *British Journal of Psychotherapy* vol. 13, no. 3.

Yariv, G. (1999), 'Eternity in an hour: experiences of time related to psychotherapy sessions',

Journal of Analytical Psychology, vol. 44.

Zinkin, L. (1998), 'All's well that ends well - or is it?', in H. Zinkin, R. Gordon and J. Haynes (eds), *Dialogue in the Analytic Setting,* London and Philadelphia: Jessica Kingsley Publishers.

Section IV
Confidentiality and Publication

10
The Reporting of Clinical Material: ethical issues

Barbara Wharton

Introduction

In an earlier version of this chapter (Wharton, 1998, p. 205) I commented on the dearth of good quality clinical papers being submitted for publication in analytic journals, a state of affairs which had also been noted by Tuckett (1995, p. 655). A piece of research conducted in 1989 (Klumpner and Frank, 1991), initially with the aim of finding out 'what people – both psychoanalysts and those critical of psychoanalysis – mean when they refer to psychoanalytic research', had revealed that, of a sample of papers most frequently cited over a given period, none contained 'any significant amount of primary clinical data'. Reflecting on the reluctance of writers to publish clinical data, these authors concluded: 'Confidentiality turned out to be our thorniest problem.' Moreover they were left with 'the distinct impression that confidentiality is not simply one issue, but several' (op. cit., p. 539).

Assuming that the problem posed by confidentiality to potential writers of clinical papers is primarily a fear of litigation, it is fair to say that this fear has also prompted a much more careful consideration of the ethical implications and consequences for the patient, the analyst, and the analysis. It can no longer be taken for granted that publication is permissible as long as one is not found out – that is, as long as the patient is unlikely to read what has been written about him, and as long as his relatives and friends would not recognise him. There are deeper ethical issues to take into account related to the nature of analysis, the analytical relationship, and the patient's trust.

Traditionally, of course, beginning with Freud's well-known case studies, and to a lesser extent Jung's, the presentation of clinical material has been the principal method of making known what is an essentially private process – that is, of teaching analysis, and of sharing analytical ideas with colleagues. Published clinical papers make it possible to share ideas among a wide professional audience and also to convey to any members of the general public who care to read such accounts something of what analysis is about. Presenting clinical material in supervision has become the chief means, after the personal analysis, by which apprentice analysts learn their craft. Although formal supervision comes to an end with training, many practising analysts continue to discuss their work with peers. This acts as a check on an isolated and isolating procedure; it encourages the analyst towards a more objective perspective and it relieves the loneliness of the consulting room.

The need for open discussion among colleagues is not one of mere convenience: it is an ethical requirement. Analysts need to work in an atmosphere of greater openness in which what they do is subjected to the scrutiny of their peers, and so that they can be seen to be accountable. Otherwise confidentiality is in danger of falling into its own shadow, that of secrecy, or, in the current idiom, 'cover-up'. In a wider sense, too, analysts have an obligation to promote education and research in psychoanalytic theory and technique, both at a small-group level, at the institutional level, and at an international level, so that patients may benefit from the most advanced thinking and discoveries in the field and from our improving ability to treat them. Moreover there is increasing political pressure, in an environment of proliferating therapeutic methods, to explain and justify publicly a treatment which is expensive in terms of both time and money. Formal public research in psychoanalysis is now being undertaken in this country at a number of centres: the work being done in the Research Training Programme at University College London (Emde and Fonagy, 1997) is one example.

In the last ten years the problems surrounding confidentiality have, if anything, increased. The new data protection laws, both in this country and in the USA, have opened up a completely new range of problems which it is not within the scope of this chapter to cover in detail, but the ethical issues with which they confront analysts are relevant in relation to confidentiality. These laws mean that analysts and psychotherapists can be legally required to give information about their patients in a court of law. Bollas and Sundelson (1995) have taken up the serious questions raised by such legislation with regard to the practice of psychoanalysis and analytical psychotherapy: they point out that this method of treatment depends on the patient's freedom at all levels to free associate and to say whatever offers itself to be said, and on the analyst's freedom to maintain an evenly hovering attention. The action of analysis takes place in the psychic sphere, in an atmosphere of mutual trust, where fantasies and fears can be experienced, verbalised and thought about without being enacted; the threat of external interference threatens or even destroys these possibilities. Between the two extremes of voluntarily writing papers on the one hand and enforced reporting on the other, lies a minefield of ethical issues and dilemmas which are now fortunately being discussed more freely. It is becoming increasingly clear, and urgent, that as a profession analysts and analytical psychotherapists need to work out an ethical stance on these problems which will ensure that the privilege of their position is respected, preserved and properly understood (cf. Minutes, October 2000).

As Klumpner and Frank discovered, not only was clinical material itself sparse, it was also 'sketchy', 'overgeneralised', and its 'assumptions were not testable'. What, then, are the requirements of clinical reports and what affects their quality? The consensus seems to be that they need to be sufficiently specific, detailed and veridical, free from 'conscious and preconscious narrative smoothing', which can result from the reporter's wish to prove his point (Spence, 1998, p. 643), to provide the reader or listener with enough unbiased evidence to reach his own conclusions. Such detailed and 'true' reporting sharpens the questions of anonymity and of how far 'disguise' can be used.

Anonymity, Confidentiality, Publication and the vas bene clausum

Jung used the alchemical metaphor of the *vas bene clausum* to express the privacy of the analytic container. The contents of the *vas* had to be prevented from leaking into the outside world in a potentially dangerous way, and also had to be protected from the intrusion or admixture of harmful elements from the environment. This image illustrates one aspect of the need for confidentiality: clinically, analysts know that for analysis to work the setting must be protected and the boundaries preserved. With the well-being of the patient uppermost in mind, the analyst has an ethical duty to maintain an environment which will be optimally conducive to the patient's ultimate health. However, the *vas bene clausum* can suggest an absolute: the hermetically sealed vessel of the alchemists. But it is unlikely that Jung intended it in this absolute way. For Jung the *vas* was an extremely rich and multi-faceted symbol, and seems to have included the principle of permeability. One of the images associated with it is the womb, which stands for vital processes of flow and interchange, as well as containing and holding. In case the reporting of clinical material suggests a leaking out of something private, it is instructive to consider the meaning of the word. 'Clinic' has come into English through Latin from the ancient Greek word meaning a bed or couch. A subsidiary meaning of 'clinic' now, according to the *Oxford English Dictionary*, is 'the teaching of medicine or surgery at the hospital bedside'. Thus clinical events can be seen as taking place within a boundaried setting (around the patient's bed) but they are not, nor can they by definition be, confined to the two-person privacy of the surgeon or physician and the patient; the onlookers/students are part of the clinical process. At the same time there is something of a paradox here: we know that patients come to analysts with the expectation that what they say will be treated confidentially and that that is an important building-block in the formation of trust.

There are two distinct aspects of confidentiality: anonymity and confidentiality proper. First and most obviously, the patient must be protected from exposure which might make him, his family, or friends recognisable to a third person reading the material. It is not difficult, through the omission of names and other identifying biographical details, to achieve this level of anonymity. Omitting details might be regarded as a kind of disguise, but heavier disguise – in the sense of substituting such details – can merge into misrepresentation.

Many professional bodies, in fields other than analysis, subscribe to the principle of protecting a patient's anonymity. Guidelines issued by the American Psychological Association (1992) and the American Psychiatric Association (1995) advocate the use of disguise, which could include the omission or changing of identifying details, to 'preserve the anonymity of the individuals involved', to 'ensure that such persons are not individually identifiable', and further that 'discussions do not cause harm to subjects who might identify themselves' (Goldberg, 1997, p. 435). Recently, however, the International Committee of Medical Journal Editors (ICMJE) has reiterated their contrasting 1995 statement, firming up on two particular issues: that no attempt be made to disguise or misrepresent details, and that the patient's informed consent be obtained (see Tuckett, 2000b; and Minutes October 2000, for a discussion of this issue). It is interesting that the medical view differs from the psychological one on the matter of disguise; I will discuss this further below. While it is useful to take account of the guidelines related professions are setting themselves, it is also important to be clear about the discrete characteristics and requirements of our own profession. We cannot simply assume that what is relevant and advisable in medicine, or in clinical psychology, is necessarily applicable in psychoanalysis. In the United Kingdom there have recently been disturbing reports about the organs and tissues of deceased persons being removed for research purposes without the consent of relatives; these reports have naturally aroused much anxiety and distress in the medical profession and in the general public. Perhaps analysts should consider how far psychological material is comparable to organs and tissues. Perhaps we might even consider whether there could be the equivalent of a 'donor card' for psychological material to which patients could be invited to subscribe on a voluntary basis.

Reading the recommendations of the American Psychological Association and of the ICMJE one could be misled into thinking that disguise and consent are alternative strategies with the same aim. In this connection it is important to keep in mind the distinction between anonymity and confidentiality. Disguise would be aimed at preventing the patient being recognised by his relatives and friends, that is, at protecting his anonymity. The medical ban on the use of disguise has the purpose of avoiding misunderstandings which could lead to erroneous conclusions; the subsequent inclusion of identifying details would mean that the patient, and even his family, were unprotected. This might be acceptable in the medical field, but in the psychological field a different view would have to be taken; here the patient's anonymity and the privacy of his family have to be safeguarded. To that end the omission or changing of all proper names and external identifying characteristics would be uncontroversial; other external identifying features can also probably be omitted without detriment. The option of substitution carries more risk of misleading or even of distorting dynamic factors. A case is cited by Klumpner and Frank (1991) of an analyst presenting her work with a child who was described, for the purpose of disguise, as suffering from gastric ulcer; the analyst later let slip that the child was in fact diabetic (op cit., p.539). This is a very obvious example of the potential of disguise to mislead, which could have serious consequences. Identifying features such as a physical condition which, as in this case, might well have psychological implications, does present a particular difficulty. Each case would require careful consideration and an individual judgement. In general, however, there is a strong argument that the more the focus of the reporting is on the patient's inner world and on the analytic interaction, the less important external identifying features become, and the less disguise is needed. By the same token, however, because the inner-world material is both unique and known to the patient, it would be highly unlikely that the patient could be disguised from himself, even if such an intention were ethically justified. Indeed, because the action of analysis hinges on this intimate, inner material, preserving it in as undistorted a form as possible is in itself of the highest ethical importance.

Ways of avoiding or circumventing problems of confidentiality have included adapting already published case studies (thus shifting the ethical responsibility elsewhere!), or using examples from literature. These, however, cannot be a satisfactory substitute for clinical material since they lack the essential elements of the direct personal interaction. Some alternatives to straightforward disguise have been discussed by Gabbard (2000): making composites of several patients is a method which is apparently sometimes used for teaching purposes. Its drawbacks would be that it would still constitute a breach (or breaches) of confidentiality, and would also seriously undermine the principle of veracity – of adhering to the dynamics of a 'true' case. A further alternative is 'transfer of authorship', an intriguing solution which involves persuading a colleague to write up someone else's case material or to allow his name to be appended to an article he has not written. Gabbard points out that the use by supervisors of their supervisees' clinical material is a variant of this practice; it would presumably require seeking two lots of consent. It is hard to believe that such a strategy could be taken seriously: for example, how could a third person describe the subtleties of transference and countertransference? Yet another variant, that of anonymous authorship, has recently been put forward by William Young (2000). Young points out that a strong identifying factor in a patient's recognising material is the analyst himself. Publishing anonymously would also remove much of the narcissistic gratification which is a powerful motivation for writing, and would seriously challenge the analyst to write for the benefit of colleagues and of future patients. The disadvantage of that solution would be that it would remove both scientific and ethical accountability from the author, thus possibly compromising the scientific value of the work. In a subsequent contribution to the discussion, Valerie Sinason pointed out that the strategy of omitting authors' names as a means of protecting patients' confidentiality was adopted a few years ago in a book on child psychotherapy; the contributors were listed in alphabetical order, but their names were not attached to their papers. She comments that sometimes seeking consent from parents of children in treatment could actually be dangerous (Sinason, 2000).

***

To turn now from the theme of preserving the anonymity of the patient to that of confidentiality proper: the issue at stake is whether it is ethically justifiable to reveal information that has been given in confidence and that might not have been given had not privacy been assured. If revealing such information can be justified in certain circumstances, what would those be, and would it be necessary and/or possible to impose safeguards?

It is sometimes argued that, provided the patient is protected from recognition by others, and is unlikely ever to be aware of what has been said about him, publication without his consent or conscious knowledge may be permissible. However, such an argument raises the question of basic honesty in the therapeutic relationship and of how such concealment can be reconciled with the fact that analysis is founded on recognising the potential power and effect of unconscious knowledge. What is communicated unconsciously to the patient and to what effect?

Colman makes a valid point that analysts constantly withhold information from patients (Colman, 2000). This judicious restraint is necessary both for the patient's well-being and for the process of analysis to be possible. Some of the information withheld is in any case not directly relevant to the patient. However the use by the analyst of material entrusted to him by the patient in confidence does seem to present a special case. What the analyst does with that material, his assimilation of it, his thinking about it and his writing about it are very much concerns of the patient, although again what is communicated to the patient, and when, is a matter for the analyst's judgement. However, if an analyst wishes to publish (make public) that material, conveyed in private and with an assumption of privacy, he will have to confront more profound ethical problems than are implied by 'restraint'.

There are some who argue that breaching analytic confidence, even with consent, cannot be justified. Some believe further that the absolute privacy of analysis is essential to the process, so that any compromise damages the analysis irrevocably: in an almost concrete way it would be like breaking the *vas*. Britton describes how an analyst who writes about a patient, even with the patient's consent, may still be left with a feeling of guilt at betraying, if not a confidence, then an 'affiliation'; the analyst is in some sense using the patient for his own ends. As Britton puts it:

> The communications internal to one relationship have become the means of furthering the development of another relationship. (Britton, in Ward (ed.), 1997, p. 12)

At the same time, however, he recognises that one's allegiance to a patient is counterbalanced by, and sometimes in conflict with, one's allegiance to colleagues, expressed in a commitment to share knowledge. In addition we need regularly to move away from the intensely subjective view which we mostly take with patients in order to achieve a more objective view through discussion.

A further issue to be taken into account is that published clinical material is read not only by other professional colleagues, and one's patients, but also by prospective patients. Casement briefly raises a query about the discouraging effect the possibility of exposure might have on the latter group (Casement, 1985, p. 226). Perhaps, however, prospective patients might be equally encouraged by the possibility of being thought about carefully, sensitively and respectfully in the way that is demonstrated in a good clinical account, especially if the principle of obtaining the patient's consent is spelled out. A different disadvantage I have met is that some would-be patients use the fact of having read clinical accounts defensively, as a way of avoiding their own experience, but this problem is not insurmountable – it can be analysed in due course.

Seeking Consent

If clinical material is to be made available – and it seems that it alone can provide an adequate basis for the discussion of analytic theory and practice – the difficulties around obtaining the patient's consent will have to be faced. Freud was quite clear that his patients relied implicitly on the confidentiality of the analytic setting:

It is certain that the patients would never have spoken if it had occurred to them that their admissions might possibly be put to scientific uses. (Freud, 1905, SE VII, p. 8)

He was equally clear that 'to ask them themselves for leave to publish their case would be quite unavailing' (Freud, ibid.). In the event, according to Deutsch, Dora did find out about the publication of her case and was said to be proud of the fact (Deutsch, 1957, cited in Lipton 1991, p.967).

The matter of consent is far from straightforward. First, as Goldberg points out (Goldberg, 1997, p. 436), it is not at all clear what 'consent' means in an analytic context. A physician or surgeon can inform a patient of the possible consequences of a physical treatment which are to an extent known and predictable. In the analytic setting the situation is vastly more complicated because it is affected by the transference/countertransference. There are two stages in the 'operation', the request for permission, and the publication itself, and for the first the patient must inevitably be unprepared. I make a distinction between the two stages because I want to emphasise that the mere fact of seeking consent is a powerful interference in the analysis, and it is one introduced by the analyst. We might formulate 'informed consent' in the analytic context as consent issuing from a thorough discussion and analysis of the patient's feelings and fantasies in relation both to the request and to the proposed publication itself. The consequences of neither of these events can be predicted since they depend on the meanings attributed consciously and unconsciously by the individual patient at any given time. The meanings will be discovered, if at all, only as time elapses.

One way to avoid interfering in the ongoing analytic process would be to postpone publication until after the treatment has ended. But would that mean publishing without permission? Or seeking a 'blanket' permission before the patient leaves, thereby possibly obscuring the immediate issues of ending, and also losing the opportunity to discuss the patient's feelings fully? Or approaching the patient for permission after he has left, thus again omitting the possibility of discussion and also risking interrupting the post-analytic healing process which may take many years? Another possible approach is to secure the patient's consent at the beginning of treatment. This way the cogent objection to disrupting the analysis when it is under way is met. To do this, however, would be to burden the patient with a weighty request before he has had a chance to develop a relationship of trust with the analyst, and probably before he has any real sense of what analysis means. Aron points out that it would put the meeting of the analyst's needs in the forefront, before the patient has had 'at least some experience [of] having their therapeutic needs met' (Aron, 2000, p. 240).

It should be considered whether the need for consent varies in different circumstances. For example, does a spoken report differ from a written report in this respect, or does the size or nature of the audience or readership affect the need to seek consent? Even when presenting material to a small group of colleagues one is entrusting the patient and oneself somewhat paradoxically to the confidentiality of a group, and one's colleagues cannot always be relied upon. Lipton tells a cautionary tale of a case being presented to a study group a member of which, without the original analyst's permission, published the material in a paper he was writing which was subsequently read and recognised by the patient's father (Lipton, 1991, p.982). It seems fairly clear that to seek permission for discussing a patient with a colleague or in a small peer group would be not only impracticable but over-restrictive and even detrimental to the patient, but not doing so entails a risk.

My own experience in seeking the consent of patients for publication is that it has certainly created a disturbance, and that in itself has usually made them angry. For some patients the interference has had particularly troubling personal meanings, echoing past abusive relationships in which the good of the child had in some way been subordinated to that of the caretaker. It has to be acknowledged that in writing a paper for publication the analyst is indeed giving his own needs (for narcissistic gratification, or for professional advancement) a high priority. The working-through of such situations has invariably resulted in benefits to the patient in terms of greater insight, increased freedom of emotional expression, and an enrichment of the analytic relationship. An excellent illustration of this process is the Fosshage protocol which gives a detailed account of part of the working-through of a patient's reaction to the analyst's request for permission to publish her material (Fosshage, 1990).

The process of interrupting the analysis to request permission for publication puts considerable strain on the transference relationship and underscores the fact that the analyst has to exercise a fine judgement about whether a patient can tolerate it. An aspect of the strain is that the patient is put in touch with the analyst's mind in a way which is different from what he normally experiences. He is wrenched out of his natural transference and is called upon to relate on more equal terms, albeit temporarily; this might be described as a move from subjectivity to objectivity – the patient is invited to stand beside the analyst and observe himself more objectively than is normally required by the therapeutic alliance. While there may be a considerable gain to the patient in this, it can also be experienced as a profound loss, akin to the loss of infantile dependence or the loss of innocence. Clearly the timing is important and has to be gauged carefully. There may be times during an analysis when broaching the subject of writing a paper would be unwise, or indeed damaging, and there may be patients whom one could not expect to be flexible enough, or to have the particular kind of ego strength required, for such a project.

Writing is disturbing to the analysis in other ways too: there is a danger that the analyst's preoccupation with a particular theme might disturb his free-floating attention and cause him to focus unduly on that theme to the neglect of others. An interesting phenomenon which I and others have noticed is that often, when one is writing on a particular theme, patients conveniently produce material that fits in with it (cf. Hubback, 1997). On the positive side this might suggest an unconscious attunement between analyst and patient; more negatively it could be seen as the patient's material being shaped unconsciously by the analyst. Moreover, the state of mind required for analysing is very different from that required for writing, and in my experience it is not easy to move freely from one to the other. For that reason I try to confine writing to analytic holidays. When I am so caught up with an idea on which I am working that patients themselves become an unwelcome distraction I know that something is amiss!

Being invited to be the subject of a paper obviously plays into a patient's narcissism and exhibitionism, and the analyst will have to decide whether this can be worked on analytically. Patients of whom I have asked consent have invariably felt gratified at the sense of being singled out or made to feel 'special'. This has sometimes been tempered by the discovery that they are not the only ones to be written about in a paper. Some patients who have *not* been written about have expressed envy towards the more 'favoured' ones. Writing papers is thus also a means by which painful sibling rivalries are re-evoked, and again by a direct action of the analyst – a further aspect of the disturbance. There are other fantasies, too: the patient may feel specially chosen to be the analyst's oedipal partner, and the subsequent paper becomes a kind of 'baby' they have made together; alternatively, the paper can be felt as something like an umbilical cord which is never cut, joining the analyst and patient forever, or as a womb-like container in which the patient is held, never to be expelled. Here it becomes clear that it is only patients with a sufficiently robust symbolic function who can be expected to manage the stress of knowing they have been written about. If they have this, it should be possible to analyse their fantasies. If they do not, there could be too great a danger of delusion.

Part of the feeling of being singled out is the patient's fantasy about being invited to help the analyst and here there is a danger of compliance: the desire to remain special may get in the way of impulses to thwart the analyst. Certainly none of the patients whom I have approached for permission to write about them has refused it; I think their reactions have been thoroughly analysed, and that their agreement was not due to compliance, but I cannot be certain. There may also be a fantasy of helping others, including future generations of patients, as Stoller has discussed (Stoller, 1988); he writes movingly of a patient who felt that the writing of a paper about her gave meaning to a life which otherwise seemed to her wasted and meaningless. I have found with some patients that the writing and discussion have given them a fresh perspective on their life, helping them to discern patterns and a sense of movement in what previously seemed random or chaotic; as one patient put it: 'You are helping me to put all the bits in the right order.' It is a positive aspect of the objectivity, mentioned above. The 'making of a story' – in a general sense, regardless of whether it takes the form of a written paper – as a joint enterprise undertaken by analyst and patient can be an important ingredient in healing.

I have alluded briefly to some risks in writing about patients with their knowledge which have been readily perceptible. Another risk is the operation of unconscious envy in the patient which can undermine subsequent work; this might range from an envy of the analyst's ability to write, to an envy of his capacity for understanding and insight: the very resources on which the patient depends for his healing. There is also envy of the joint enterprise itself, which may be seen as a manifestation of the particularly malignant form of envy which Proner has described as envy of one's self (Proner, 1986, 1988). Envy can be very persistent and remarkably resistant to analysis, fresh layers of it repeatedly revealing themselves. Even when permission has been granted the analyst needs to be clear about what that permission means to the patient – whether it is a 'gift in perpetuity', so to speak, or for the purpose of a particular paper at a particular time; whether, that is, it is a kind of loan, for which permission would have to be sought again on any subsequent occasion when the analyst wished to use the material.

In seeking permission for writing I have simultaneously offered the patient the opportunity of commenting on and possibly amending the material, and amendments have sometimes been worked out in discussion and incorporated. Knowing that the patient would read the material has sharpened my awareness of my use of language. Lipton points out that 'the language has to be accurate, but it need not be traumatic', and he gives an example of using a circumlocution ('she took things out on herself') rather than describing a patient as 'a masochist' (Lipton, 1991, p. 975). Everyday language is usually much more meaningful and acceptable to patients than technical terms, which can feel pathologising and 'clinical' in the worst sense. Thinking about the language one is using can also alert the analyst to become more aware of any countertransference hostility towards the patient in question, which might have been a factor in choosing to write about that patient in the first place (cf. Gabbard, 2000, p. 1,076). It seems important to me that the patient feels he is still the 'owner' of his material. Once the transference meanings have been understood as far as possible, I want the patient to know that it is *their* story that is being told, and not to feel that I have stolen from them in any external, non-transference sense. A patient described to me the painful experience of having been written about unknowingly by a previous analyst and of feeling that her material had been stolen from her, and used in ways which she did not recognise as belonging to her. The analyst's formulations seemed like a hurtful falsification against which she had no redress, in spite of the fact that some of the formulations made by that analyst now seem to be partly corroborated.

Several of my patients have reacted strongly to discovering, in what I have written, thoughts about them, or formulations, which I have not (yet) communicated to them directly. This has variously been experienced as my hiding something from them which they had a right to know, cheating them, or doing something behind their back, and again they have been justifiably angry. It has also enhanced the fantasy of the analyst's omnipotence and omniscience in an unfortunate way, putting the analyst in the position of the parent who 'knows best'. Again, a thorough working-through has been necessary. Sometimes a patient has realised spontaneously that these thoughts have been communicated, but indirectly, in that they have formed the basis of numerous interpretations. However, whether or not the patient reaches that realisation, it is important that such thoughts or formulations be discussed and possibly modified before publication. To discover them after publication would be potentially much more traumatic. However, it is also true that the thinking that goes into a paper can lead to new understandings which cannot be passed on to the patient immediately but have to await an appropriate time. The ambiguity of the situation is evident: on the one hand is the possible disadvantage of the analyst's being out of step with the patient, while on the other is the particular energetic intellectual and emotional focusing necessary for writing a paper, which goes beyond the day-to-day reflective thinking and can only benefit the patient in the long run.

It may be objected that the measures described here fall too much into the category of gratification, or manipulation, that they are non-analytic, and that the patient's anger and other possible negative reactions are stifled as a result. That may be partly true. But since the whole procedure of writing a paper, and of seeking permission for publication, is extra-analytic, I feel I owe it to patients to protect them from unnecessary pain within this circumscribed area, while at the same time analysing their responses, feelings and fantasies as far as possible.

Technical Aspects of Clinical Reporting

Although I have called this section 'technical aspects' I believe that the quality of clinical reporting is also an ethical issue. Out of respect both for patients and for scientific endeavour reporting needs to be as accurate and as 'true' as possible, though the meanings of 'accurate' and 'true' in this context will need to be elucidated. I propose therefore to discuss the kind of clinical material likely to be most effective for present purposes. To place these remarks in context I will first give a brief overview of the history of clinical reporting in psychoanalysis.

The tradition of case studies goes back of course to Freud. His *Fragment of an Analysis of a Case of Hysteria*' ('Dora'), the first of his five case histories, was published in 1905, the subsequent ones in 1909 ('Little Hans' and the 'Rat Man'), 1911 ('Schreber') and 1918 (the 'Wolf Man'). Another outstanding case study in the history of psychoanalysis is Klein's *Narrative of a Child Analysis* (1961).

It is interesting to compare the comments of Freud and Klein on their concerns and aims in publishing their case material. In his Prefatory Remarks to 'Dora', Freud states that his purpose was to 'substantiate' (Freud, 1905, SE VII, p.7) the theoretical views he had proposed in 1895 and 1896 (in *Studies on Hysteria* (Breuer and Freud) and in 'The Aetiology of Hysteria'). He regarded it as 'awkward' that he had had to publish 'the results of his enquiries without there being any possibility of other workers in the field testing and checking them' (ibid.). His purpose was to 'demonstrate the intimate structure of a neurotic disorder and the determination of its symptoms'; he did not aim to '[reproduce] the process of interpretation to which the patient's associations had to be subjected, but only the results of that process', and he acknowledges the 'incompleteness' of this procedure (op. cit., pp. 12, 13). Klein, on the other hand, states her first aim to be that of '[illustrating her] technique in greater detail than [she had] done formerly' – 'the day-to-day movement of the analysis and the continuity running through it'; however, she also intends that 'the details of this analysis [will] clarify and support [her] concepts' (Klein, 1961, Preface, p. 11). Thus in Freud we see the beginnings of a tradition of using analytical case material to illustrate and to give substance to theory. It is also relevant to note the distinction implied by both Freud and Klein between general theories of personality or of development on the one hand, and theories of practice on the other – what Susan Budd has called the 'how-to-do-it level' (Budd, in Ward (ed.), 1997, p. 33).

Both Freud and Klein are aware of the problems inherent in remembering and recording material. It is significant that the treatment of Dora spanned only three months and that of Richard (the subject of the *Narrative*) only four. The volume of material did not therefore reach the unmanageable proportions of analyses which might have lasted years. Freud explains that he wrote the study of Dora in the two weeks following her departure, 'while my recollection of the case was still fresh and was heightened by my interest in its publication' (Freud, 1905, SE VII, p. 10). He is careful to point out, however, that he recorded the wording of Dora's dreams immediately after the session in which they were recounted; 'they thus afforded a secure point of attachment for the chain of interpretations and recollections which proceeded from them' (ibid.). Klein had made 'fairly extensive notes' after each session, which she prepared for publication fifteen years later; according to Elliot Jaques who helped her, this entailed a process of 'carefully editing in style, but not in content, so as to leave intact the picture of how the work had gone at the time' (Klein, 1961, Foreword).

Freud touches on another important issue, that of the shaping of an account. Although 'the record is not absolutely – phonographically – exact, ... it can claim to possess a high degree of trustworthiness'. He then adds, interestingly, 'Nothing of any importance has been altered in it except in some places the order in which the explanations are given; and this has been done for the sake of presenting the case *in a more connected form*' (Freud, 1905, SE VII, p. 10, my italics). Here he seems to foreshadow a theme developed in the 1980s by Donald Spence: the shaping of case reports into a cohesive narrative; but Spence recognised that the process he called 'narrative smoothing' not only makes reports easier to read but also risks falsifying them (Spence, 1997, p. 78). Klein, too, is aware of problems of accuracy in recording, acknowledging that she might not always be quoting literally either the patient's words or her interpretations, and that the sequences might not always be correct. However, she rejects the possibility of taking notes during a session as being too disturbing for both participants, and she dismisses out of hand the idea of 'a recording machine, either visible or hidden' as being 'absolutely against the fundamental principles on which psychoanalysis rests, namely the exclusion of any audience during an analytic session' (Klein, 1961, Preface, p. 11).

Klein also takes up the highly relevant issue of the nature of evidence in psychoanalysis as compared with that required in the physical sciences; she suggests that the attempt to record exact data in psychoanalysis reflects 'a pseudo-scientific approach' since the 'intangible factors' of the 'workings of the unconscious mind, *and the response of the psychoanalyst to them*', including the 'intuition of the analyst' (op. cit., p. 12, my italics) cannot be quantified or classified.

Freud and Klein were thus concerned with many of the issues which still preoccupy us today: how to remember, how and what to record, and its status as evidence, as well as the central problem of the inalienable privacy of analysis which, in Freud's words, 'brooks no listener' (Freud, 1915, SE XV, p. 17).

An obvious problem about recording sessions afterwards is the fallibility of the analyst's memory. The inevitable delay risks the further blunting or distorting of recall. Lustman comments wryly on the irony of the analyst's placing so much trust in his own memory: 'I consider it peculiar that analysts who every day deal with the vagaries of memory would trust their own memories in terms of scientific data' (Lustman, 1963, p. 69). Wallerstein and Sampson quote the well-known incident recorded by Kubie (1958, pp. 232-3), which is also cited by Spence (in Ward (ed.), 1997), of the supervisee who mistakenly 'remembered' that his patient had requested that the tape-recorder be switched off at a certain point in a session; when the recording was listened to it was discovered that the supervisee himself had suggested switching it off, a fact he had completely distorted.

At the level of attempting to produce an accurate record, Wallerstein and Sampson discuss the methods used to circumvent the first and overwhelming difficulty: that no third person can be present to observe the proceedings in the consulting room. Such methods would include audio- and video-recording. However, apart from the intrusiveness of these methods, it must be questioned whether such recording, while 'accurate' in a verbatim sense, would convey the subtleties of feeling and meaning which are the essence of analysis. The content of an analytic session is intensely private and personal, frequently bewildering, hard to grasp and to formulate; the most important events take place in the minds of the two participants and can only be inferred. Without an account of the analyst's thoughts and feelings, or, as Spence has described it, a commentary by the analyst 'naturalising' the text (cf. Spence, 1981), the record is near meaningless.

Theory: its uses and influence

The scientific validity of traditional case studies is another issue discussed by Wallerstein and Sampson – that is, how far they can be used to support general theories of the mind. One disadvantage of the 'clinical retrospective method' used in case studies is that causes are inferred after the fact; linking a patient's present symptoms with past events often seems to suggest satisfying sequences of cause and effect, but the fact that human behaviour is so complex and multiply determined makes it impossible to reverse the direction – to predict the future consequences of present events. Moreover, human behaviour is also over-determined: that is, the same (overt) behaviour might be the manifestation of different psychological states in different people, or in the same person at different times.

In what sense and to what degree a case study can validly be held up as proof of a theory has been variously questioned (cf. Wallerstein and Sampson, 1971) as the pressure to uphold the scientific nature of psychoanalysis has increased in the face of challenge. Attempts continue to be made to produce evidence which can be 'tested and checked' by an observer. There are different ways of approaching theory, however: one can use it to generalise and to classify in order to make comparisons and predictions and to build up a general theory. In this case one would need reliable 'evidence', verifiable across different cases, to support the theory. In a recent contribution Tuckett, citing Widlöcher (1994), implicitly raises the question of what clinical reporting is for, suggesting that it might be seen less as a method of 'proving' theory and more as a means of enabling clinicians to learn from each others' experience (Tuckett, 2000a, p. 404). Clinical reports provide a means of stimulating thinking both in the writer and in the listener/reader about what actually happens in an analytic interaction and its possible meanings, why any given intervention works or does not, and indeed what leads us to believe it has or has not worked. Such ongoing thinking is essential to the continuing progress of analysis as a method of treatment.

Theory can be thought of as a way of perceiving the patterns in an individual person's life and development, of building up a theory about that particular person. Such a theory still calls for verification but the evidence unfolds with the patient's material, and is much less subject to problems of comparison and generalisation. Of course, care needs to be taken with regard to how theory is used, even a theory about a particular patient. It can be useful as an aid to thinking about a patient but should not be used as a Procrustean mould into which the patient is expected to fit. I am frequently surprised to discover how different each patient is – how, for example, even when the affect being expressed, or the developmental stage being enacted in the transference, is known by the same name, the quality of it varies subtly from one patient to another, or in the same patient at different times, and elicits subtly different responses. Jung seemed to have this in mind when, in the context of writing about the powerful bond of the transference/countertransference relationship, which he described as 'a combination resting on mutual unconsciousness', he stated:

Each new case that requires thorough treatment is pioneer work, and every trace of routine then proves to be a blind alley ... and sometimes it sets tasks which challenge not only our understanding or our sympathy, but the whole man. (Jung, 1946, CW 16, para. 367)

Jung seems to be suggesting not only that a new theory is necessary for each patient, but that the working through of the transference neurosis is a task intensely personal to the two people concerned, and indeed that each case is unique.

The notion of the observed being affected by the observer is now a commonplace one, even in the field of physics. It is expressed by Jung in the vivid imagery of the alchemical metaphor, the chemical mix in which both elements are changed. As Editor of the *Zentralblatt* he was sensitive to the possibility of the reporting of clinical material being influenced by the writer's point of view; in 1935 he wrote:

The empirical intellect, occupying itself with the minutiae of case-histories, involuntarily imports its own philosophical premises not only into the arrangement but also into the judgment of the material, and even into the apparently objective presentation of the data. (Jung, 1935, CW 10, para. 1042)

A major issue which we cannot afford to ignore is the extent to which theory influences the analyst's every perception, observation, and response. This was well illustrated in a collection of papers published in 1990 in the journal *Psychoanalytic Inquiry* in which a number of analysts from different theoretical backgrounds commented on a detailed clinical protocol of four analytic sessions presented by James Fosshage (Fosshage, 1990). The attention to detail clearly highlighted the different mental models being employed, consciously and unconsciously, by the various contributors. A similar project was carried out by the *International Journal of Psycho-Analysis* in 1993 when a series of responses by different analysts to two clinical presentations, by Dennis Duncan and Theodore Jacobs respectively, was published. Significantly, Jacobs's presentation was entitled: 'The inner experiences of the analyst: their contribution to the analytic process' (Jacobs, 1993).

Spence strikes a warning note when he writes of the 'damaging possibility' of the analyst's influence on the analysis, even on the patient's 'free' associations which are 'sometimes (and perhaps frequently) ... directed by the analyst's own agenda'. He suggests that the analyst 'can impose a story line on the patient's productions and ... turn them into supporting evidence for received theory' (Spence, 1997, p. 78). The influence of theory is unavoidable: we simply have to be more alert to it. Theory that is only partially digested can be particularly problematic, as Duncan describes (Duncan, 1993); and a theory we might be trying to develop, or our theory of a particular patient, can become obstacles to maintaining the open mind that analysts need.

Theory influences both what we select to respond to in the patient's material and how we respond to it. The Fosshage protocol illustrates clearly how the selection of one element in a patient's statement rather than another leads to the material developing in a particular way. This selecting is something that analysts are doing all the time in analysis – many times in every session. It does not invalidate the process, but we need to be aware of its effects and to be alert to the signs that theory might be obscuring rather than illuminating our experience of the patient.

Selectivity

Selection is inevitable in writing about clinical material if only to enable the analyst to handle and organise the large amount of data at his disposal. Moreover, the analyst selects the patient he is going to write about: he chooses someone who illustrates the theory he wishes to develop; he will naturally elaborate on certain relevant material, perhaps to the neglect of details which might suggest other views. He will probably tend to focus on sessions which he feels he understands rather than those which leave him in doubt or confusion. It is often much more difficult to remember a session one did not understand, partly because the material does not hang together, and partly perhaps because it is painful to recall the sense of confusion and of not understanding. For similar reasons it is also difficult for the analyst to present material he does or did not understand, and material he feels he might have mishandled. He may fear an adverse effect on his reputation, or the internal discomfort of feeling incompetent or not in control.

It is difficult to institute safeguards against error either of observation or of judgement in the analytic situation; no third party can be present to check the analyst's perceptions. It is true that it is the analyst who has first-hand knowledge of the patient and the experience of the analysis to date – all that gives him a 'privileged competence' compared with the 'normative competence' of his audience or readers (Spence, 1981). He is faced, however, with a major challenge of how to leave room in his presentation for other points of view: this means putting forward his evidence in a sufficiently 'loose' way to enable his listeners or readers to take hold of it and to turn it round, as it were, so that other aspects become visible and other viewpoints possible. It is not easy for the presenter to check his natural desire to give a well-rounded, highly polished paper which will elicit praise and admiration, offering instead a more open-ended presentation in which not every loose end is tied up and every conclusion drawn. As Jung remarked in his 1935 Editorial: 'An hypothesis does not rest only on the apparent testimony of experience, it rests also on the judgment of the observer' (Jung, 1935, CW 10, para. 1041). The task is how to present clinical material in such a way as to give the observer, that is the listener or reader, enough evidence of a sufficiently unbiased nature to form his own judgements. This leads to the question of what is the most useful focus of reporting to enable that to take place.

What Should Be the Focus of Clinical Reporting?

The agonising over the scientific value of clinical reporting and its validity for research purposes – what Klein called the 'pseudo-scientific approach' (see above) – has been based on the false assumption that it is valid to apply to analysis an epistemology more appropriate to the natural sciences, in which observable facts are less ambiguous. Ricoeur points out that 'facts in psychoanalysis are in no way facts of observable behaviour. They are "reports"' (Ricoeur, 1977, p. 837). Even a dream recounted by a patient is a report of that dream, not the dream itself; it has been sifted by consciousness, and subtly changed and 'distanced' by intervening events. Above all it is that particular dream he has remembered and is recounting, at that moment, in that way, in the context of the transference relationship at that particular time. In Ricoeur's words we are '[forced] to situate the facts of psychoanalysis inside a sphere of motivation and meaning' (ibid.).

Ricoeur reinforces his argument by pointing out that within the context of psychic reality, which is the stuff of analysis (as contrasted with material reality which is the focus of the natural sciences), dreams carry the same psychic validity as myths, fairy-tales, symptoms, illusions, hallucinations: 'their reality is their meaning' (op. cit., pp. 841-2), that is, they all have a symbolism or a symbolic basis. Much of the work of analysis lies in piecing together the symbolic fragments (cf. Stein, 1957), re-membering, re-assembling, and weaving into a cohesive form the events of a person's life. At the time they happened, traumatic events by definition could not be accorded the meaning which would have enabled them to be integrated, with the result that they were either repressed, grossly distorted, or they have lain around in the landscape of the psyche like erratic blocks, apparently immovable and unconnected with their surroundings, but carrying within them a meaning and a history if only it can be recognised. The discovery of meaning in analysis is not a mere 'philological' (to use Ricoeur's word) attribution of meaning but the uncovering of the motives and causes which gave rise to the original distortion. It is also firmly rooted in the transference/countertransference relationship. As in the course of analysis the patient re-visits significant areas of his life, different nuances of feeling, fresh insights, and new perspectives on memory emerge as they are elicited or illuminated by transferences. Spence gives a vivid example of this phenomenon, the 're-transcription of memory', in his 1997 paper.

The search for what counts as a 'fact' in the universe of analytical discourse is a crucial one. Despite the efforts of those who believe that the words themselves, mechanically recorded, represent the analytic data, there is an increasing shift towards recognising that the words are not enough, and that the complex processes by which we try to formulate and convey the meanings behind the words, must be included in the focus of study.

The movement towards conceptualising and acknowledging the data of analysis as more interior and more subjective than the externally verifiable observations of the natural sciences has been gaining momentum over the years. Wallerstein and Sampson quote Sargent as '[arguing] that the *essential* data [of analysis] are not behaviours or verbalisations but rather the patient's intrapsychic organisation as "seen" clinically through these, i.e. the essential data are the clinical judgements [of the analyst]' (Sargent, 1961, in Wallerstein and Sampson, 1971, p. 31). Sargent is suggesting in other words that we need to get behind the analyst's eyes, to understand what goes on in his mind. In 1960, the year before Sargent wrote that, Winnicott, too, in his paper 'Counter-transference', highlighted the importance of this factor: 'in between the patient and the analyst is the analyst's professional attitude, his technique, *the work he does with his mind*' (Winnicott, 1960, p. 161). Winnicott goes on to explain that he is not talking about a primarily intellectual process but about his feelings and somatic sensations in relation to a patient and how he thinks about these. His statement links closely with Wyman and Rittenberg's 1992 formulation, cited by Tuckett, of the ingredients of a clinical presentation as 'what the analyst felt, what the analyst thought about this, and what the analyst said and why'. Tuckett adds that it is also necessary to be clear about the model the analyst is working with (Tuckett, 1993, p. 1,178).

If the theory of analysis is 'the codification of what takes place in the analytic situation and, more precisely in the analytic relationship' (Ricoeur, 1977, p. 836), enquiring about the proof of the theory entails asking two questions: What truth is claimed by the theory? and What sort of verification or falsification is possible?

The nature of truth as it can appropriately be applied to the analytic experience is what Ricoeur describes as a 'saying-true'. One of the essential characteristics of analysis is, as he has pointed out, that it is restricted to what can be said: this is both a constraining factor, often frustrating to patients, and an enabling one, because it aims to free analysis from cumbersome action; analysis can then, like poetry, take us deep into feeling. Ricoeur comments that the truth of analysis is 'closer to that of Greek tragedy than to that of modern physics' (op. cit., p. 858). The 'saying-true' of analytical discourse is to do with 'self-recognition, recognition of the other, and recognition of the fantasy' (p.862). This self-recognition results from being freed from self-accusation and self-blame, though it is not a complacent self-acceptance which negates the need or the possibility of change. Indeed, as Ricoeur argues, one of the criteria for the verification and validation of the analytic process is that change takes place. The talk of which analysis consists eventuates in the formulation of interpretations which, when assimilated and digested, bring about the release of new energies for change.

The 'saying-true' is also to do with '[reorganising] the facts of a person's life into a meaningful whole which constitutes a single and continuous history' (op. cit., p. 861). 'Saying-true' is close to Spence's idea of 'narrative truth', which is to be distinguished from historical truth. The historical truth of a person's life cannot be established through analysis. But in so far as the story created by patient and analyst is 'persuasive and compelling' to those who have made it, it has the characteristics of narrative truth (Spence, 1982, p.49). In the context of 'saying-true' the patient is able to enunciate the truth of his feelings, both to himself and to another person – the longing for the mother one can never have, or for that relationship with the parent which is permitted only to the other parent – and to uncover the fantasies which lie behind them. The 'saying-true' of analytical discourse is an outcome of the work undertaken jointly by analyst and patient to find words and make links. Interpreting has traditionally been seen as the analyst's task and/or prerogative. However an interpretation is often, and perhaps ideally, less a pronouncement by the analyst and more a formulation that is worked on together, consciously and unconsciously, by both partners. While Spence rightly points out that 'the engaged therapist is in no position to "study", in any systematic manner, the conditions under which interpretation leads to change' (Spence, 1986, p. 12), since the therapist is more deeply engaged in his subjective involvement with the patient than 'study' would allow, it is also worth considering, as Wallerstein and Sampson have suggested, that an interpretation is an experiment in miniature, 'a working hypothesis to be tested by certain explicit or implicit predictions' (Wallerstein and Sampson, 1971, p. 12). From the fate of the interpretation, not so much its immediate reception but its subsequent long-term effects, the analyst can deduce much information about the patient's state of mind and stage of psychic development. The phrase 'worked on', which I used above, even when it happens unconsciously, seems to imply too much directedness for the process by which an interpretation 'grows'; there is a 'coming together ... of a mass of apparently unrelated phenomena' whose shape, sometimes gradually, sometimes suddenly, becomes apparent, and 'which are thereby given coherence and meaning not previously possessed' (Bion, 1967, p. 127, quoted in Tuckett, 1993, p.1,182).

Tuckett recognises the extreme subtlety with which these links are formed, deriving both from the patient's past and from the here-and-now experiences of analyst and patient; his contrasting of 'construction (implying present unconscious phantasies and informing structures) [with] reconstruction of past events' is helpful here. Kris (quoted in Wallerstein an Sampson, 1971, p.16) had suggested that 'interpretation works not by "producing" recall, but by completing an incomplete memory (thereby implying that validation consists of the judgement of the goodness of fit)'. Perhaps one could say, following Ricoeur, that the memory can be completed because the analysis provides a safer context for experience: events are no longer unspeakable (they can be said), and are no longer experienced in isolation (they are said to another person); moreover, they can be fantasised and thought about and their symbolism allowed to reveal its meaning without risk of material enactment; they can thus be woven into an integrated story of a life (cf. Ricoeur, 1977, p.85).

However, the subtlety and complexity of the formation of these links, as it happens in the analysis, make it very difficult to convey the process to another person in all its elusive detail; the frustration of which Tuckett speaks, of 'trying to tell someone else about it and discovering that what we say sounds much less convincing than it felt in the session when it was formulated' (Tuckett, 1993, p. 1,182) is an experience that many analysts will share, but perhaps it should not be surprising. It is not just a question of remembering detail and being able to reproduce it. We have to take into account that, conscious as we aim to be, there are still many aspects of an intimate relationship – and particularly of special moments in that relationship of coming together and, in analysis, of an interpretation finding a 'home', of what Jungians would call *coniunctio* – which remain unconscious and inexpressible, subtleties of feeling and 'fit'.

Renik points to the correspondence between the analytic situation in which the analyst offers the patient an interpretation and the situation in a clinical presentation or a case report where he offers an interpretation to colleagues. In both cases the interpretation is offered for judgement or testing of its validity. It is an arresting parallel but there is a fundamental difference: the analyst is in a close emotional relationship with the patient, and the interpretation is more an attempt to 'touch' the patient in a feeling sense than a rational statement offered for his intellectual assent. Renik's further comment that the analyst's interventions to the patient should aim to be what in the field of philosophy are apparently known as *'pensées pensées'*, 'thoughts communicated so as to reveal how the thinker arrived at them' (Renik, 1994, p.1,249), is an interesting one. This is a kind of self-revelation which has a particular value. I have sometimes found myself intuitively spelling out the steps which have led me to an interpretation as I give it. Perhaps the reason it is effective is that the patient is enabled to see, and feel, the links himself, step by small step; thus the interpretation does not come as a shock, nor does it sound like a magical pronouncement by the analyst. Each interpretation contributes to the making of the patient's story which consists in finding a fitting narrative to which the patient can assent emotionally – the 'saying-true' of Ricoeur.

In his definition of a 'clinical fact' Tuckett brings together a number of the factors that have been mentioned: the analyst's subjectivity and the dependence of the clinical fact on the operation of the analyst's mind and feelings. He establishes that two conditions need to be clarified in order to produce a definition of a clinical fact, these being the instrument of observation, which he terms 'psychoanalytic sensibility', and the object or focus of that instrument in the analytic session – the words used, the feelings and other information the analyst picks up from the patient, together with his own feeling responses and what he makes of them. Clinical facts are the product of the interaction of those two conditions (cf. Tuckett, 1995, p. 657).

Conclusion

There is a growing consensus among analytic thinkers and writers that the kind of clinical communication which is valuable in promoting analytic thought and discussion is that which sets out to provide as much detail of the analytic interaction as is needed to show how the analyst arrived at an interpretation, and in such a way as to leave room for the listener or reader to judge whether the conclusion is valid or reasonable and whether there might be alternatives. The translator of Freud's Prefatory Remarks to 'Dora' used the word 'substantiate' to describe his purpose in writing up that case. That means not to 'prove' but to 'give substance to' abstract formulations and to ground them in truthful observation and reporting. Renik's use of the word 'truthful' in this context rather than, say, 'accurate', is significant: it leaves room for the analyst's 'irreducible subjectivity' while at the same time insisting on the use of 'specific, phenomenological language' (Renik, 1994, p.1,247), the language of feeling and experience.

Now we come full circle. The more detail we give of the interaction with the patient and of our own thought- and feeling-processes, the more we expose ourselves. In writing about a patient, an analyst also 'writes *himself up*'(Ward, in Ward (ed.), 1997, p. 8; original italics), laying bare the workings of his own mind, and putting himself on the line both professionally and personally. Our concern to safeguard confidentiality for the patient's sake might contain a sizeable proportion of anxiety about giving away too much of ourselves. Tuckett suggested this a few years ago in an editorial in the *International Journal of Psycho-Analysis*, commenting that the lack of 'high-quality clinically based contributions ... is often explained away with reference to not-always-convincing rationales concerning the need to maintain the patient's confidentiality' (Tuckett, 1995). I believe that confidentiality in respect of patients should be regarded with the deepest seriousness and I would hesitate to reduce it to a 'rationale', but it may be that we can take our concern too far. Is it possible to be too rigid – even obsessional – about it? What anxieties might lie behind the need to make confidentiality an absolute? Taking up an absolutist position on an ethical matter should make us suspicious. It may be that a major part of the anxiety concealed by our apparent certainty is a fear of exposing not so much our patients as ourselves, and it has to be recognised that the more the analyst focuses on the inner world and the analytic interaction, as I have advocated here, the more he reveals of himself. But an absolutist position also provides a kind of (false) security: it can feel like a firm base on which to anchor ourselves, where we are protected from the pain of conflict. It is also a dangerous position because it paralyses further thought and growth.

It is not possible to reconcile the opposing needs for the patient's privacy and confidentiality on the one hand, and on the other for open discussion, for education, and for promoting the development of analytic thinking and technique. Freud was well aware of the conflict between the analyst's duty towards his present individual patient and towards 'the many other patients who are suffering or will some day suffer' (Freud, 1905, SE VII, p.8) and he considered it a 'disgraceful piece of cowardice' to neglect the latter (Freud, ibid.). It is a conflict we still have to struggle with.

An ethical position in relation to confidentiality and consent seems to demand at least a basic honesty towards our patients, as well as towards scientific enquiry; disguising material in any way other than omitting or altering the simplest external details runs counter to this. Moreover in any substantial account of inner world material the patient could not be disguised from himself. If it were agreed that the patient's consent for publication should be sought if at all possible, we would have to acknowledge that there seems to be no good time to do it. What is most important to take into account is the individual potential of each patient: we are in the position of having to gauge the tolerance of each one for knowledge which we know they will find difficult. The ultimate guiding principle must, as always, be the clinical needs and well-being of the patient. He would need to be at a stage where he could manage the psychological pressures related to the discussion of consent, and there are patients for whom this would never be the case.

A continuing failure to publish clinical data however will have a profoundly serious effect on the future development of analysis as a credible method of treatment. It is clear that we need to establish ground rules that hold in balance the conflicting demands of present patients and of the profession and future patients. We need to devise a means of fostering a culture in which the publication of analytical clinical material for educational and research purposes is taken for granted. This might mean, as has been recently suggested (Minutes, October, 2000), building a statement about such publication into the analytic framework as it is explained to the analysand at the beginning of treatment, alongside guidelines about holidays, the regularity of sessions, payment for missed sessions, and so on. An analogy might be found in the assumption in a teaching hospital that patients may be 'used', with, according to best practice, their permission, and subject to safeguards, for teaching purposes: the 'clinic', as defined earlier. Such ground rules should, as Tuckett suggests, 'push forward patients' rights and professional accountability while at the same time ensuring that these are tackled in a sufficiently complex way so that they do not stifle the drive to discover and transmit accounts of good practice' (Tuckett, 2000b, p. 1,067).

Note

Throughout this chapter, for the sake of simplicity the pronoun 'he' is used in a generic sense to refer to patients of either gender.

References

Aron, L. (2000), 'Ethical considerations in the writing of case histories', *Psychoanalytic Dialogues,* 10, pp. 231-45.

Bion, W.R. (1967), 'Commentary', in *Second Thoughts*, London: Maresfield Library, Karnac Books.

Bollas, C. and Sundelson, D. (1995), *The New Informants. The Betrayal of Confidentiality in Psychoanalysis and Psychotherapy.* London: Karnac Books.

Britton, R. (1997), 'Making the private public', in I. Ward (ed.), *The Presentation of Case Material in Clinical Discourse,* London: Freud Museum Publications.

Budd, S. (1997), 'Ask me no questions and I'll tell you no lies: the social organization of secrets', in I. Ward (ed.), *The Presentation of Case Material in Clinical Discourse,* London: Freud Museum Publications.

Casement, P. (1985), *On Learning from the Patient,* London: Tavistock [Routledge].

Colman, W. (2000), IJPA Internet Discussion Group, Bulletin No. 399.

Duncan, D. (1993), 'Theory in vivo', *International Journal of Psycho-Analysis* 74, I.

Emde, R. and Fonagy, P. (1997), Editorial: 'An emerging culture for psychoanalytic research?' *International Journal of Psycho-Analysis* 78, 4.

Fosshage, J. (1990). 'Clinical protocol'. *Psychoanalytic Inquiry,* '0.

Freud, S. (1905), *Fragment of an Analysis of a Case of Hysteria* ('*Dora*'), Standard Edition, vol. VII,

London: The Hogarth Press.

—— (1915), *Introductory Lectures*, Standard Edition, vol. XV, London: The Hogarth Press.

Gabbard, G. (2000), 'Disguise or consent. Problems and recommendations concerning the publication and presentation of clinical material.' *International Journal of Psychoanalysis* 81,6.

Goldberg, A. (1997), Editorial: 'Writing case histories', *International Journal of Psychoanalysis* 78, 3.

Hubback, J. (1997), Personal communication.

Jacobs, T. (1993), 'The inner experiences of the analyst: their contribution to the analytic process', *International Journal of Psycho-Analysis* 74, 1.

Jung, C.G. (1935), Editorial, Collected Works of C. G. Jung, vol. 10, *Civilisation in Transition*, London and Princeton: Routledge & Kegan Paul and Princeton University Press.

—— (1946), 'The psychology of the transference', Collected Works of C. G. Jung, vol. 16, *The Practice of Psychotherapy, London and Princeton: Routledge & Kegan Paul and Princeton University Press.*

Klein, M. (1961), *Narrative of a Child Analysis*, London: Virago (1989).

Klumpner, G.H. and Frank, A. (1991), 'On methods of reporting clinical material', *Journal of the American Psychoanalytic Association*, 39.

Kubie, L. (1958), 'Research into the process of supervision in psychoanalysis', *Psychoanalytic Quarterly*, 27.

Lipton, E. (1991), 'The analyst's use of clinical data, and other issues of confidentiality', *Journal of the American Psychoanalytic Association*, 39.

Lustman, S. (1963), 'Some issues in contemporary psychoanalytic research', *The Psychoanalytic Study of the Child*, 18.

Minutes of the meeting on confidentiality issues in publishing clinical material, London, October 2000.

Proner, B. (1986), 'Defences of the self and envy of oneself', *Journal of Analytical Psychology*, 31, 3.

—— 1988), 'Envy of one's self: adhesive identification and pseudo-adult states', *Journal of Analytical Psychology*, 33, 2.

Renik, O. (1994), 'Publication of clinical facts', *International Journal of Psycho-Analysis* 75, 5/6.

Ricoeur, P. (1977), 'The question of proof in Freud's psychoanalytic writings'. *Journal of the American Psychoanalytic Association*, 25.

Sargent, H. D. (1961), 'Intrapsychic change: methodological problems in psychotherapy research', Psychiatry, 24.

Sinason, V. (2000), IJPA Internet Discussion Group, Bulletin No. 396.

Spence, D. (1981), 'Psychoanalytic competence', *International Journal of Psycho-Analysis* 62, 1.

—— (1982), 'Narrative truth and theoretical truth', *Psychoanalytic Quarterly*, 51.

—— (1986), 'When interpretation masquerades as explanation', *Journal of the American Psychoanalytical Association*, 34.

—— (1997). 'Case reports and the reality they represent: the many faces of *Nachträglichkeit* in I.Ward (ed.), *The Presentation of Case Material in Clinical Discourse*, London: Freud Museum Publications.

—— (1998), 'Rain forest or mud field', *International Journal of Psycho-Analysis* 79, 4.

Stein, L. (1957), 'What is a symbol supposed to be?', *Journal of Analytical Psychology*, 2, 1.

Stein, M. (1988a), 'Writing about psychoanalysis:1. Analysts who write and those who do not', *Journal of the American Psychoanalytic Association*, 36.

—— (1988b), 'Writing about psychoanalysis:2. Analysts who write, patients who read'. *Journal of the American Psychoanalytic Association*, 36.

Stoller, R. (1988), 'Patients' responses to their own case reports', *Journal of the American*

Psychoanalytic Association, 36.

Tuckett, D.(1993), 'Some thoughts on the presentation and discussion of the clinical material of psychoanalysis', *International Journal of Psycho-Analysis,* 74, 6.

—— (1995), 'The conceptualisation and communication of clinical facts in psychoanalysis'. *International Journal of Psycho-Analysis,* 76, 4.

—— (2000a), Commentary on 'The case history' by Robert Michels, *Journal of the American Psychoanalytic Association,* 48.

—— (2000b), 'Reporting clinical events in the Journal: towards the construction of a special case', *International Journal of Psychoanalysis,* 81, 6.

Wallerstein, R. and Sampson, H. (1971), 'Issues in research in the psychoanalytic process'. *International Journal of Psycho-Analysis,* 52, 1.

Ward, I. (ed.) (1997), *The Presentation of Case Material in Clinical Discourse,* London: Freud Museum Publications.

Wharton, B. (1998), 'What comes out of the consulting-room? The reporting of clinical material', *Journal of Analytical Psychology,* 43, 2.

Widlöcher, D. (1994), 'A case is not a fact', *International Journal of Psycho-Analysis,* 75, part 5/6, p. 1,233.

Winnicott, D. (1960), 'Counter-transference', in *The Maturational Processes and the Facilitating Environment,* London: Hogarth Press, 1972.

Young, W. (2000), IJPA Internet Discussion Group, Bulletin No. 394.

11
Finding a Space for Ethical Thinking about Matters of Confidentiality

Jan Wiener

Sir Robert Morton: I wept today because right had been done.
Catherine Winslow: Not justice?
Sir Robert Morton: No. Not justice. Right.
It is easy to do justice – very hard to do right.
Terence Rattigan, *The Winslow Boy*

Introduction

Mary Warnock (1998, p. 75) makes the point that 'public morality, the insistence on justice and equality, is dependent for its working on the conviction of at least some individuals that it is worth being virtuous rather than vicious, honest rather than dishonest, good rather than bad; that one must try individually as well as collectively, to act for the best'. She goes on to say that 'what is private is the inner sense of and interest in morality itself, in giving priority to the private over the public'. It is this paradox, or central tension, if you like, that is the subject of this chapter. There is a delicate balance between what may be seen to be in the public or the private good, and sometimes we have to be prepared to forgo what we might like to do for the sake of other people.

In private practice, analysts are only rarely faced with situations in their clinical work that lead to ethical or legal decisions to break professional confidentiality. For this reason, it is perhaps easy to turn a blind eye to the issues. However, we do have a responsibility to think about our personal, moral and ethical views about confidentiality. For those of us who work analytically, a unique feature of our method is that we work with fantasies, making definitions of objective truth difficult and, because of this, the issues are likely to pose particular problems and paradoxes that are by no means easy to resolve.

The Nature of Confidentiality

The subject of ethics has absorbed writers for centuries and it is complicated because our morality is a strange mixture of received tradition and personal opinion. For the purposes of this chapter, I would like first to make a distinction between what I think of as ethics with a small 'e' and ethics with a big 'E'. Ethics with a small 'e' is what Solomon (2000) believes underlies the foundation of our humanity. It is the ethical or analytical attitude that pervades the room each day when analyst and patient meet, and which affects what we say to our patients and how we say it. The emphasis in this chapter, though not exclusively so, is more on ethics with a big 'E': those relatively rare occasions during analysis when we find ourselves contemplating action, in this case, breaching the vas bene clausum and the ensuing struggle for the analyst to manage their ethical and unethical impulses.

Matters of confidentiality come under the rubric of ethics. Jung himself was more interested in ethics, with what is right and what is good, than he was with morality: 'having learnt by long and often painful experience the relative ineffectiveness of trying to inculcate moral precepts, he [*the psychotherapist* – my italics] has to abandon all admonitions and exhortations that begin with "ought" and "must"' (Jung, 1949, CW 18, para. 1408). As members of the analytic profession, we have a commitment to provide high standards of service to our patients within self-regulating organisations that control entry and provide codes of ethics to guide working practice. Ethics places great stress on the importance of respecting our patients' rights to confidentiality, emphasising its link to the relationship of trust, so crucial to creating a space for unconscious exploration. In the field of medical ethics, we find a sophisticated and fertile literature to contemplate. From the first Hippocratic oath to present-day ethical codes developed by the General Medical Council in the UK, doctors have been exhorted to preserve the confidentiality of their patient information. The Hippocratic oath – the first professional code of ethics – states that 'all that may come to my knowledge in the exercise of my profession…which ought not to be spread abroad I will keep secret and never reveal'. For analysts, two thought-provoking questions arise from this oath. First, the reasons why knowledge 'ought not to be spread abroad' and second, our capacity to put our hands on our hearts and promise that we will always 'keep secret and never reveal'. The main problem when applying ethical principles in clinical practice is when two or more of them seem to be in conflict. For example contacting a patient's GP when a severely anorexic patient is becoming dangerously underweight could be seen as 'for the patient's own good' but in another way, restricts her freedom of choice.

In our culture, there has been a move away from paternalism (the doctor knows best) towards autonomy (the patient knows best). Values have changed. There is now greater pressure to disclose, to reveal what we do, but at the same time ethical and legal controls to protect the privacy of our patients are becoming ever more stringent. This seems to me to foster a central paradox, a double bind that analysts inevitably internalise: should we disclose or keep secret? Is the welfare of the individual more important or the greater public good? Fulford (2001, p.16) thinks that 'the ethical difficulties we face in mental health practice are driven not by immaturity of ethical theory but by differences in human values'. He thinks that there is now a gap between ethical theory and practice and that we should stop chasing after ever more criteria of confidentiality but look rather to process, with a greater reliance upon clinical integrity, even though this may result in radically different views on ethical issues. Warnock

(1998, p.107) would agree when she remarks that 'the subject matter of ethics demands that one become emotionally as well as philosophically committed to one's beliefs'. To my mind these paradoxical cultural changes are Jungian opposites demanding analytical understanding and any resolution is dependent on finding an *ethical space* to process specific forms of countertransference relevant to confidentiality that are palpable in the analytic relationship. Ethical codes and regulations are unlikely to be sufficient.

Confidentiality is not easy to define as, psychologically speaking, there are subtle differences between privacy, secrecy and confidentiality. *Privacy* is a universal professional principle, a fundamental right that allows individuals to decide the manner and extent to which information about themselves is shared with others. In Bollas's view, 'we live in an era where human privacy is fast becoming a cultural artefact. If the invasion of human privacy continues at its present pace, the psychoanalyst's anguish will seem quaint at best and delusional at worst' (Bollas, 2001, p.117).

Secrecy frequently imbues the events, thoughts, feelings or fantasies which patients choose to tell us and which are often associated with guilt or shame. There are what may be considered to be ordinary secrets and extra-ordinary secrets. Ordinary secrets are part of the fabric and texture of our day-to-day work, to be listened to sensitively and non-judgementally. Secrets are likely to include personal and intimate revelations from our patients' inner and outer world, including sexual experiences and fantasies, betrayals, secret longings and events or thoughts that may generate strong feelings in both patient and analyst. There is no reason to break confidentiality. However, if patients are becoming psychotic, threatening to harm themselves or someone else, telling us they are abusing a child, imagining raping or torturing someone, or telling us they are infected with the HIV virus and infecting lovers, then we are in the area of extra-ordinary secrets. The boundaries between fantasy and reality become blurred for both patient and analyst and we may well ask ourselves the questions: Should I be doing anything about this? Why is the patient telling me this now? Should I be encouraging the patient to report this to the authorities?

Confidentiality is about the commitment to maintain boundaries and to take no action. For analysts, the temptation to take actions to break the boundaries of the analytic container is dependent on personal and moral principles, codes of ethics, clinical judgement and, not least, the role of the law. But – and this is central to the argument – if patients do not implicitly or explicitly believe that the thoughts, fantasies and feelings they bring to analysis will be confidential, they will not come. A shadow is cast over our profession as a whole.

Different Kinds of Disclosures

The structure of our profession and the culture of contemporary practice mean that there is, in my view, no such thing as absolute confidentiality. One GP and ethicist, Warwick (1989), has argued that confidentiality in healthcare is no longer tenable and a principle of non-confidentiality should be substituted instead. We will all talk about our patients sometimes, hopefully without damaging the analytic relationship and, more likely, in the interests of furthering its growth. More relevant considerations are the distinctions between *revealing* and *reporting;* between a *choice to reveal* and an *obligation to report*; and, finally, between those revelations that could be seen as *benign,* and those likely to be considered more *malign,* probably constituting acting-out by the analyst. It is in the sifting of these distinctions that the seeds of disquiet and paradox may stir.

(a) Revealing
We reveal personal information about our patients when we seek supervision for our work, when we consult with colleagues, give talks or publish articles and books which contain case examples from clinical work. We can, I think, make a distinction between these kinds of revelations and what I shall later define as *reporting,* but the question as to whether they are ethically justifiable nevertheless needs to be addressed.

The analytical psychologists and psychoanalysts who have written on this subject express a surprising variety of points of view. Aron (2000) points out that discussions about the ethical considerations in writing up clinical accounts are really at a preliminary stage in our discipline and we have only begun to fathom the unconscious issues brought into play by these problems. Other authors are bolder in the expression of their personal views. Wharton (1998, p. 217) thinks it is *ethically justifiable* to reveal information from the consulting room, as it is useful to share clinical material as a means of learning our craft, to relieve the loneliness of the work and to promote discussion of new ideas in the field. Bollas and Sundelson (1995) would also agree as long as we take great care to preserve the anonymity of our patients. Budd (1997, pp. 30-1) thinks we can be too precious about the ethics of publishing: *we have to find a way of communicating case material.* Gabbard and Williams (2001) think that the ethical need to protect our patients can co-exist with what they call *the scientific need to maintain the integrity of clinical reporting.* Britton (1997, p. 12) explores with elegance the analyst's psychological conflicts associated with the act of publication. He names the guilt about publication *betrayal of affiliation,* 'what had seemed like the mental content of a private relationship has become the raw material for other minds'. However, he points out convincingly how it would involve a different kind of betrayal if he did not write at all:

> there are circumstances where objectivity is felt to be the death of subjectivity and others where subjectivity is felt to threaten the demise of objectivity. (Britton, 1997, p. 12)

Gabbard (2000, p. 12) acknowledges the 'not quite impossible' conflicts in this area and recommends five strategies whereby authors can deal with the dilemmas posed by writing about clinical work: thick disguise; patient consent; an emphasis on process material; the use of composites, combining several patients into a single case example; and, finally, the use of a colleague as author.

My personal ethical attitude dictates that I do consult with a colleague if I am in difficulty in my analytic work. This chapter, although without clinical revelations about my patients, is a testament to the fact that I agree with Britton. Not to write would feel like a betrayal of my profession. However, there is a special kind of thinking involved when I am writing or when I think a patient should be consulting with their GP. My own defences, narcissism in the case of publishing clinical material and omnipotence when a patient may for a while require more help than I can provide, force a particularly strenuous inner struggle between the subjective and the objective, between unconsciousness and knowledge about what is ethical. Warnock puts it well:

> the human desire to further one's own interest is extremely and often overwhelmingly strong ... the ethical arises when someone begins to see that he must postpone his immediate wishes for the sake of the good. And 'the good' here embraces both his own goodness and the goodness of the society of which he is a member'. (1998, p. 87)

(b) Reporting
To report means to reveal the identity of a patient to another, to other healthcare professionals such as GPs and psychiatrists, to social services, to the police or, in some cases, in court. It could be said that we are under increasing pressure to report, given the general public's attitude to analysis. There is now less faith in understanding and reflecting with the individual in mind, but rather more faith in punishment and protecting society. Analysts may be mindful of this and the conscious and unconscious pressures to 'mind their backs'.

Few of us would disagree that the role of affects is central in the analytic relationship. The countertransference – that is, our own thoughts, feelings and body responses to our patients – are crucial to the work. It could be argued therefore that if we are to practise effectively, we must be protected from intrusions and the destructive effects of the law, including the requirement to report. The intrusion of the law on the analyst's frame of mind, the thought police, can lead to the practice of defensive analysis:

> the screen of receptive listening no longer exists...the clinician will bear an increasingly menacing internal object; the heavy footsteps of the state. (Bollas and Sundelson, 1995, pp. 90-1)

A central paradox exists when reflecting on our attitudes to confidentiality. The same sharing of information can be seen on the one hand as:

- in the interests of responsible, ethical analytic practice
- in the interests of child (or other adult) protection; the public interest in mind
- good multidisciplinary 'working together'
- compliant with child abuse reporting laws

but on the other hand as a:

- betrayal of patients' rights to privacy
- betrayal of clinicians' personal rights to privacy
- violation of the rights to practise our profession
- violation of the principles of privilege granted to other professionals such as the clergy, lawyers and journalists

Bollas and Sundelson (1995) think that to break confidentiality by reporting is to betray the central tenet of our method and therefore we should never abrogate confidentiality but bear the anguish that this uncomfortable position will generate. Truth is often subjective and provisional and, when it comes to reporting, is likely to be experienced by our patients as a betrayal of what we ask of them: to trust us and, implicitly, to talk openly and honestly about whatever is on their mind. Mosher (1999) discusses the great significance of the US Supreme Court Decision in 1996, in the case of Jaffee versus Redmond, to recognise and establish the principle, after half a century of effort, that communications between patients in psychotherapy and their psychotherapists are in need of protection – the kind of protection that is presently given to the communications between lawyers and their clients. It will be interesting to observe whether such privilege will gain favour in the UK.

The Sanctum, the Citadel and the Souk

Many of us work in a variety of different settings and while our ethical attitude to our work remains constant, the nature of the context is likely to affect our models of confidentiality and the subtlety of conflicting principles (Wiener, 1998).

(a) The Sanctum

Private practice is the setting where we have the individual in mind. We are living and working with unconscious processes and the images and affects from the inner world. Patients are encouraged to say whatever is on their mind, psychic truth is highly valued and distinctions between fantasy and reality our building blocks for exploration. A secure frame is an essential precondition if the sanctum – that place where two selves, patient and analyst, have the potential to relate to each other authentically – is to be entered. Here, 'consulting' and 'supervision' and occasional 'management' actions are generally in the interests of good practice – the frame has some elasticity – but 'reporting' could be seen as a major betrayal of trust and can have implications for all other private practice patients.

(b) The Citadel

Hospital psychotherapy clinics require a strong-walled citadel environment to preserve therapeutic integrity and to deal with the large numbers of referrals and political pressures to modify the methods we believe in. It is accepted good professional practice to consult with clinic colleagues and seek regular supervision, most particularly with difficult borderline patients who often present in the National Health Service in the UK. The unspoken ethic of confidentiality is rather like a moat around the citadel. Within the portals, patient files are freely consulted. Cases discussed with identities disguised but contact with neighbouring citadels is restricted. The door of the citadel opens from time to time for information on a 'need to know' basis to pass out to referrers. Assessment and end-of-treatment reports are common practice, not abrogation of confidentiality.

(c) The Souk
In the UK, the metaphor of a *souk*, or Arab bazaar (Wiener, 1996), captures the atmosphere of primary care, where family doctors work together with psycho-therapists, health visitors and practice nurses in multidisciplinary surgeries. Teamwork is essential and a model of confidentiality not of a patient/therapist couple but one operating within the bounds of the practice team is most usual. Therapists must modify two sets of cherished training beliefs if they are to adapt: first, that information is profitably shared with GPs in patients' best interests and second, that a more flexible work style is essential.

The Analyst's State of Mind: locating an ethical space

Jung's (1952, CW 12, p. 219) metaphor of the vas bene clausum, the well-sealed vessel, is a precautionary measure very frequently mentioned in alchemy, and is 'the equivalent of the magic circle... to protect what is within from the intrusion and admixture of what is without as well as to prevent it from escaping'. Jung (1935, CW 18, p. 410) describes this magic circle as 'a kind of holy place or temenos to protect the centre of the personality'. Here he introduces the idea of an analytic frame or container, to use the more usual word, which creates a space inside it in which something vital, a relationship between two selves, patient and analyst may evolve. The frame may seamlessly expand or contract a bit, or vary in its permeability at different times during analysis with no adverse effects for patient or analyst or their relationship. But when the analyst feels under pressure to reveal or report, knowing that this may have an adverse effect on the analytic relationship, the frame becomes brittle, potentially breakable.

This brings us to the nub of the issue. How may we think about the analyst's state of mind when in the grip of a countertransference experience of anxiety leading to a wish to report or reveal what is emerging in the analysis? At such moments, rare though they may be, we struggle to make an ethical space to unpack our countertransference responses. This is normal practice. However, this is not a normal situation but rather a special form of countertransference experience constellating particular archetypal inner psychic processes. Uncon-scious processes continue in day-to-day work untrammelled by decisions as to whether to break the bounds of confidentiality. Then the therapist is plunged into a liminal place, in the sway of an archetypal experience where the pressure from psychic opposites can be intense. Jung (1936, CW 9(i)) points out that 'the chief danger in succumbing to the fascinating influence of the archetypes is most likely to happen when the archetypal images are not made conscious'. The quality of these experiences means that the codes of ethics developed by our particular societies are likely to be insufficient when faced with ethical dilemmas such as:

Should I write now about an aspect of a patient's analysis? How will he or she feel about it? How will it affect the work?

- Is my patient breaking down? Do I need to consult a colleague, suggest they visit their GP?
- An anorexic patient is dangerously losing weight. Should he or she be in hospital?
- I am frightened for my own safety when a patient is talking about acting out violent fantasies. What, if anything, should I do?
- A colleague seems to be unaware of the debilitating effects of a prolonged physical illness on his state of mind. Should I report him to our ethics committee?

These are uncomfortable situations and we may wish to avoid them, to defend ourselves against our beliefs and wishes. We are caught in a psychic area where distinctions between inside and outside, between what is subjective and what is objective, between fantasy and reality are blurred. The guardian of our everyday beliefs fails and the analytic frame is under threat so that, inevitably, the nature of the analytic space within it is affected. Our impulse to act automatically inhibits any space for reflection. We may collude with a patient and do nothing, or alternatively act too hastily. Generally we talk to a colleague to bring these opposing forces closer together but at these moments, analyst and patient become embedded in a larger set of values. We are citizens with responsibility as well as analysts. Such an experience generates a tension between our moral principles and our ethical principles; a conflict between the code of ethics we adhere to and our own personal, internal ethical attitude. There is a need to find a *third area,* an ethical space, in which meaning and therefore new thinking can emerge (Gordon, 1993; Ogden, 1994). However, as Figlio (2000, pp. 17-18) points out, this is not necessarily an easy task, 'the split self, under the force of excessive projection, invades others and undermines their sense of themselves. This can reduce the analyst's responsibility and consequent reliance on principles and rules'.

I first discovered a reference to the concept of ethical space when I read the philosopher, Roger Poole:

thinking is doubly ethical. First, it involves transforming the terms of a thinker's own system into terms which can be grasped, comprehended and redeployed in one's own system. And then in a second moment, thinking has to refuse certain terms in the original system, to become independent enough not only to understand the law, but also to change it. (Poole, 1973, p. 145)

This idea of a double process is similar to Britton's helpful distinction between *belief* and *fact*, necessary distinctions when it comes to decisions as to whether or not 'to act':

> the status of belief is conferred on some pre-existing phantasies, which then have emotional and behavioural consequences ... initially it is treated as a fact. The realisation that it is a belief is a secondary process, which depends on viewing the belief from outside the system of the belief itself. (Britton, 1998, p. 9)

An ethical space may form when there is an intermediate area of experience (Winnicott, 1971) that is outside the system of the belief itself. Secondary process thinking becomes possible and inner and outer reality may be separated yet remain interrelated. Britton names this third position from which to view subjective beliefs in order to find internal objectivity, *triangular psychic space*. It is a third position in mental space where 'the subjective self can be observed having a relationship with an idea'. I believe this comes close to my own conception of an ethical space. Nussbaum (2001, p. xxxvii), in her book *The Fragility of Goodness*, challenges us to inhabit this ethical space actively, 'as a contested place of moral struggle, a place in which virtue might possibly in some cases prevail over the caprices of amoral power, and in which, even if it does not prevail, virtue may still shine through for its own sake'.

The ethical decisions we make determine the state of our mental life (Symington, 1996). There are always ethical and unethical forces at work and it is precisely when these anti-analytic impulses surface that we are most likely to search for shelter behind impersonal dictums as to what we 'should' do, neglecting our more personal subjective feelings which can also validly inform any decision as to whether to break confidentiality. A collusion with inertia is often the path of least resistance. Issues of confidentiality confront us with our own ethical dilemmas and the need somehow to find a third position where conflict and paradox, structures and feelings, concern for our patients, our model of work and ourselves may helpfully interact. When beliefs come to be trusted, thinking becomes possible, meaning is found and decisions as to whether or not to 'act' facilitated.

Conclusions

These thoughts about dilemmas linked to the breaking of confidentiality do not provide any answers but rather raise problems and paradoxes that need to be discussed. At these moments we should practise what we advocate in our day-to-day work, to think about the issues with care and concern for the welfare of our patients. Our own codes of ethics and the law are not always containing. They are sometimes destructive to our method of work and paradoxically, we may have to turn a blind eye to legal intrusions in order to do our work properly. In today's culture of increasing litigation and vilification, I wonder how easy this is to put into practice?

How we respond (or do not respond) when faced with an ethical dilemma is likely to depend upon our clinical integrity, the meaning we attribute to our beliefs about what to do, the setting in which we work and our capacity to find a third position, an ethical space, from which to view the relationship between our moral principles and our personal ethical attitude so that the subjective and objective can become more companionable bedfellows. There will, however, always be some element of subjective choice. This process is likely to be facilitated if there are etiquettes and institutional structures to help contain us but, ultimately, they will not prevent the inevitable internal struggle for each one of us between the chaos arising from our archetypal shadow, narcissism and omnipotence, and the wish to behave ethically in the face of adversity. To my mind, this view is in line with the change of emphasis in postwar philosophy from the problems of knowledge to the problem of meaning. Postmodernism is skeptical about the existence of objective reality and has destroyed ethical certainty. It celebrates uncertainty and the lack of universally shared moral values. The postmodern human condition espouses the individual state of mind, and moral choices have to be made without the reassurance of philosophical foundations, relying rather on *self*-monitoring and *self*-evaluation. Surely it is in this domain that Jungian analysts with their concepts of the collective unconscious and the self, have a particular contribution to make.

This chapter is regretfully without clinical examples to illustrate my ideas about finding an ethical space and the analyst's internal processes of discovery during their search for Britton's triangular psychic space. I say regretfully because I am in agreement with David Tuckett (2001, p. 647) in his valedictory editorial in the *International Journal of Psychoanalysis*, when he suggests that

> only by finding a language to share and discuss clinical findings *and* their theoretical conceptualization adequately can we hope meaningfully to classify both the different types of psychoanalysis and the difference, if any, between each of these so-called psychotherapy practices, as well as what the consequences are of the different practices.

Tuckett's objective for a scientific paper is 'to clarify an argument and then evaluate it'. The reader of this chapter may accept my theoretical arguments, taking for granted that they emerge from my clinical experience and several years on the Ethics Committee at the Society of Analytical Psychology. However, there is no written supporting clinical evidence because neither of the two people I asked gave me their permission, even in a disguised form, to publish their ethical dilemmas and subsequent decisions that were made. I have wondered about their reasons, since in the past, patients have given me permission to publish disguised vignettes from their analyses, although it has often stirred up powerful feelings. Perhaps in this case, the potential anxieties about exposure and betrayal are correspondingly greater for an ethical matter where the *vas bene clausum*, that very precious container of the analytic relationship, is under threat?

I have used the sanctum, the citadel, and the souk as metaphors to characterise three different work settings using subtly different models of confidentiality. I am tempted to stretch these metaphors to describe the analyst's inner psychic drama when working with issues of confidentiality. We turn to the sanctum, that inner private place of feelings, of intuitions and of thoughts – the centre of the self – to search for subjective knowledge to foster an ethical space for reflection that facilitates ethical behaviour. Along the way, we hope for support from a strong-walled citadel to contain this intra-psychic process but we will certainly have to struggle in the chaos of the souk, that shadow force, the source of what is most unethical within us. It is to this inner process that the barrister, Sir Robert Morton, refers in Rattigan's *The Winslow Boy* when he stresses that it is easy to do justice but much more difficult to do the right thing.

Note

An earlier version of this chapter was published in the *Journal of Analytical Psychology*, 2001, 46, pp. 41-63.

References

Aron, L. (2000), 'Ethical considerations in the writing of case histories', *Psychoanalytic Dialogues*, 10: 231-45.

Bollas, C. (2001), 'The misapplication of "reasonable mindedness": Is psychoanalysis possible with the present reporting laws in the USA and the UK?', in C. Cordess (ed.), *Confidentiality and Mental Health*, London: Jessica Kingsley Publishers.

Bollas, C. and Sundelson, D. (1995), *The New Informants: Betrayal of Confidentiality in Psychoanalysis and Psychotherapy*, London: Karnac Books.

Britton, R. (1997), 'Making the Private Public', in I. Ward (ed.), *The Presentation of Case Material in Clinical Discourse*, Northampton: Freud Museum Publications.

Britton, R. (1998), 'Belief and Psychic Reality', in *Belief and Imagination: Explorations in Psychoanalysis*, London: Routledge.

Budd, S. (1997), 'Ask me no questions and I'll tell you no lies', in I. Ward (ed.), *The Presentation of Case Material in Clinical Discourse*, Northampton: Freud Museum Publications.

Figlio, K. (2000), 'Ethics and psychoanalysis', in Joan Raphael Leff (ed.), *Ethics of Psychoanalysis*, The Centre for Psychoanalytic Studies, Colchester: University of Essex.

Fulford, K.W.M. (2001), 'The paradoxes of confidentiality: A philosophical introduction', in C. Cordess (ed.), *Confidentiality and Mental Health*, London: Jessica Kingsley Publishers.

Gabbard, G.O. (2000), 'Disguise or consent: problems and recommendations concerning the publication and presentation of clinical material', *International Journal of Psychoanalysis*, 81, part 6, 1071-87.

Gabbard, G.O. and Williams, P. (2001), Editorial: 'Preserving confidentiality in the writing of case reports', *International Journal of Psychoanalysis*, 82, pp. 1067-8.

Gordon, R. (1993), 'The location of archetypal experience', in *Bridges: Metaphor for Psychic Processes*, London: Karnac Books.

Jung, C.G. (1935), 'The Tavistock lectures', Collected Works of C.G.Jung, *The Symbolic Life*, vol. 18, London and Princeton: Routledge and Princeton University Press.

Jung, C.G. (1936), *The Archetypes and the Collective Unconscious*, Collected Works, vol. 9(i), London and Princeton: Routledge and Princeton University Press.

Jung, C.G. (1949), 'Forward to Neumann: Depth Psychology and a New Ethic', Collected Works of C.G. Jung, *The Symbolic Life*, vol. 18, London and Princeton: Routledge and Princeton University Press.

Jung, C.G. (1952), 'The symbolism of the mandala', Collected Works of C.G. Jung, *Psychology and Alchemy*, vol. 12, London and Princeton: Routledge and Princeton University Press.

Ogden, T.H. (1994), *Subjects of Analysis*, London: Karnac Books.

Mosher, P.W. (1999), Psychotherapist-patient privilege: the history and significance of the US Supreme Court's decision in the case of *Jaffee v. Redmond*. Unpublished paper.

Nussbaum, M.C. (2001), *The Fragility of Goodness: Luck and Ethics in Greek Tragedy and Philosophy*, Cambridge: Cambridge University Press.

Poole, R. (1973), *Towards Deep Subjectivity*, London: Allen Lane.

Rattigan, T. (1996), *The Winslow Boy*, London: Nick Hern Books.

Solomon, H.M. (2000), 'The ethical self', in E. Christopher and H.M. Solomon (eds), Jungian Thought in the Modern World, London: Free Association Books.

Symington, N. (1996), *The Making of a Psychotherapist* London: Karnac Books.

Tuckett, D. (2001), Editorial: 'Towards a more facilitating peer environment', *International Journal of Psychoanalysis* 82, pp. 643-51.

Warnock, M. (1998), *An Intelligent Person's Guide to Ethics*, London: Duckworth.

Warwick, S. (1989), 'A vote for no confidence', *Journal of Medical Ethics*, 25, 183-5.

Wharton, B. (1998), 'What comes out of the consulting room: The reporting of clinical material', *Journal of Analytical Psychology*, 43 (2): 205-23.

Wiener, J. (1996), 'Primary care and psychotherapy', *Psychoanalytic Psychotherapy*, supplement vol.10. Conference proceedings: Future Direction of Psychotherapy in the NHS: Adaptation or Extinction.

Wiener, J. (1998), 'Tricky beginnings: assessment in context', in ? Alister and C. Hauke (eds), *Contemporary Jungian Analysis*, London: Routledge.

Winnicott, D.W. (1971), *Playing and Reality*, London: Routledge.

Section V
Applications: Thinking Analytically
about Ethics in Different Settings

12
Ethical Issues for Psychotherapists Working in Organisations

Mannie Sher

Introduction

This chapter addresses the key ethical issues for psychotherapists who are employed by, and work in, organisations that provide psychotherapy services.

Working in organisations raises issues of how psychotherapy practitioners relate to the objectives, goals and methods of the departments, sections or units in which they work, and beyond that with the broad aims of the larger employing organisation. This chapter makes the assumption that psychotherapists will inevitably be faced with the need to balance the key organisational issues such as employer liability, allocation of resources, accountability and authority, with the ethical demands imposed on them by the psychotherapy profession in areas such as confidentiality, research and publication, disclosure, access to records and information technology. It has often been the case that the relationship between psychotherapist and organisation is defined as one of a conflict of interests, rather than a forum in which a number of different interests, values and practices may be debated and reconciled by mutual agreement. Such agreements as emerge out of those debates are likely, then, to stand a better chance of working in the interests of everyone involved – patients (to avoid clumsiness in the usage of terms, this chapter shall define the user of psychotherapy services as 'patient', although in some settings the term 'client' is used) professionals and organisations – because the agreements will be supported by systems with converging interests.

It is not an uncommon view that the practice of psychotherapy in organisations and in the private sector are so different in character as to make them unrecognisable from one another. The research that went into the writing of this chapter revealed a completely different picture in terms of ethical requirements and codes of practice. Surprisingly, the ethical issues, debates and final agreements were identical for psychotherapy practised in organisations and in private practice. Naturally, there are differences in context, method and task of psychotherapy practice, but all the essentials of the ethical position are the same – confidentiality is a core issue which forms a central pillar in the psychotherapist's duty of care towards the patient; responsibility towards children at risk over-ride all other considerations and no psychotherapist, medical or non-medical, can claim protection in a Court of Law under the principle of *privileged communication*.

Ethical Frameworks

It is a truism that all professional relationships are predicated upon differential power positions between the professional and the user. Moreover, this applies to the relationship between the user and the organisation through which the service is provided and is complicated by the fact of there being three parties to the transaction. However, that is also the case in private practice where the practitioner's professional organisation/association is never far from both parties' minds. The way the power relationships are played out lies in the tension between the patient's need for help and care and the need for both of them for a form of protection against exploitation. The patient approaches or is referred to the professional or the professional's organisation in order to seek the benefits of specialist knowledge and skills in a particular area of human functioning in which the patient believes themselves to be deficient. The patient hopes that as a consequence of the intervention by the professional their situation will improve. A particular characterisation of the professional, acquired through their socialisation as they pass through training programmes over many years, is that they will develop solid commitments to work for the benefit of their patients and that they will not abuse the power that their greater knowledge and skill bestows upon them. Differentials of power in the psychotherapy situation are self-evident in so far as patients appearing before psychotherapists are usually very troubled, fearful, vulnerable and dependent. They are likely to have experienced rejection, abuse and victimisation. Psychotherapists will be committed to an ethical framework that holds that the interests of the patient will always be paramount; that patients will not be exploited, financially or sexually; that psychotherapists will observe the principles of confidentiality, will act competently, and ensure the maintenance of their competence through continued professional development.

But how do these ethical principles stand up in practice where there is a tension between professional practitioners and their employing organisations? In cases where there is a conflict of interest how does it affect the psychotherapist's commitment towards the individual patient? Where the psychotherapist is not engaged directly by the patient – e.g. when the psychotherapist is employed by an organisation such as the health service, the prison service, education department of local government or voluntary organisation – the psychotherapist's duty of care would normally be orientated towards both the patient and towards the employer, but their ethical duties would be more strongly biased towards the patient. Where the psychotherapist works for an organisation, it is incumbent upon them to explain very carefully to the patient the nature of the 3-way relationship between patient, psychotherapist and organisation.

Psychotherapists working in organisations are likely to be subject to the demands and constraints of a number of codes of ethics. The first is the ethical framework of their psychotherapy training organisations. The second is the framework of their core profession. The third is the framework of their employing organisation that is usually within the public sector but could also be in the voluntary sector. In certain situations, there could be a degree of conflict between these different ethical frameworks. It is the purpose of this chapter to outline these possible conflicts of interests and to describe how psychotherapists and organisations alike deal with them.

Psychotherapists working in hospitals will have a duty to the Chief Executive of the Trust to ensure the best and most effective use of public resources. However, as psychotherapists, they will have an ethical duty to care for their patients, e.g. to seek investigations and services provided by other specialists and organisations if considered necessary. At what point does the psychotherapist make a decision between a duty of care to the patient and duty not to expend resources unnecessarily? A psychotherapist has a duty of confidentiality to the patient regarding the material that emerges during the psychotherapy work, but others in the Trust may have other duties in respect of the patient, e.g. to prevent the spread of infectious diseases, protect children or increase the clean-up rate of crimes. These issues raise ethical controversies between different care organisations and between different disciplines practising psychotherapy, e.g. social workers, psychologists, prison officers, nurses and doctors.

Confidentiality

From their first days as psychotherapy trainees, psychotherapists are educated to the strong injunctions regarding confidentiality. This part of the ethical code is drummed into trainees as the most important ethical foundation of the psychotherapy enterprise. On the other hand, psychotherapists, but especially trainees, need to talk to others – supervisors, colleagues and other professionals – all for good professional reasons. Supervision is an elemental part of training and development; others may simply need to talk about what is bothering them after a difficult session. Psychotherapists will tell their patients at the beginning of psychotherapy what the limits of confidentiality are. The statement will include that the work is confidential to the organisation. It will be explained that confidentiality is not absolute and there may be times and situations where others may have a right to know what happens in the psychotherapy treatment. For example, letters may need to be written to patients' GPs or psychiatrists informing them if a crisis is looming.

Patients may be under the care of other services, in particular the primary care services and possibly the psychiatric services. Patients would be asked for permission to contact these if necessary. In all these eventualities, the important principle on confidentiality requires patients to be told about possible links to other professionals and services and for patients to provide written permission for when and if communication with these services becomes necessary.

Psychotherapists may be asked by patients or by others to provide letters in cases involving insurance claims, divorce or custody of children. In general, psychotherapists will avoid writing letters. Instead, they will try and understand with the patient why they are being drawn into the patient's life in this way.

There are pressures on the concept of confidentiality that arise from working in organisations and in working with specific age groups such as adolescents and children. Even in organisations that do not provide psychotherapy directly to children there will be obligations on psychotherapists if there are risks of harm to minors. This situation may conflict with the psychotherapist's duty of care to clients. For example, if a paedophile tells his therapist about abusing a child who is not located in the psychotherapy system, the therapist would have a duty to inform someone. That duty may be viewed differently by the different disciplines. The Children's Act of 1989 states that everybody has a duty of care to children and this duty of care overrides their duty of care to their patients. This principle operates in any setting where the psychotherapy takes place, even if the minor may not be located there. This is a serious issue in the work with paedophiles because they may be reluctant to talk in their therapy if they believe that the therapist's overriding duty of care to children may compel them to act. The psychotherapist working with paedophiles has a conflict regarding their individual patient as a perpetrator of terrible things, and regarding the same individual as a victim of terrible things. The way this is understood leads to a swing between a collusive empathy, which can obscure the individual patient, on the one hand, and a sadistic countertransference, on the other. The hope is that by exploring the patient's past experiences as a victim, it might enable him to be aware of the damage that he has done to his victim. So, in the way that patients were damaged as victims, by getting an emotional grasp of the effect their victimhood has had on them, they might have some emotional grasp of the effects that they have had on their own victims. The obligation to act on hearing of abuse to minors may prevent this important working through of these dynamics. The aim of psychotherapy is, after all, to engage with the patient's internal conflicts in order to prevent future acting out. Containing the conflicts of ethics that the duty of care to minors at risk imposes upon the psychotherapist working with a paedophile adds to the burden of the therapeutic task. But the very containing of conflicts may actually constitute the psychotherapy task.

Working in a 'safe' environment is a *sine qua non* for psychotherapy practice, safe here meaning to have as few impingements from the outside world as possible, including freedom from anxiety of infringing both the law and the psychotherapist's ethical codes. Sadistic countertransference enactments that are involved in telling how horrible the patient's crimes were, and how dangerous they are themselves, are unethical and represent a recapitulation of the abuse that the patient had experienced in earlier life. On the other hand, it is equally unethical to collude with paedophiles who are in the process of trying to seduce the psychotherapist. The contract between patient and psychotherapist is that they are engaged in a process based on the understanding of the meaning of seduction and punishment through the use of interpretation. The expectation is that others are not to be involved.

There are parallel debates within organisations providing psychotherapy and the kind of debate that takes place between the personality of the patient and that of the psychotherapist. There are different complex networks within organisations that may have anxieties about the psychotherapy community within it. For example, some may want to see the gradual dismantlement of confidentiality within the psychotherapy setting in the organisation. The Human Rights Act (1998) has drafted into it the notion of the statutory requirement to disclose risk, rather than a statutory requirement to consider whether risk should be disclosed, so that it would be a breach of the law not to disclose any risks. The difference between a general organisational psychotherapy provision and the psychotherapy encounter itself, is that what is said in an organisation is a matter of public record because it is legally defined as a public place, so by this definition psycho- therapy records are public documents. Disclosures made in organisations are available to others, and there is no boundary as there is in a psychotherapist- patient relationship. In the work with paedophiles this principle can be circumvented by telling the patient to be vague about 'time, place or person' in relation to previous crimes on the grounds that the police are not interested in pursuing investigations where they do not have specific information on 'time, place or person'. Psychotherapy, therefore, whether in private practice or in organisations, provides a transitional space in which people can talk about current or previous offences that have not been cleared up or for which they have not been prosecuted. If patients talk about such cases, but do not mention 'time, place or person', the matter need not be pursued. If patients do mention 'time, place and person', psychotherapists should encourage them to disclose this to the authorities and so wipe the slate clean. The hope is that, as a result of the therapeutic work, the patient would come to a position where they themselves would want to wipe the slate clean.

It is a fact that in many organisations that provide psychotherapy services, the staff in those services are drawn from different disciplines while still retaining some of the statutory responsibilities of those disciplines. So social workers, nurses or prison officers acting as psychotherapists may be obliged to disclose to the police things that they hear, but others, like doctors or psychotherapists, are not obliged. This points to differences in ethical codes between the disciplines and organisations.

The basic ethical implication is that organisations are responsible for setting up the psychotherapeutic settings, where people are meant to feel free and be encouraged to disclose their free associations. In the process of these associa- tions, they may disclose things that it is not in their interest to disclose. But with some types of patient, crimes may have been committed, a body may be buried somewhere and there is no closure for grieving relatives. There is a difference in magnitude in terms of the severity of undisclosed risk and the crime clean-up rate.

Organisations create structures for therapeutic work to take place in the safest possible way. Inevitably, questions about boundaries and ethical issues have to be resolved especially in relation to records and confidentiality and the relationship between the statutory responsibilities of different disciplines. Different disciplines may be bound by different ethical codes and the organisation somehow has to work towards resolving them, although in some situations the different professional ethical codes may have advantages. Since achieving one fully integrated ethical system is difficult, managers and professional staff of psychotherapy services have to work at these issues all the time, in order to minimise conflicts and tensions. Resolution of these issues emerges through multidisciplinary and multi-agency debate, and in a broader context, in the debate with government, leading to a consensus view as to what is needed in terms of ethical codes. However, sharp differences of opinion on confidentiality are emerging. The UK government has foreseen the possibility that the confidentiality issue as it pertains in the criminal justice system, might be extended across the National Health Service and other care professions. The professions object to this, and the government is currently rethinking the situation, but the new Mental Health Act may nevertheless contain the provision of statutory disclosure that pertains at the present time. Psychotherapists operate in a statutory disclosure environment because policy-makers believe that there is a need in the public domain for the care professions to have a statutory duty to disclose risk. The point that psychotherapists are seeking to impress upon policy-makers is that confidentiality is absolutely essential in order to facilitate free association disclosures, even if they reveal things that people have not been committed for, e.g. an uncleared-up crime. Because the therapeutic discourse takes place in an organisation that may be bound to disclose, the issue of confidentiality affects the work considerably.

Although confidentiality is at the root of all psychotherapy practice, it is not absolute because everyone is subject to the law. The law requires all professions to release information in certain circumstances. Psychotherapists need to recognise that they are never going to get full protection for psychotherapy information. We can argue that we do not need that protection. But psychotherapists need to make sure that psychotherapy information is recognised by government departments as something to which they do not have a right of access. It is important that policy- and law-makers understand that if they undermine the principle of psychotherapy confidentiality, the result will be a destruction of healthcare generally. Psychotherapists have a duty, not only to their patients directly but within the institutional setting within which they are working, to look at the way information is handled. This could be the way physical records are held and computers are organised, but also the way in which the organisations, whether hospitals, prisons or voluntary organisations, respond to queries and check their methods and systems to make sure that there is no unnecessary sharing of information.

Psychotherapists must be pragmatic. It is pointless for them to espouse conspiracy theories, nor should they support absolutist positions that nothing should ever be disclosed under any circumstances. Current thinking is that patients and their carers and helpers should be the ones who decide who else should share their information. There needs to be a partnership between patients and psychotherapists regarding decisions on patient care. The view of psychotherapists has always been for there to be full and frank discussions on every aspect of disclosure when other parties have requested information for whatever reason.

Supervision

All organisations have systems of supervision in place for psychotherapists. Reasons for supervision often emphasise the deepening of the supervisee's insight and awareness of the therapeutic process. But the management aspects of supervision of psychotherapists in both statutory and voluntary organisations are often overlooked. Supervisors are entrusted with the dual task of promoting the individual development of the psychotherapy trainee and ensuring that policies, ethical standards, values and practices of the organisation are being followed. Supervisors may carry development roles, but they also work within certain authority structures.

Supervision in organisations has a different definition attaching to it than supervision that is part of professional development and training. In the statutory organisations, supervision has elements of hierarchy and management control attached to it. Distinctions are also made between supervision and consultation.

In training organisations and private practice supervision is regarded as absolutely essential. These organisations will consider the continuation of supervision as part of professional development and therefore an important ethical principle. These organisations will require weekly supervision for all their trainees and less frequent supervision for qualified psychotherapists. Psychotherapy trainees seeing training patients may have two separate individual supervisors weekly. Supervision is regarded as a discipline in its own right and these organisations will have training for supervisors – not something that any psychotherapist can do. Supervisors are expected to take responsibility for the conduct and management of the cases they are supervising as well as developing the thinking part of psychotherapy theory and practice. Supervision has a firm authority base in training, seniority, skill, wisdom and managerial responsibility. If necessary, supervisors can instruct trainees and can make recommendations to pass or fail them. In this way, they play a part in the management of the training organisation. The supervisors are accountable to the management of the organisation and are expected to voice their concerns, if they have any, about trainee psychotherapists.

In psychotherapy carried out in organisations, the nature of supervision carries two frames. One is supervision in order to help the practitioner do better clinical practice, and the other is to ensure that junior personnel are held within a framework of quality control. Senior psychotherapists within a clear hierarchical structure will do the supervising of junior personnel. Case discussion among psychotherapists of equal seniority would be called consultation, because they would be peers and one would not have authority over the other.

Codes of Practice for Different Disciplines

Codes of Practice or Codes of Conduct are elaborations on Codes of Ethics. These are discussed in the context of working in organisations where conflicts or differences in Codes of Practice for psychotherapists may be present. Psychotherapists diagnosing and/or treating patients do so on the understanding that they are acting on behalf of the organisation providing the service. Consequently, they are bound by the Codes of Ethics and Practices of the organisation on whose behalf they are working with their patients. In some organisations, notably voluntary psychotherapy organisations, all distinctions between the disciplines are removed or regarded as irrelevant and they work under the broad heading of psychotherapist. They do not perform any disciplinary function and as such they would all be bound by the organisation's unitary Code of Ethics.

In others, different disciplines may have different duties of care, as between, say, those that exist for forensic psychologists and those that exist for psychotherapists. These two disciplines contain the kernel of the whole debate between the interests of the individual and the interests of third parties. In some cases the organisation may work under Civil Service Ethical Codes and Codes of Conduct. These Codes of Conduct may conflict with the psychotherapy Codes of Conduct that demand free speech. Free speech is a *sine qua non* of psychotherapy. Psychotherapists attempt to speak the truth and the truth of what is in mind at a particular time. However, in some organisational contexts, it may be prudent not to say what is in mind if it leads to an official complaint. In organisations where psychotherapists in training are drawn from different disciplines, there could be conflict between a psychotherapist's discipline of origin role and their psychotherapist role. If, for example, psychotherapists or patients express strong feelings in what is considered to be discriminatory, offensive or abusive language, they could be exposed to investigation and admonishment for allowing things to take place that are psychotherapeutically normal practice. There is potential confusion for registrars, nurses, social workers and prison officers (the latter being trained in methods of control), who as a result of working psychotherapeutically, incorporate new attitudes and practices. But the strength of therapeutic work derives from the different Codes being debated and coming together in the best interests of the patient as part of a multidisciplinary process. For example, psychotherapeutic work in personality disorders units in high-security healthcare settings involves people whose core profession is health – doctors, nurses, psychologists – and prison officers, who are primarily concerned with custody. These professions work in new clinical situations where personality disordered people are able to manipulate them. Looking at it positively, these professionals can make a contribution from a very structured custodial point of view. They are actually able to maintain the boundaries very effectively and keep a clear prospective of what the boundaries are.

Authority and Accountability

Authority structures and dynamics are always present in organisations, and it is part of the responsibility of organisations to discuss and debate them in order to produce appropriate working conditions. Psychotherapists, too, have to address the ubiquitous tension in authority relationships that occur between the employer's legal liability and the psychotherapist's professional ethical requirements.

Some organisations, especially voluntary ones, attempt to deal with the therapeutic and authority functions by separating supervision and management roles, believing that in this way they can avoid confusion. The supervisor has a separate role, which in theory frees them to concentrate on dynamic clinical issues alone. From the perspective of this role, supervisors avoid potential conflict between the trainee's training requirement and what may be in the patient's best interests. Some voluntary organisations may depend in part upon fees paid by patients. Indeed, their charitable status requires them to offer treatment in return for low fees. But as they struggle to meet their financial obligations, organisations may ponder how long should they go on treating someone who is paying a very low fee. Can the organisation afford to let the patient stay in treatment for years, which may be what the psychotherapist says they need? The length and frequency of treatment is left to the professional judgement of the supervisor and trainee psychotherapist, but there is a question whether the organisation can support their decision. There is always a tension over whether training requirements and clinical needs will dovetail sufficiently. The organisation's ethical obligation is not to take on more patients than it can deal with, but it often does so if patients are willing to remain as long-term treatment cases for its trainees.

Statutory Organisations

The issue of legal liability arises because statutory organisations are part of the systems that are legally defined and determined. In some psychotherapy services, the doctors might be employed by a Trust, the psychologist by another authority, and the social workers or probation officer come from yet another. All of them may provide services to the one patient and each claims the right to make decisions. Other organisations may be structured differently, where, for instance, the staff are all employed by the same service. In such cases, there would be a unified structure in the management line, which may, nevertheless, provide a diversity of conduct and codes. In the case of a medical psychotherapist employed in a non-medical setting, or in a medical, but non-psychotherapy setting, the clinical governance of the doctors would need validation by a doctor who may not be available within that structure. There could be a problem in operating with diverse ethical codes that would not be reflected in the different accountability structures. The medical psychotherapist in that case could be accountable to the Chief Executive of that organisation and also be accountable to other senior doctors in another service who are not psychotherapists who have to validate the work of a medical psychotherapist. It leads to a complicated picture of organisational authority and accountability.

Ethical Implications of Research and Publication in Organisations

Organisations have a duty to evaluate performance and to seek more effective methods of delivering goods and services. Evaluation involves researching the efficacy of treatments, which in turn involves patients directly or indirectly. Patients' records and other methods may be used. All evaluation methods involve sensitive matters around consent, confidentiality and the potential for identification, archiving and publication.

In most psychotherapy training organisations, evaluation of the performance of individual therapists is made through supervision reports. Evaluation of the organisation as a whole is by means of auditing every few years.

There are three areas of research: audit, empirical research and descriptive research. Descriptive research relies on the use of clinical material. This normally requires the written permission of the patient, who should be shown the written material and give a signed release that he or she is in agreement with it. It is the duty of all organisations that undertake research to ensure that patients fully understand what is being done.

Empirical research is governed by hospital ethics committees that are locally structured committees protecting patient rights. The ethical standards for research and consent are set out by hospital ethical committees.

Audit activities do not give rise to major ethical issues. The variety of different audit structures ensures anonymity. Gathering pre- and post-treatment data on a variety of psychological diseases based on large numbers of cases is not regarded as having ethical dimensions because it relies on pooled, collective data – it is not individual data. The ethical implication of audit within the public services generally has not been raised.

Disclosure and 'Psychotherapist Privilege'

There is an overlap between the issues of disclosure, 'privileged' communication and confidentiality. Disclosure and psychotherapists' 'privilege' are important issues for psychotherapists working in organisations, especially in their dealings with other statutory bodies, like the Courts, social services departments, the National Health Service, education departments, etc. The extent and limits of 'privilege' are different for different organisations and professions.

Legally, psychotherapists do not enjoy 'privileged' communication. Psycho- therapists may be approached by patients' solicitors seeking reports and asking for letters and clinical notes. Psychotherapists should not write anything to anybody without first seeking permission from the patient. Sometimes the patient may want the psychotherapist to write a report and this may cause difficulties to arise. Even when the patient asks the psychotherapist to write, minimal information should be given. Psychotherapists know, of course, that if they refuse to disclose, they can be subpoenaed, and would be subject to the same penalties as anybody else. Bollas and Sundelson (1995), are worried that psychotherapists may be obliged to report on all manner of clinical details that would gradually and ultimately erode the principle of confidentiality on which all psychotherapy work is based.

'Privilege' for all psychotherapists may seem desirable, but it could also backfire. The patient, knowing that the psychotherapist would not disclose, could talk endlessly about a deviant situation, and continue acting out sadistic fantasies, say, towards a minor, behaving similarly in the transference towards the therapist, and never feeling inclined to stop. In such a situation, the psychotherapist and patient, instead of existing in a safe environment, could become tied up in a merciless trap without end. 'Privilege' and trust could be seen as two sides of the same coin. Therefore, issues like 'privilege' and confidentiality always have to be qualified; neither is absolute. Psychotherapists, like all other professionals, except legal representatives, do not have 'privilege'. However, health information in the UK is regarded as being 'special' not 'ordinary'. Courts do not generally regard health information as being privileged but it is set aside as 'special' because of its sensitivity. All health information is regarded as having special status but certain categories are particularly sensitive, e.g. mental health. Courts will be sympathetic towards psychotherapists who seek private audience with a judge to explain the sensitive nature of psychotherapy material and who are willing to divulge it privately to a judge.

Access to Records

There is much uncertainty regarding the ownership of psychotherapy notes. These are generally regarded as the property of the employing authority. The conditions of their storage, protection and use will have implications for psychotherapists. There is the question of what notes – the brief notes that are placed in the formal file? Detailed notes of each session that are usually used for supervision purposes? Or *aides mémoire* that psychotherapists sometimes rely on to refresh their memories of the immediate past sessions and which are not usually kept in the formal case note files? In the current position where patients have rights of access to their records, which notes would they have access to? All categories of notes? Or only the formal records?

Organisations (and private practitioners, too) have strict rules about the storage and protection of records, how they may be used, where they may be taken and who may access them. These rules are firmly laid down. Patients are recognised as having the right of access to their records. But if patients want to see their records, it is expected that the therapist will discuss the reasons widely with the patient and explore with them what it is they want to achieve by seeing their records.

Organisations may have two or three sets of files. First, there may be a kind of 'everything' file which has everything in it concerning the individual's crossing-into-the-institution process. A second file may contain only treatment details. Normally, there is a very tight confidentiality barrier between the two sets of records and the rest of the organisation. Bizarre situations can emerge to the detriment of the individual's overall care if certain information is not allowed to be shared, just as there may serious infringements of rights if certain information is shared. The arrangement of multiple files is a way of dealing with splits in organisations. Some information can be shared with others on a need-to-know basis, and others not. In some cases, a third record may be kept, which is a therapy record that is for the private use of the psychotherapist. But the different levels of confidentiality and access should be made explicit – what the content of the files is, their use, and who has access them. The 'everything' file is a public record that other professions can access. The treatment file would be accessible by members of the multidisciplinary team only. Patients would have access to all records. Ownership of the records is usually in the hands of the organisation, and therefore the organisation and the individual psychotherapists have individual and collective responsibility to ensure their safekeeping under lock and key.

In the past the argument ran that patients' records were owned by the Secretary of State. It is now agreed that ownership of the paper is irrelevant, but what matters is who controls them on a daily basis. Records departments or administrators and receptionists are the agents, but it is effectively the psychotherapist and patient who are the people who should control the records. Release of information from the notes should only be done with the patient's consent, except on rare occasions where the law requires the release. Patients should have access to their records, with one caveat: that they do not have rights to information concerning other patients that might be in their notes. Requesting to see a patient's notes is usually a matter of helping the patient to understand what is in the notes.

Consent and Coercion in Psychotherapy Treatment

A chapter on psychotherapy and organisations needs to include situations where patients do not enter treatment voluntarily but where the psychotherapy treatment is part of a court order or prison sentence. Patients never receive treatment involuntarily. They may be imprisoned involuntarily but their treatment is entirely voluntary and they can discharge themselves at any stage. The only compulsory treatment that might be considered is when an individual has a psychotic breakdown and is in need of psychiatric treatment. If they wish to carry on psychotherapy treatment but are judged too ill to continue with the treatment, they will be compulsorily discharged and moved to another place where they can receive the appropriate psychiatric treatment. Patients may be discharged from psychotherapy treatment compulsorily for a transgression of the law. But usually patients have two or three chances before being discharged.

Where psychotherapy treatment facilities exist within a framework of compulsory detention as, say, in a gaol, there will inevitably be a debate about whether patients should ever be compulsorily discharged from treatment. Some will want a policy that will be part of the constitution; others will want each situation to be regarded as different and judged on its own merits. There is a dialectic between an aggressive wish to have a set of rules that will follow in certain circumstances, e.g. compulsory discharge if found positive for drugs, and a case for flexibility in clinical application, e.g. when someone who takes drugs, acknowledges this, and thus demonstrates that they are working on the issue. But where someone is caught several times in possession of drugs, they would be much more likely to be compulsorily discharged.

The Mental Health Act has very limited authorisations, but more important is the issue with children who refuse treatment and/or are incompetent and where the court orders treatment or where the parents authorise it. In cases where children are given treatment without consent, there are grave concerns that their right to refuse treatment is being overridden. On the other hand, it is argued that the child's competence and ability to understand, and therefore to give consent, may be limited.

Patients may talk to their psychotherapists about their wish to die, their fears of dying, the pain, leaving their loved ones, etc. Only two medical societies at the World Medical Association are in favour of recognising that occasionally suicide could be a sane act and that suicide is not something that one should always stop. Being open and talking through the issues helps patients. The psychotherapeutic principle is that by talking through a fear, patients may get to feel better. The psychotherapist is on the side of the patient's survival, attempting to understand with the patient those aspects of his current feelings that impel him towards self-destructive acts, with the intention that this would make such enactments less likely.

The psychotherapist has to decide whether it is best to listen and explore the issues. If the psychotherapist has doubts about the patient's competence, if the patient is acutely depressed or chronically ill, the psychotherapist may consider intervening under the Mental Health Act. When someone is sane and competent and not depressed, the psychotherapist might take a different view and talk to the patient exploring the issues around living and dying before choosing whether or not to intervene. Although psychotherapists have no greater ability to prevent suicide than other members of society, they are nevertheless in a more privileged and qualified position, are more likely to be faced with information about their patients' suicidal impulses and therefore could respond earlier in the development of these impulses in their patients.

Information Technology

Organisations are continually thinking through the implications of technological innovations to ensure the protection of their patients while remaining consistent with their organisational responsibilities. They are obliged to observe the requirements of the Data Protection Act and the Human Rights Act and there is concern that computers and the way that data is kept on computer may compromise the principles of confidentiality. But on the whole, organisations attempt to comply with the law on information technology (IT).

IT functions can be divided into three areas: the first is the typing of reports; the second is data gathering as part of ongoing audit and evaluation work where individuals would be subject to various parameters to identify their changes and various other empirical measures; and the third is the general computerisation of the records of everyone using the services. Organisations generally are obliged and are willing to be compliant with the Data Protection Act provided that broader issues of maintaining confidentiality are assured. Information, encrypted or otherwise, has to be secure without compromising the reasons why information is kept electronically in the first place – rapid access, research, audit, multidisciplinary and multi-agency working. For obvious reasons, organisations rely more extensively on IT than private practice, where usual methods of record keeping may feel more secure.

Voluntary and training organisations are also obliged to comply with the law on IT and they try to limit written records to factual accounts of events: telephone conversations, attending sessions, letters written. The actual content of sessions is handwritten and is kept by practitioners for supervision purposes. Material is written in such a way as to be unidentifiable. Session reports and six-monthly progress reports of the psychotherapy do not usually get computerised.

Conclusions

This chapter has attempted to address as many of the ethical elements in psychotherapy practice that have relevance to psychotherapy treatment situations as they are practised in organisations. Although, at first glance, there may appear to be significant differences between traditional private practice and the more complex arrangements of psychotherapy in organisations, the result of these investigations reveal a surprising similarity between the ethical requirements in the two contexts. To be sure, organisational contexts – clinics, hospitals, prisons, etc. – are geared up to provide treatment for patients with greater degrees of pathological disturbance which is usually acted out through violence, paedophilia, and other manifestation of borderline personality structures, where the issue of detention and withdrawal of human rights, the necessity to work with multidisciplinary and multi-agency arrangements, make for differences of degree on key questions. But irrespective of context, the main ethical issues are the same – confidentiality, protection of minors, and prevention of crime. Psychotherapy practice in whatever context, holds that the duty of care towards the patient is paramount and this duty includes the keeping of confidence regarding their patient's information, exercising care in the matter of communications between professionals, record-keeping and protection of records, and consultation with patients on all matters concerning their treatment.

Acknowledgements

This chapter is the result of conversations with people who are at the forefront of the debate on ethics in the work of their organisations and professions. I have learned much from them and I appreciate their willingness to entrust me with their ideas and dilemmas, which by definition are in a continuing state of non-resolution. They are all committed to the development of ethical principles in working environments that are complex and difficult. They are also committed to working out the exigencies of collaborative work between professionals from different disciplines. I would like to thank the following: Robert Hale, Lesley Murdin, Vivienne Nathanson, Ginney Riley, Honor Rhodes and Rosie Wilkinson. I also thank Julie Wilson and Mara Gorli for their good humour while typing the transcripts from difficult-to-hear tapes.

References

Bollas, C. and Sundelson, D. (1995), *The New Informants: Betrayal of Confidentiality in Psychotherapy and Psychoanalysis* Karnac Books, London.
Hale, R., Minne, C. and Zachary, A. (2000), *Assessment and Management of Sexual Offenders.* New

Oxford Textbook of Psychiatry, vol. 2, edited by Ibn-Lopez Gelder and ? Anderson, Oxford University Press.

Human Rights Act (1998), published by The Stationary Office, ISBN 0 10 544298 4.

Royal College of Psychiatrists, Council Report CR85 (2000), Good Psychiatric Practice: Confidentiality Sacombe Press, Hertfordshire.

Supreme Court of the United States (1996), Jaffee, Special Administrator for Allen, Deceased v. Redmond et al., Certiorari to the United States Court of Appeals for the Seventh Circuit, No. 95-266. Argued February, 1996. Decided June 13, 1996.

Scoggins, M., Litton, R. and Palmer, S. (1998), 'Confidentiality and the law', Counselling Psychology Review, vol. 13, p.141.

The British Psychological Society (1993), 'Ethical principles for conducting research with human participants', The Psychologist, January 1993.

The Master of the Rolls (1996), 'Confidentiality – an inter-disciplinary issue', Inaugural Spring Lecture.

13
Ethical Issues in Working
with Children and their Families

Judith Trowell and Gillian Miles

Introduction

Over the last decade psychoanalytic work with children has had to recognise pressures and changes in society, and expectations have changed. There is now a demand from adults for openness of records, a recognition that children and young people have a right to give their own consent and that their case records need to be respected and accorded confidentiality. What is recorded about different members of a family is no longer accessible to all members of the family. Again, whereas in the past the professionals believed the records to be their own clinical account, it is now seen as a shared document to which both parents and children have a right of access, and a right to question the accuracy of the account. The implication of this has been that psychoanalytic psychotherapists have had to struggle to use language appropriately, language that is accessible whilst not losing the complexity of the work, grappling with unconscious issues such as unconscious phantasy, splitting, projective identification, transference and countertransference.

The Legal Framework

Psychoanalytic work with children and families raises many issues and there is a complex legal framework that surrounds it. The Children Act 1989 became active in October 1991, closely followed in December 1991 by the ratification in the United Kingdom of the UN Convention on the Rights of the Child. This convention contains forty-two substantive rights for children, covering their needs and aspirations, civil rights, freedom of expression and religion, social welfare rights and the right to education and good health care, and should be the current context for our children and young people.

The Children Act spells out the powers of the courts in England and Wales to determine or advise on the future of children in matrimonial disputes (private law), care proceedings largely arising from Child Protection concerns, education where there is non-attendance, and secure provision where a child or young person is a danger to themselves or others (public law). This Act has importance, therefore, within the lives of many children and young people.

In the General Medical Council guidance to doctors, contained in 'Seeking patients' Consent: the Ethical Considerations', there is the statement: 'You must assess a child's capacity to decide whether to consent to or refuse proposed investigation or treatment before you provide it.' A distinction is then made between a young person aged sixteen years or more, who can be treated as an adult and presumed to have the capacity to decide, and a child less than sixteen years, who may have the capacity to decide depending on their ability to understand. This follows the Gillick case (*Gillick v. West Norfolk and Wisbech Area Health Authority & Another* (1986, AC 112)), where it was established that those less than sixteen years of age who were competent and had capacity could request treatment in their own right. In spite of this, psychoanalytic psychotherapy is rarely offered if there is no adult with parental responsibility to give consent. In matrimonial disputes, if both parties have parental responsibility then it is usually wise to seek the consent of both parents. An emergency consultation can be offered without parental consent but ongoing therapy really requires parental consent.

However, where a child less than 16 years of age withholds consent and the person with parental responsibility also withholds consent, clinicians still have to consider the child's best interests and may need to seek the views of the court. Quite frequently now courts are ordering therapy, and this is an interesting development.

The Human Rights Act 1998 has been in effect since October 2000 and the relevant parts for children and families are: Article 6, the right to a fair hearing; Article 8, the right to respect for private and family life; Article 5, the right to liberty and security of person. All these articles have implications for professionals working with children and their families. But given that the principle of the 'best interests of the child' is still seen as paramount, problems should not arise given thoughtful sensitive practice, well recorded.

Two pieces of legislation are currently under review, the Adoption Act and the Mental Health Act. The Adoption Act will have some impact since the emphasis on fast tracking adoption and the pressure to see adoption as the placement of choice may conflict with the wishes, feelings and possibly the needs of the child. Professionals may have difficulties, as there are consent and confidentiality issues involved. The Mental Health Act is only used for a small number of young people when they are withholding consent to treatment (usually of acute psychosis, serious self harm or anorexia nervosa). If these young people have been in therapy, again issues of consent and confidentiality may arise, and the therapist will need to be honest and straightforward about their views and actions. It is now recognised that it would be most helpful, when the Mental Health Act is being used for a child or young person, if there were a guardian for the child as there is in Children Act cases. This person could speak for and support the child, and the therapist could then maintain their therapeutic role.

Clinical Issues

Child Protection (1)
There is a considerable difference between those cases where child protection

concerns arise for the first time during treatment, and those coming for help where child protection is already known about prior to commencing treatment.

A child in psychoanalytic psychotherapy talks and plays freely, may talk about dreams, and phantasies may emerge. The therapist may suddenly or gradually find themselves wondering if some reality is being conveyed. Unless there is intense anxiety, the therapist must take time to allow the issue to clarify, and also to have supervision and discuss the concerns with the staff member responsible for the case. If the concerns remain or increase, then usually the child is told that worrying matters have come up that need to be shared. At the start of therapy, during the introductions with the child and family, it is usually stated that what is talked about stays in the room, the child's confidentiality is protected. Some therapists do add 'unless there is something really worrying that I need to share.' Either way, the therapist needs wherever possible to let the child know if they think matters are too worrying.

Emotional abuse is difficult to assess. In one way, one could say that all children who need therapy have been abused, damaged or traumatised. Most often, this was not deliberately abusive but occurred by omission rather than by commission. Sometimes, however, the level of emotional cruelty or neglect is such that assessment and intervention may be needed alongside the therapy.

Physical abuse usually prompts quite speedy action, where there is excessive bruising or where, more rarely, cigarette burns may be seen. Most physical abuse initially goes to casualty or the paediatrician.

Sexual abuse is a real worry and problem, since sexual phantasies are very much part of therapy, including sexual thoughts and feelings about parents, siblings, authority figures. If contact sexual abuse – when the body is touched inappropriately – is talked about then a quite speedy response is needed. Non-contact abuse – flashing, observing bodily functions, pornography — are more difficult and merit a more thoughtful response. Telephoning the social services is always felt to be a betrayal of confidentiality and may go against the child's stated wishes; they may not consent. It needs to be borne in mind that a child who shares such information usually wants the abuse to stop, even if other *sequalae* are not wanted. Hopefully, the social services and the police, if need be, will explore and assess the case sensitively and the child is then protected by the offer of services, by the removal of the alleged abuser or, more rarely, the child is taken into care.

Once such protective intervention has taken place, if the therapist has alerted the statutory services, then the therapy is changed. Hopefully, the child and the therapist continue to work together. The transference and countertransference is interfered with and this needs to be acknowledged; the therapist wished to protect the therapeutic relationship, and now has to manage her own and the child's fear that it is damaged irreparably. This is usually not so: the child or young person can understand the therapist's anxiety, concern and wish to ensure there was no serious problem. Slowly the therapeutic alliance and therapeutic work can continue. External reality intrudes into work with children and adolescents quite often: school trips, exams, family crises, for example, are all events which have to be worked with in the therapy. However, it is always important to allow the phantasies, the unconscious communications, to develop. Often, in situations of possible abuse, the therapist becomes so anxious and fearful about the possible consequences of their intervention that they temporarily lose the capacity for containment, or the capacity to allow the child's understanding consciously or unconsciously to emerge.

Once the child protection issues have emerged then there are case conferences, the assessment framework, the possibility of court reports and then ongoing case reviews. Here, there can be a difference of opinion: some therapists do not want and will not be involved in any of these meetings and procedures, and another member of the multidisciplinary team is asked to take this on, often the psychiatrist; others see the need for the child to know that all the professionals are working together and feel that they should be involved. A therapist can attend case conferences, court or case reviews. There is no need to disclose the content of the sessions but a valuable professional opinion about the child can be helpful. Their involvement, if only intermittent, can also help professionals in the community, such as teachers and social workers, to understand how therapists work and how their efforts can complement each other in trying to help the child.

Where cases are very difficult or very contentious, the case records, process notes, audio- or videotapes may be subpoenaed. This means that the judge insists that all case material can be used in court. It is wise when making records, including process notes, to be aware of this and keep fact (interaction) separate from opinion, reflections, and countertransference material. Similarly, if there is a Part 8 Review of a case where a child has died or there has been a serious incident, then case files can be frozen and scrutinised and professionals can be interviewed to explore their practice. Similar issues can also apply to looked after children, where there may have been child protection concerns. It must always be remembered that when a child is in care, the social worker has parental responsibility and needs to be involved in a parental capacity.

Parental Issues

When a child is in psychotherapy parents are also offered sessions to hear about parental concerns and to maintain the family perspective for the work with the child.

The professional working with the parent/carer has a difficult and complex task. Parents need to come to bring the child to their treatment but they may also want help in managing the child. Sometimes they can see that exploring their own concerns and past can be helpful in understanding themselves and the child. More rarely, parents recognise that they need psychotherapy for themselves. In any of this work, the worker with the parent may become worried that child protection issues are emerging, usually in relation to the child in therapy, sometimes in relation to other children. This inevitably produces conflicts for the therapist working with the parents, concerning who is the patient who needs to be protected. Just as the child's therapist may ignore the implications of what is being said or enacted, so the parent's therapist can turn a blind eye, not wanting to know. They may at last face the issue and raise it with the parents, the parents may themselves be very worried and may then be able to acknowledge the problem. This may then be worked on, and a decision will need to be made whether or not to inform the social services. If difficulties persist, it is usually wise to let the social services know and together decide how to proceed. The parent's therapist should continue to offer sessions, even if some are missed. The social services may investigate and, if the situation is seen to be adequately safe for the child, leave the therapist to continue and report back. If the social services remain concerned following the investigation, they may intervene.

The parent's therapist also has to consider involvement in case reviews and court as well as contact with the child's school and the general practitioner. Hopefully, the child's therapist will be in touch with these outside agencies but the parent's therapist may carry this forward. Throughout these professional contacts, maintaining confidentiality, seeking consent, and being as thoughtful and open as possible is essential.

Where parents and carers are seen frequently, problems may emerge that are cause for concern: parental mental illness, drug or alcohol abuse, domestic violence, criminality, or the use of pornography. The parent's therapist needs to be thoughtful and sensitive but also needs to clarify when work can proceed and when other professionals need to become involved. Often, if a parent is under the care of an adult psychiatrist and is on medication or methadone maintenance, then work can continue, although it is generally more supportive work rather than psychotherapy. Criminality, violence and pornography may not intrude directly but the work can easily be corrupted or become so sadomasochistic that its usefulness needs to be reviewed. These cases are not easy, the child in treatment often desperately needs help, but it is important that the clinic and the therapy are not used as a cover for illegal activities.

Confidentiality Issues in Ongoing Treatment

Within the treatment situation other confidentiality issues arise when parents or carers wish to know about their child's therapy. When the process of therapy is explained at the outset, the parents will have been told that the content of the child's therapy sessions is confidential. Again, we might add, that it is confidential unless matters arise in the course of therapy which lead to concerns about the child's welfare, when the child's therapist might need to break this confidentiality, inform the parents, and possibly other professionals. Such issues might be the possibility of abuse, or concerns about the child's state of mind.

However, we would also expect any parent to be concerned and want to know about the progress of their child's therapy. Where there is a separate worker for the parents, there is the possibility of a dialogue between the parent worker and the child worker, to ensure that major concerns are communicated: for instance, external events or family problems. The child's therapist may also want to be kept informed of the child's progress as reported by the parents, and join the parents' worker and the parent for review sessions from time to time. However, at all times the confidentiality of the content of the child's therapy will need to be protected. Equally, there will be issues from the parent's sessions which it may be important for the child's therapist to know about. Both therapists will need to respect the fundamental confidentiality surrounding the content of their work, whilst being able to share concerns of importance for the child's best interests and the furtherance of the therapy. Much will depend on the basic trust built up between the workers, the parents and the child, and it is of central importance that this trust is maintained. In sharing their concerns, both therapists will need to bear in mind the impact of transference and countertransference issues in their work with parents and child, and the possibility of mirroring family dynamics. Similarly complex confidentiality issues are present when parents are separated or divorced, and seen in their role as parents. Where there is no parent worker, the child's therapist will need to take on the task of maintaining contact with the parents around the child's therapy, at the same time respecting the confidentiality of the child's sessions.

Adolescent Issues

Adolescents also can raise worrying concerns. As indicated earlier, mental illness, attempted suicide and anorexia nervosa may become so worrying that the young person requires medical treatment. There is then the debate about the appropriate use of the Children Act and a care order, or the Mental Health Act and a section.

The therapist frequently hopes the therapy will improve the situation, and many adolescent patients are treated successfully, but a few need more help. It is sometimes hard for the therapist to recognise this, and with or without consent they break the young person's confidentiality and contact parents and other professionals.

When young people are experimenting with drugs, alcohol, sexual partners and internet pornography, confidentiality can usually be sustained. Adolescent turmoil is normal; it is when the behaviour becomes fixed or escalates in dangerousness that real worry may need to be expressed. Adolescents are very sensitive to confidentiality and consent and this must be done very carefully. If the issues are explored over time, they may be able to continue to attend, but some may not. Where young people are abusing young children, particularly sexually, there are serious problems. If both are children, then the abuser who is the patient needs to be cared for and protected, but so does the child victim. More is now known and understood about adolescent abusers, and we are aware that if nothing is done to help them with this behaviour it can become an addiction and persist and develop. Rarely do adolescents grow out of it. It is very important to address this problem fully with the young person and to give them all the help available. It is also helpful to inform the social services.

Matrimonial Disputes

When marriages break down, and parents fight over the children and money, both become very emotionally charged areas. Increasingly, the children in these situations are being brought to clinics for assessment and therapy. It may then emerge that the parent wants a report on the emotional damage caused by their ex-partner, or wants a report to support reducing or terminating contact with the non-resident parent.

If this is referred to a clinic as a piece of court work, then it is clear that a report will be written and all sessions may contribute to the report. Confidentiality and consent must be clarified at the start of therapy. It is far more difficult when a request for a report was not declared at the start and emerges well into therapy. It may also emerge that the non-resident parent did not know about the therapy and, when told, they may refuse consent, since according to the principle of parental responsibility they should have been involved in the decision to treat. This can be very difficult and disruptive to deal with in retrospect. Any child taken on for assessment and treatment must have had two parents, and it is sensible to check at the start the whereabouts, status and views of any absent parent. This parent should always be contacted if at all possible. After a divorce has been settled, contact issues continue, and both parents always need to be borne in mind.

Recently there has been an increasing awareness of domestic violence and the associated risk of emotional as well as physical damage to the child. However, as with sexual abuse, one partner can use the issue to attack and try to eliminate their ex-partner. Of course, the child may be very troubled and distressed by what they have witnessed, and their behaviour may have deteriorated, but this can be used by one parent against the other. Sessions with the child may reveal real issues but may also reveal the child's distress at the breakdown of the parents' relationship. The therapist will need to be thoughtful and to explore with the child or adolescent how to proceed. Parental pressure should be resisted, but it will need to be firmly stated when the child's situation is unacceptable.

Consent to Treatment

All these issues are clinical concerns that arise in therapy when decisions need to be made to break confidentiality or act without consent. There is, of course, a more fundamental issue – when parents want therapy for a child but the child or young person does not agree. Children can be brought to treatment against their will, adolescents less easily so. It used to be possible to insist that a child come to the therapy room and remain there but this is no longer acceptable practice. Children can be encouraged – perhaps an adult who is seen as a safe person can accompany them and sit in the room or outside the door – but it is no longer possible to restrain a child and keep them in the room against their will. Similarly, if during a session the child wants to leave or wants to stop the therapy, this presents a difficulty. The child can be encouraged to remain: perhaps they can understand the purpose of the therapy and see that whilst part of them wants to leave, another part wishes to stay and recognises that they need help. But, ultimately, if the child does not consent to treatment then the child can leave. If therapy is seen to be so important, one must consider compulsion – the Mental Health Act.

This is a significant change in practice and can be painful and distressing for the therapist, who knows only too well how much in need of therapy the child may be. But, sometimes, the children are right, and they know that they cannot manage therapy at this time or that the therapist is not the person to work with them.

If the therapist does restrain the child, they will have to explain what has happened to the parents. Some children do make allegations against their therapist of physical or sexual abuse. Any such allegation must be taken seriously and investigated properly. Male therapists are somewhat more vulnerable to such allegations.

Complaints

Formal complaints can be made against therapists. Such complaints may follow difficult sessions, or may arise when the parents or the child are experiencing serious uncertainty about the form of the intervention. Often, in therapy, the child can deteriorate, become more depressed, more difficult, may even become more disturbed. If this has not been explained as a possible outcome prior to the start of therapy, then the parents may complain. When consent is sought, the possibility of psychological deterioration for a while should be explained, so that consent is given with as much information as possible.

Another source of complaint is the writing of clinical papers without the consent of the patient. The subject of consent to publish and the breaking of confidentiality in this way are current issues that are being vigorously addressed and debated. Clinicians learn from each other through clinical case studies but patients can be very distressed if they read about themselves. This must be taken seriously, and careful thought given as to how to proceed. Children and their parents can also be very distressed when they read court reports. There is sometimes an assumption that National Health Service staff are bound by the old view of medical confidentiality. This no longer applies, and it is wise to warn children and their parents if one has to write a report, particularly if the request comes during ordinary clinical work.

Case Notes

With the Data Protection Act and the Access to Health Records Act, patients have the right to see their computer and paper files. As already indicated, these records can be subpoenaed by the judge in a court case. When this happens, however, the practitioner can have a lawyer make representation in court so that only the lawyers in the case are allowed to see the file, and this only after the judge has read it in chambers to decide if it is relevant for them to read.

Some children return as adults and ask to see their file, when they are trying to make sense of what has happened to them. Often, the relevant clinician is no longer in post and, rather than just consent and break the past confidentiality of the child and therapist, it is often more useful to offer an appointment with the person, taking them through the file, and perhaps reading with them from therapy reports or assessment sessions.

Where it is thought that access to records might damage a person's mental health, such access can be refused. However, it is usually better in such situations to see the person and to try to understand why they want to find out about themselves.

There is a real issue about access to children's or family files. Case records often cover the whole family, parents and several children. One parent may then demand to see the file, which contains information about their partner or ex-partner, shared in confidence. It is not appropriate for one adult to see material relating to another. The child's record is also held on behalf of that child. The child might consent to their records being seen, but may not. An individual can see anything on file which relates to them if it is unlikely to damage their mental health. It is, therefore, important when writing for the file that this is borne in mind. If files can be arranged in sections then each individual can be given a space of their own, which would facilitate this process. Confidentiality must be maintained unless there is individual consent, or unless access to the file is ordered by the judge in court or by the Secretary of State.

Research

Research and scholarly work are essential if knowledge is to be shared and increased. As we have indicated, whilst case studies are vital for furthering knowledge, they raise important issues of confidentiality and consent. Research and evaluation involve more complicated procedures around confidentiality. Normally, research projects must be considered by a local ethics committee, and consent will be a serious consideration. The whole process of the research and necessary consent must be explained clearly and agreed to by the child/ren, parents and anyone else with parental responsibility.

Smaller projects for audit and evaluation may use anonymised or aggregated data or information but may be enlivened by case vignettes. Similarly, some evaluation involves multiple case studies. When embarking on research it is important to consider the issue of consent. The project and what is proposed should be explained clearly to the individuals involved in order for both parent(s) and child to give their signed consent It is important to consider the issue of consent and to explain the project and what is proposed clearly to the individuals involved, for their signed consent. Some are very reluctant to consent to 'research', fearing they will be guinea pigs, whilst others are happy to help others whilst receiving help themselves. When obtaining consent in all research projects, much will also depend on the clarity and spirit with which the aims and objectives of the research are explained, since the researcher may well feel unduly reticent when requesting participation.

Difference

Psychoanalytic psychotherapy, whether for children, adolescents, parents or families, tends to be seen as arising from a particular class, the middle class, and a particular culture, white or Jewish European. It is not seen as sensitive to difference: to other races, religions, non-European languages, to disability or sexual orientation. Respecting these differences involves care with issues of consent and confidentiality, and also sensitivity in the use of language. Bad aspects of a person being connoted as 'black', or deep depression described as 'a black hole' can be seen as racist. Certain races and cultures are sensitive to comments about 'primitive'. Devout religious individuals and their ideas and beliefs should be respected, and those individuals with disability have to be seen as individuals first, with the disability second; they must be seen as individuals with their strengths and weaknesses, rather than as damaged. Differing sexual orientations should not be seen as a problem to be cured but as an aspect of the person to be worked with and accepted, just as heterosexuality is accepted.

Consent in this area of difference is concerned with working with the person in need of help and accepting them as an equal; not as someone seeking to become part of the white middle-class European society but as someone wanting to understand themselves and work through some of their difficulties. Do we, the therapists, consent to treat them on this basis?

Issues in Private Practice

Most of this chapter relates to work in the state sector, health, social services and education, where most children, young people and families are seen. Many are also seen in the voluntary sector, and a small number of children and families are seen in private practice. Rather more adolescents are seen privately.

Clinicians in private practice are not bound by the same rules as in the state sector in relation to child protection. However, all professionals have their own code of practice and code of ethics. Case records in private work are often more disorganised. However, there can also be complaints in the private arena, and court reports can be ordered. Children assessed in private practice for a court report must be treated in the same way as in the public domain; any letters and documents are the property of the court, and can only be circulated with the permission of the court.

One of the major problems in private practice arises when a child is in treatment but there is no one to see the parents or carers, so the same clinician sees both parents and child. In some cases, this works well. In other cases the child, rightly, sees the clinician as on both sides and also, wrongly, then believes the clinician cannot be trusted. The child fears the therapist will share the content of their sessions, and will be acting on behalf of the parents. In reality, it is hard to work psychotherapeutically with both child and parent. Parents, of course, need to be seen as parents of a child in therapy but working in parallel is very difficult. If the work with both is psychodynamic psychotherapy, the transference and countertransference issues and the need for confidentiality mean that clinical thinking can become confused and boundaries blurred.

Conclusion

As has been shown, there are many areas of ethical concern in working with children and their families. In 'Moral Agendas for Psychoanalytic Practice with Children and Families' (Trowell and Miles, 1999) we argue that psychoanalytic psychotherapy is both a particularly potent and creative way of working, but that it also arouses strong feelings which can be difficult to control until the therapeutic process consolidates. We live in a society where nuclear families predominate, with little by way of extended families or community support. Within such tight family structures feelings are inevitably very strong, and it is therefore not surprising that many emotive issues and dilemmas can arise. Consenting to this form of therapy is always a leap into the unknown and the need for confidentiality means that family members can be left not knowing what others are saying, thinking and feeling. With a treatment that uses transference, countertransference, and unconscious communication as its key agents of change, that activates and examines such emotions as anger, envy and sexuality, there are bound to be clinical issues that arise, and all too easily some aspect of the work can slip out of control.

It is therefore essential to consider carefully issues of consent and confidentiality during assessment, during therapy and in any possible subsequent documentation in work with children and their families.

Note

(1) In the discussion that follows we acknowledge the contribution of Margaret Hunter, whose book, *Psychotherapy with Young People in Care*, contains a very helpful chapter on confidentiality (Hunter, 2001). We also recognise that our thinking in this area was developed within the context of a conference, out of which Michael King edited a book of papers (King, 1999).

References

Access to Heath Records Act 1990, The Stationery Office.
British Medical Association (2001), *Consent Rights and Choices* In *Health Care for Children and Young People*, BMA, London.
Children Act 1989 (1991), HMSO.
Data Protection Act (1998), The Stationery Office, ISBN 0 10 542998 8
Department of Health (1999), *Mental Health Act(1983) Code of Practice (1999)*, The Stationary Office, London.
Department of Health (2000), *Framework for the Assessment of Children in Need and their Families*, The Stationary Office, London.
General Medical Council (1999), *Seeking Patients' Consent: the Ethical Considerations*, GMC, London.

Gillick v West Norfolk & Wisbech Area Health Authority & Another, AC112 (1986).

Human Rights Act (1998), The Stationary Office, London.

Hunter, M. (2001), *Psychotherapy with Young People in Care*, Hove: BrunnerRoutledge.

King, M. (1999) (ed.), *Moral Agendas for Children's' Welfare, London: Routledge.*

Trowell J. (2001), 'Confidentiality and child protection', in C. Cordless (ed.), Confidentiality and Mental Health, London: Jessica Kingsley.

Trowell, J. and Miles, G. (1999), 'Moral agendas for psychoanalytic practice with children and families', in M. King (ed.), *Moral Agendas for Children's' Welfare, London: Routledge.*

UN Convention on the Rights of the Child (1988), ratified by UK 1991.

Section VI
The Ethics of Supervision

14
The Ethics of Supervision: developmental and archetypal perspectives

Hester McFarland Solomon

Introduction: integrating the ethical attitude in analytic practice

This chapter argues that the provision of ongoing supervision, peer supervision, or consultation helps to ensure, amongst other important functions, reliable access to ethical thinking in analytic practice. This does not in any way preclude the importance of, or suggest the lack of, an ongoing active internal capacity for ethical thinking or an internal supervisory function that comes through the processes of internalisation of the analytic attitude during the course of training and post-qualification professional development. I am, however, advocating the expectation that analytic practitioners be aware of the need for constant attention to the ethical dimensions of their clinical work, and that this may best be fostered by supervision as a present factor in clinical practice.

The struggle to keep ethical thinking integral to clinical work and to the theory-building that develops out of clinical experience requires sustained diligence and is particularly needed in those areas of our analytic and therapeutic practice where we are likely to be the most tested as clinicians. The function of the ethical attitude in clinical practice is not simply a matter of a set of rules that can be forgotten as long as they are not contravened in the clinical setting. I have argued in other contexts (Solomon, 2000b; and chapter 3 of this volume) that the ethical attitude is integral to all our activities and relationships as human beings as well as clinicians, and especially to that most intimate, intense and demanding of relationships, the analytic relationship. Since the time of the Hippocratic Oath, professional Codes of Ethics and Codes of Practice state the practitioner's commitment to ethical practice and the principles that underpin it.

In this chapter, I will explore the role of supervision in helping to maintain ethical thinking and practice in clinical work. I refer to the terms supervision (in which a younger practitioner, often a trainee, seeks regular, often weekly, supervision on one patient seen intensively, and where a fee is paid to the supervisor by the trainee), consultation (which usually refers to two colleagues, one senior and one junior, who discuss, regularly but not necessarily weekly, patients or clinical issues, and where the senior colleague receives payment from the junior one), or peer supervision (often in a small group of colleagues who are more or less at the same level of clinical experience and where payment is not involved, who meet regularly but not necessarily weekly). Unless there is a specific point of differentiation to be made between these modalities, for the purposes of this chapter I will use the term 'supervision' to cover all three.

Crucial to my argument is the view that the analytic attitude is in essence an ethical attitude, and that the achievement of the ethical attitude is tantamount to the achievement of a developmental position. Here, 'developmental position' is meant in much the same way that Klein or Bion had in mind when they referred to the paranoid-schizoid or the depressive positions as stages in the developmental process. Much of the argument of this chapter will revolve around the notion that the ethical attitude, like the paranoid-schizoid and depressive positions, is not a once-and-for-all achievement but rather is part of an internal human dynamic that is experienced alongside and in relation to more primitive and sometimes more dangerous states of mind. Hence, just like the depressive position, the achievement of an ethical attitude can be considered in developmental terms which requires mental effort, in particular, conscious effort, to sustain. This perspective has much to offer when we think of the importance of an ongoing supervisory function in the practitioner's clinical work as offering a place where that conscious effort is shared and reinforced.

The view that I set out in this chapter incorporates the role of both developmental and archetypal perspectives in the understanding of the achievement of ethical thinking through the supervisory function. Alongside the triangular developmental perspective of achieving of an ethical attitude, in whatever way that may be accomplished (this chapter focuses on the role of supervision in this achievement), there lies the archetypal nature of the triangular relationship underpinning the achievement of the mental capacity for ethical thinking.

Achieving an Ethical Attitude: a developmental model

It is a truism that it is not possible to be ethical in a vacuum. The ethical function is a relational function involving the assessment of subjective and intersubjective states. Jung pointed out (CW 10, paras 371-99) that it is ubiquitous and hence has a collective dimension, while at the same time being experienced most vividly at the personal level. In thinking about the development of the young mind and how an ethical attitude might come into being, the Kleinian model shows that, because of the massive onslaught of internal and external stimuli on its limited mental capacities, the infant is at first suffused with psychotic states of mind that may cause profound anxieties, particularly if the holding environment is deficient and unable to process such states. These anxieties are primarily managed defensively through splitting and projection. Communicating, relating and using the other psychodynamically often take place through projective identification (Klein, 1946). Hence self and other are mixed up, and parts of each are allocated to different and separate psychic locations, either internally or externally, in the self or in the other. Klein called this the paranoid-schizoid position, where the perception and experience of the bad and good parts of the self and the other are not psychically found together, and where relating is at the level of part objects, because the young mind is not as yet capable of holding together opposite affective states. In a later development, called the depressive position (Klein, 1935), the infant or child is more able to experience the other as a whole object, separate from the self, and containing both good and bad aspects. Thus the child's feelings of love and hatred for the object, which had previously been split off and experienced as separate, are now capable, at times, of being held together in the infant's mind, giving rise to feelings of ambivalence towards the object, as well as feelings of guilt and the wish to repair the damage that the self might have wrecked on the object in the previous, part object mode of relating. In elaborating how this dynamic occurs, Britton (1998) has made a helpful contribution in offering a model which involves the circularity of the dynamic movement between the paranoid-schizoid and the depressive positions, such that each new cycle builds on the experience of the previous ones. Schematically, this has similarities with Fordham's model of deintegration and reintegration (Fordham, 1957).

In thinking in developmental terms about what are the conditions that foster an ethical capacity (Solomon, 2000a; 2000b; chapter 3 of this volume), I have suggested that it is through the combination of the infant's or child's earliest experiences of devotion and reflection by the parental couple, who maintain the ethical attitude in relation to their infant or child. It is this combination that is eventually internalised by the child and is activated as the self and ego develop in dynamic relation, eventual internal parents in the psyche. The first stirrings of a nascent ethical capacity occurs as the infant experiences being the recipient of the non-talionic responses of the parental couple in the face of his or her various states of distress, including rage and dread. Under the right conditions, the infant's experience of the parent's non-talionic responses is eventually internalised and identified with, and becomes the basis for gratitude. The idea of the ordinarily devoted parent, mother or father, represents a deeply ethical mode in their instinctual and unconditional devotedness to another – their infant – overcoming their narcissistic needs and frustrated rages, their shadow projections, and resisting by and large the impulse to skew their infant's development through requiring undue acquiescence.

Later they will leave this state of primary preoccupation and devotedness and will begin the processes of socialisation which are so necessary a part of ethical development – the capacity to say, in different ways, 'no', thereby establishing boundaries and an expectation of self- regulation, including an expectation to regulate behaviour in relation to others. Thus, to the image of ordinary devotedness to a nascent self I am combining the notion of the discriminating and thinking function of the masculine principle, thus evoking a notion that appears in various guises in psychoanalytic and Jungian analytic literature: that of the creative potential of the third, whether a third person, a third position, or a third dimension. The activation of an archetypal potential for eventual ethical behaviour will be thus reinforced in ordinary good enough situations by caregivers capable of sharing acts of thoughtful devotedness and of empathic and devoted thinking about their infant. This has a clear parallel with what happens in the consulting room, where the analyst's willingness to go on sacrificing their own narcissistic needs through the sustained activity of thoughtful devotedness to the patient that we call the analytic attitude protects the patient so that they may develop and grow according to the needs of their self.

From Dyad to Triad: the eventual achievement of triangulation

I am conjecturing that the internalisation of and identification with the agapaic function of the parental figures in their empathic holding as well as their thinking and discriminating aspects can trigger or catalyse a nascent ethical capacity in a young mind, the first steps of which include those primitive acts of discriminating good and bad which constitute the foundations of splitting and projection. Early (as well as later) splitting and projecting may therefore be instances of primitive moral activity, what Samuels (1989) calls original morality – the expulsion from the self of what is unwanted and felt to be bad into the other, where it is identified as bad and eschewed. Even in situations where the good is split and projected, it is in the service of maintaining a discriminating, but highly defensive, psychic structure. This is a two-dimensional internal world, in which primitive psychic acts discriminate good from bad experience, and split the bad from the psyche by projection into the caregivers – a first, primordial or prototypical moral discernment prior to the state where there is sufficient ego strength for anything resembling mature moral or ethical behaviour to arise. This constitutes the very preconditions for the creation of the personal shadow, which eventually will require a further ethical action of reintegration when the person has achieved an internal position of moral and ethical capacity.

As we posit, following Fordham (1969/1994), the self as a primary integrate, autonomous but very much in relation to another or others, so we are alone as moral beings while at the same time finding our moral nature in relation to others. To truly find another represents a transcendence of narcissistic ways of relating in which the other is appropriated for use in the internal world, denying the other's subjective reality. To live with the implications of this capacity to recognise and relate to the truth of the other is a step in the development of – and perhaps eventually beyond – the depressive position. The depressive position is usually considered to contain acts of reparation through guilt and fear that the object may have been damaged and therefore may be unable to go on caring for one's self (Hinshelwood, 1989). As such, acts of reparation remain contingent on preserving the other for the benefit of the self. The ethical attitude envisaged here goes beyond this contingency and suggests a non-contingent realm of ethical behaviour. This situation has direct implications for what transpires in the consulting room between the analytic couple (see chapter 3 of this volume).

This represents a two-stage, dyad-to-triad process which reflects the two-stage developmental process in the infant (the neurophysiological implications are also considered in Solomon, 2000a) in which the neural development of the infant's brain post partum must be matched by a parallel nurturing provision such that (i) at first infant and mother are highly attuned (a 'me/me' relationship); and (ii) where, later, there follows complementary and compensatory discriminations (a 'self/other' relationship. The differentiation could then be between when to be 'caring' and flexible and when to be 'tough' and resilient, both of which have implications for the interactions in the consulting room. Just as the analyst can have a two-stage developmental relationship with their patient, so the intensive dyadic work would have a counterbalancing relationship created by the triangular space of supervision.

In this developmental framework, it is evident that there evolves a gradual demarcation between self and other, including an enquiry about how the self individuates from out of a projective and identificatory mix-up between self and other through to a fuller experience of the reality of the self's subjectivity in relation to the reality of the subjectivity of another. This is the beginning of the capacity for triangulation, that 'theory of mind' (Fonagy, 1989) which the child has achieved when he or she is aware that their thoughts and those of the other are separate and not available directly to each other (as assumed in states of fusion or identification), but only through reference to a third perspective. As Cavell has described:

the child needs not just one but two other persons, one of whom, at least in theory, might be only the child's idea of a third ... the child must move from interacting with his mother to grasping the idea that both his perspective on the world and hers are perspectives; that there is a possible third point of view, more inclusive than theirs, from which both his mother's and his own can be seen and from which the interaction between them can be understood.(Cavell, 1998, pp. 459-60)

Jungians would amplify this view by addressing the difficult but necessary work on the withdrawal of the projections of those negative aspects of the self, called shadow projections, leading to a gradual capacity to view the self along with the other as separate but interrelated subjectivities with multivariate motivations, including shadow motivations that project the bad outside one's self. The withdrawal of shadow projections, predicated on the realisation that the other is truly other and not assumed to be a function or aspect of the self, which otherwise might sully the gradual more mature experiences of intersubjectivity, underpins the ethical attitude. As such it is a developmental achievement that derives from an innate potential, activated at birth, and fostered by the continuous 'good enough' experience of living in an ethical environment. It represents a constant struggle through acts and attitudes that are against the natural selfish inclinations of the self, acts which are *contra naturam*, forgoing insistence on the self's limited perspectives in order to encompass a wider view, including the recognition of that which is not ethical within the self. In Jungian terms, that recognition represents the integration of the shadow back into the self: steps toward incremental advances in the self's movement towards greater states of integration and wholeness. This is the individuation process, and it is predicated on a teleological view of the self in which the self's capacity for change, growth, and development are understood and experienced as being suffused with a sense of purpose and meaning.

Triangulation: the archetypal third

In 1916, a short time after the split with Freud, when Jung was suffering what might be described as a psychotic regression in the face of his loss of Freud, who represented the centrally organising psychic function of the father figure he had never had before, Jung wrote two landmark papers that can appear to be diametrically opposite in content and form: 'VII Sermones ad mortuos' ('Seven Sermons to the Dead') and 'The transcendent function'. The former was published at the time, but not in a separate English edition until 1982, whereas the latter was not published until 1958, only a few years before Jung's death in 1961. Both reflect, in different ways, the immediacy of Jung's distressing and threatening psychic experiences that arose from Jung's self-analysis, undertaken, as Freud's self-analysis, on his own. At the same time Jung continued to function as Clinical Director of the Burgholzli Hospital in Zurich and also fathered a growing family. If the tone of the 'Seven Sermons' was that of a chilling account of the horrifyingly vivid psychic experiences he endured at the time of his 'confrontation with the unconscious' (Jung, 1961, p.194), that of the 'Transcendent function' was of a measured, scientific contribution to analytic theory-building, which he compared to a 'mathematical formula' (Jung, CW 8, para. 131), and which we could interpret as a dispassionate exteriorisation of his highly emotive internal state at the time, a kind of self-supervision. In this paper, Jung set out an archetypal, deep structural schema of triangulation in which he demonstrated that psychic change occurs through the emergence of a third position out of an original conflictual internal or external situation, the characteristics of which cannot be predicted alone by those of the original dyad. In relation to this idea, it is interesting to note that the philosopher and psychoanalyst, Marcia Cavell, who has recently put forward the idea of triangulation in a psychoanalytic context, refers to Polanyi's notion of 'emergent properties' in much the same manner as that pertaining to the dialectical nature of the transcendent function, that is, as 'properties that in a developmental process arise spontaneously from elements at the preceding levels and are not specifiable or predictable in terms of them' (Cavell, 1998, p. 461).

Whether or not he consciously drew on its philosophical origins, Jung's notion of the transcendent function is based on the idea of the dialectical and deep structural nature of all change in the living world expounded by the 19th century German philosopher, Hegel, in his great work, *The Phenomenology of the Spirit* (see Solomon, 1994). Hegel posited a tripartite schema as fundamental to all change, including psychic change, a situation in which an original oppositional pair, a dyad, which he called thesis and anti-thesis, struggle together until, under the right conditions, a third position, a synthesis, is achieved. This third position heralds the transformation of the oppositional elements of the dyad into a position with new properties which could not have been known about before their encounter – the *tertium quid non datur* in Jung's terms. Hegel called this ubiquitous struggle dialectical, because it demonstrated how transformations in the natural world happen through the resolution of an oppositional struggle and can be understood to have meaning and purposefulness. This was a deep structural patterning of dynamic change that was archetypal by nature and as developmental as a dynamic movement in time. This archetypal schema can also be thought of as the basis of the tripartite Oedipal situation, where transformation from out of a primordial pair, mother and child, can be achieved through the third position afforded by the paternal function, whether this be a real father, or a capacity of mind in the mother or in the child, or both, as Fonagy illustrates (Fonagy, 1989). It is in this sense that we might speak of the emergence of the mind of the child, the child's identity, as separate from his or her mother, through the provision of a third perspective. For Jung, this would be thought of as the emergence of the self, through successive states of transformation and individuation via the transcendent function. In the context of the function of supervision with which we are concerned in this chapter, we could say that it is through the provision of the supervisory third that both patient and analyst are helped to emerge from out of the *massa confusa* of the analytic dyad. Both change as a result as individuation progresses.

In psychoanalytic theory, the importance of the negotiation of the Oedipal threesome, that archetypal triad *par excellence*, constitutes much of the psychoanalytic understanding of developmental achievement. Freud first used the term 'Oedipus complex' in 1910, following Jung's scientific researches on the complexes using the Word Association Test (WAT). At that time, the Oedipus complex was considered to be one of many organising complexes of the psyche, but soon became the core psychoanalytic concept. Britton sums up consisely the Oedipal situation:

we notice in the two different sexes the same elements: a parental couple ...; a death wish towards the parent of the same sex; and a wish-fulfilling dream or myth of taking the place of one parent and marrying the other. (Britton, 1998, p. 30)

Britton stresses the necessity of working through the Oedipus complex in order to resolve the depressive position and of working through the depressive position in order to resolve the Oedipus complex (p. 29). He evokes the notion of internal triangulation, which requires the toleration of an internal version of the Oedipal situation in order to do this. He describes 'triangular psychic space' as 'a *third* position in mental space ... from which the *subjective self* can be observed having a relationship with an idea' (p. 13). He concludes that 'in all analyses the basic Oedipus situation exists whenever the analyst exercises his or her mind independently of the inter-subjective relationship of patient and analyst' (p. 44).

In developing Britton's idea of the Oedipal triangle as present through the internal events and relationships that occur in the analyst's mind, as links to an internal object or to psychoanalytic theory, I wish to reiterate that the external manifestation and facilitation of this internal triangular state is quintessentially present in the supervisory or consultative relationship. Here, two people, the analyst and the supervisor, are linked in relation to a third, the patient.

Within psychoanalysis, the current debate about the implications of intersubjectivity – that the analyst and patient are acting together within a treatment relationship, in which the analyst's countertransference to the patient's transference as much as the reverse (for example, Atwood and Stolorow, 1993, p. 47) offer essential information – has been enhanced by Cavell's (1998) notion of 'progressive triangulation'. Rose summarises Cavell's notion succinctly: 'in order to know our own minds, we require an interaction with another mind in relation to what would be termed objective reality' (Rose, 2000, p. 454). I hold that the provision of supervision, including the internal supervision that happens when the analyst thinks about aspects of the patient and the analytic relationship, is an important instance of 'progressive triangulation', in that it allows for ongoing interaction with another mind in relation to a third – the patient – who can be thought about because differentiated from the dyadic relating of the patient-analyst couple.

Triangular Space and Supervision in Analytic Practice

The provision and function of supervision of analytic and psychotherapeutic work with individuals, children, couples, or families, creates a needed triangular space essential to the care and maintenance, the ongoing hygiene, of the dyadic relationships. I use the term 'hygiene' in the sense that, through its provision, supervision keeps constantly activated the awareness of the analytic attitude, including its ethical component, in and through the presence of a third person (the supervisor), or a third position (the supervisory space), and that it acts as an aid in the restoration of the analytic and ethical attitudes when at times they might be lost in the maelstrom of clinical practice. Supervision is itself the representation of that attitude through the provision of a third area of reflection. The treatment, at profound levels, of the psyche in distress always involves a regressive and/or narcissistic pull back into part object relating, those primitive either/or, dichotomous states of mind that Jung and others have shown are dominated by the internal experience of the archetypal warring opposites at the basis of the defences of the self (Kalshed, 1996; Solomon, 1997). Ensuring the provision of the sustained triangular space of the supervisory situation creates the necessary opportunity for analytic reflection, where two people work together to think about a third, whether the third is an individual, a couple, or a family, or an idea or aspect within the therapist or analyst, that is relevant to their clinical work. The provision of triangular space through internal or external supervision, or both, is essential to the maintenance of the analytic attitude in the face of the multitudinous forces and pressures at work within the analytic and therapeutic situation, arising from the conscious and unconscious dynamics within and between patient and analyst alike, and the consequently inevitable, often unconscious, intersubjective exchanges between them as a pair, that would seek, for defensive reasons, to undermine analytic achievements.

To the extent that this triangular space created by supervision is necessary to the hygiene of the analytic couple (just as the paternal, reflective principle is essential to the hygiene of the mother-infant dyad, providing the space for psychological growth to occur), then supervision has an ethical as well as a clinical and didactic role to play in all analytic and therapeutic work, notwithstanding the years of experience of the practitioner. Whether supervision is provided in the same way as during training, with weekly meetings in a one-to-one situation with a senior practitioner, or in consultations with a senior practitioner at agreed intervals, or whether peer supervision in small groups is selected as the means of providing the triangular space, these are questions which are up to each clinician to decide upon, according to personal need and inclination.

In the case of the analysis and supervision of training candidates, where there are particular ongoing boundary issues and other pressures inherent in the training situation that do not usually pertain in work with non-training patients, such as the need to see a patient under regular supervision at a certain minimum intensity (three, four or five times per week), over a certain minimum amount of time (often for a minimum of either 18 months or 2 years), supervision will help to identify and work under these constraints without forgoing the analytic attitude. This will in turn foster in the candidate their own ethical attitude, as they internalise the expectation that all analytic work, including the work of their own analysts and supervisors, is in turn supervised. The trainee will then know from the very outset of his or her training that there is always a third space created in which he or she as a patient or as a supervisee will be thought about by another supervisor-practitioner pair.

Fostering the ethical-supervisory expectation is more likely to engender a generationally based commitment to the analytic attitude within a training institution, as the tradition of good clinical practice is passed down across the analytic and therapeutic training generations. Currently, there is an assumption that the aim and goals of training can often be summed up in almost the opposite way: that is, that the success of the candidate's progress through his or her training is assessed according to whether he or she is judged to be ready to 'work independently.' Of course, the assessment of the trainee's capacity for independent judgement and a sense of their own viable autonomy is an important, indeed crucial, factor in the process of assessing whether someone is ready to qualify to practise as an analyst or therapist. I am arguing here that, included in this assessment should be a judgement about the candidate's awareness of the need for, and usefulness of, the provision of a triangular space in which to discuss their clinical practice, in order best to ensure against the risks inherent in working in such intimate and depth psychological ways, including the dangers of mutual identificatory states or the abuse of power.

My contention is that, in addition to its obvious advantages, the expectation that the practitioner will ensure that they have ongoing supervision or consultation on their clinical practice is a sign of maturation, both on the part of the practitioner as well as that of the training institution, as they assess their own and others' clinical competence. This is part of the assessment process which results in the authorisation to practice as members of the training institution. There is the added dimension that some members go on to become eventual trainers, that is, training analysts, supervisors, and clinical and theoretical seminar leaders, entrusted with the responsibility for training future generations of analysts and therapists. The expectation in the trainee of ongoing supervisory and consultative provision is modelled by the trainers, fostering the candidate's respect for, and understanding of, the conditions that create and sustain the analytic and ethical attitude. This includes attention to boundary issues that can arise within and through the intensity of the intersubjective dynamics within the analytic and therapeutic relationship. (See Gabbard and Lester (1995) for a detailed discussion of boundary issues in analytic practice.) These intersubjective dynamics are inevitably released by the inter-penetrative, projective, introjective and projective identificatory exchanges within the transference and countertransference.

The recommendation that (i) members of analytic training institutions seek to establish an ongoing supervisory ethos to discuss their work, even if the provision is not systematically maintained, and that (ii) all training analysts and supervisors of the institutions have regular consultations regarding their training cases (including patients, supervisees, or training patients) represents a further development of those ubiquitous triads created by the training situation: the trainee – training analyst – supervisor; the trainee – training patient – supervisor; and the trainee – supervisor – Training Committee. The expectation of providing a space for reflection with another would benefit all parties concerned and at the same time increase clinical awareness. Without this benefit, we run the risk of identifying with those narcissistic and other pathological processes and pressures that are inevitable in analytic practice, as we are liable to treat those aspects in our patients that correspond and resonate with our own internal issues and personal histories. Hence the importance of clinical 'hygiene', of creating the third space of supervision, that can help us to maintain our connection to genuine object relating and to staying alert to the pitfalls of intense dyadic relating.

Conclusion

I have explored some aspects of the supervisory function in analytic practice in relation to developmental and archetypal perspectives. The provision through supervision of a triangular space in which clinical work with patients can be thought about creates the necessary dimensionality for psychological transformation to occur and has resonance with developmental reality and archetypal truth. The ethical aspect of supervisory provision is predicated on the notion that genuine object relating arises out of such dimensionality, in which one mind is aware of the subjective reality of another and chooses to take ethical responsibility towards the other, as the parent in relation to the child, and the analyst or therapist in relation to the patient. This is fostered in the supervisory setting, where the triangular relationship of supervisor-analyst / therapist-patient makes manifest in concrete form a universal triangular and deep structural situation which is necessary if psychological development is to occur.

It may be that the emergence of an ethical capacity represents a development on from the depressive position, in that it seeks to provide for and protect a non-contingent space or place for reflection about another, be it a person, a relationship or an idea. Such reflection may result in decisions taken with respect to another, and may be followed by actions, which include the content, form, timing and other characteristics of interpretations, as well as other, more subtle, modes of being in the presence of another, that will have a direct impact on the quality of their internal world. It is for this reason – because of the possibility of doing harm to the vulnerable interior reality of another – that the Hippocratic Oath was first established two thousand five hundred years ago with its main premise, *nolo nocere*, and why we, as practitioners, continue to seek to hone its ethos.

References

Atwood and Stolorow (1993), *Structures of Subjectivity*, Northavale, NJ: Analytic Press.

Britton, R. (1998), *Belief and Imagination*, London: Routledge.

Cavell, M. (1998), 'Triangulation, one's own mind and objectivity', *International Journal of Psychoanalysis*, 79, 3, pp. 449-68.

Fonagy, P. (1989), 'On tolerating mental states: theory of mind in borderline personality', *Bulletin of Anna Freud Centre*, 12: 91-115.

Fordham, M. (1957), *New Developments in Analytical Psychology*, London: Routledge & Kegan Paul.

Fordham, M. (1969, 1994), *Children as Individuals*, London: Free Association Books.

Freud, S. (1910), 'Leonardo da Vinci and a memory of his childhood', Standard Edition, vol. IX, London: Hogarth Press (1950/1974).

—— (1916), 'Introductory lectures on psycho-analysis: lecture XXII', Standard Edition, vol. XVI, London: Hogarth Press (1950/1974).

Gabbard, G. and Lester, E. (1995), *Boundaries and Boundary Violations in Psychoanalysis*, New York: Basic Books.

Hegel, G. W. F. (1807/1977), *The Phenomenology of Spirit*, trans. A. V. Miller, Oxford: Oxford University Press.

Hinshelwood, R. (1989), *A Dictionary of Kleinian Thought*, London: Free Association Books.

Jung, C.G. (1916), *VII Sermones ad Mortuos*, London: Watkins, 1967.

—— (1961), Memories, Dreams, Reflections, London: Collins and Routledge & Kegan Paul.

Kalsched, D. (1996), *The Inner World of Trauma*, London: Routledge.

Klein, M. (1935), 'A contribution to the psychogenesis of manic-depressive states', *The Writings of Melanie Klein. Volume I*, edited by R. Money-Kyrle, B. Joseph, E. O'Shaughnessy and H. Segal, London: Hogarth Press, 1975.

Klein, M. (1946), 'Notes on some schizoid mechanisms', *The Writings of Melanie Klein. Volume I*, edited by R. Money-Kyrle, B. Joseph, E. O'Shaughnessy and H. Segal, London: Hogarth Press, 1975.

Rose, J. (2000), 'Symbols and their function in managing the anxiety of change: an intersubjective approach', *International Journal of Psychoanalysis*, 81, 3, pp. 453-70.

Samuels, A. (1989), *The Plural Psyche*, London: Routledge.

Solomon, H. M. (1994), 'The transcendent function and Hegel's dialectical vision', *Journal of Analytical Psychology*, 39, 1. Also in Mattoon, M. (ed.), Collected Papers from the 1992 IAAP Congress, *The Transcendent Function*, Chicago.

Solomon, H. M. (1997), 'The not-so-silent couple in the individual', *Journal of Analytical Psychology*, 42, 3. Also in *Bulletin of the Society of Psychoanalytic Marital Psychotherapists*, 1 (Inaugural Issue), 1994.

Solomon, H. M. (2000a), 'Recent developments in the neurosciences', in E. Christopher and H.M. Solomon (eds), *Jungian Thought in the Modern World*, London: Free Association Books.

Solomon, H. M. (2000b), 'The ethical self', in E. Christopher and H. M. Solomon (eds), *Jungian Thought in the Modern World*, London: Free Association Books.

Index

abortion while in analysis 9
'abundant communications' 34
Access to Health Records Act 159
accountability and authority 144
adolescents and consent to
    psychotherapy 157–8
Adoption Act 153
agapaic attitude 62
Akeret, R. 35–6
American Psychiatric Association
    guidelines 101
American Psychological Association
    guidelines 101
'Analysis Terminable and Intermina-
    ble' 87
analyst
    as patient 34
    capacity for identification 8
    homosexual relationship with 53
    and loss 93
    and narcissism 8
    and patient with baby 71
    and pregnant patient 66–71
    and prosecution 61
    and receptivity 80
    refusal to testify 61
    and retirement 87
    sacrifice of personal gratification 35
    state of mind 129
    and third party 82
    trustworthiness 61
    unconscious sadism 7
analytic alliance 51
    and benign cycle 52
    and social pressures 60

analytic associations 40
analytic attitude 4–5
Analytic Experience, The 59–60
analytic organisations and ethics 44
anonymity and publication 101
anonymity of the patient 59
anonymous authorship 103
Answer to Job 85
Aristotle 16
Aron, L. 106, 126
audit 146
authority and accountability 144
authorship, transfer of 103

Bacon, Francis 15, 20
Bauman, Zygmunt 19, 24
benign cycle 63
Bion, W.R. 58–9, 117, 168
    Basic Assumptions 51
Bollas, C. 61, 100, 125, 126, 127,
    128, 146
Bomford, Rodney 63, 92
Bonaparte, M. 34
Breuer, J. 58
British Association of Psychothera-
    pists 55, 61
Britton, R. 104, 126, 131, 173
Buber, M. 23
Budd, Susan 110, 126

case material, ownership of 59
case records and the family 160
case reporting 58–9
case studies, clinical retrospective 112
Casement, P.J. 59, 104

Cavell, M. 171, 172, 174
Chasseguet-Smirgel, J. 33
child protection 153–5
child psychotherapist and parental issues 155
Children Act 152
children
    and emotional abuse 154
    and non-contact abuse 154
    and physical abuse 154
    and sexual abuse 154
Christianity and ethics 16
Christopher, E. 42
Chronos and Kairos, differences 93
Citadel 128
Cities of Refuge, Israel 62
Civil Service Ethical Codes 144
clinic, meaning of 101
clinical material, reporting of 99, 109
clinical reporting, pseudo-scientific 111, 115
code of ethics 12, 15, 44, 55, 61, 63, 65, 91, 92, 143, 167
Colman, W. 104
Coltart, Nina 42
complaints against therapist 159
confidentiality 125, 139–42
    nature of 123
    of the analytic setting 105
    and paedophiles 140–1
    and research 160
    and social services 154
consent 148
    and child's competence 148
    and difference 161
    from parents 103
    informed 56, 105
    seeking 105
    timing of 106
    to publication 58
    to treatment 55
    and young person 153
consulting room 26
'Counter-transference' 116
court order for psychotherapy 148
curing 57

customs 15

Data Protection Act 149, 159
data protection laws 100
depressive position 76
descriptive research 146
Didier-Weil, A. 84
difference and consent 161
discharge from psychotherapy 148
disclosure 146
    different kinds of 125
divorce during analysis 32
domestic violence 158
Don Quixote dream 81
Dora 105, 109–10, 118
'Dream of Irma's Injection, The' 34
Duncan, Dennis 113
dyad-to-triad 170

'Economic Problem of Masochism, The' 33
'Ego and the Id, The' 33
ego ideal 22, 31, 33, 36, 41
Emde, R. 100
emotional development 76
empirical research 146
ending, meaning of 88
epistemophilia 17
Etchegoyan, R.H. 31–2
ethical attitude 46
    achieving 168
    capacity 24–6
    and clinical setting 65
ethical frameworks 138
ethical principles 44
ethical safeguards 10
ethical space 27, 130
ethical struggle 7
ethics and psychoanalysis 32
ethics, code of 12, 15, 44, 55, 61, 63, 65, 91, 92, 143
ethics, with small or big E 123–4
ethos 15, 42

Face to Face 19
'Fight with the Shadow, The' 41

Fliess, Wilhelm 34
Fonagy, P. 100, 171, 173
Fordham, Michael 26, 41–2, 45, 87, 169, 170
Fosshage, James 106
and *Psychoanalytic Inquiry* 113
Fragment of an Analysis of a Case of Hysteria 109
Frank, A. 100, 102
free association 31, 95, 113
free speech 144
frequency of sessions 35
Freud, A. 34
Freud, Sigmund 17–18, 22, 31–4, 36–8, 41, 51, 58, 87, 94, 95, 99, 105, 109–11, 119
Mind of the Moralist, The 18
Fulford, K.W.M. 124

Gabbard, G.D. 26, 103, 108, 126
Gaillard, C. 85
General Medical Council 152–3
Gillick case 153
'God-Almightiness' 40–1, 46
Godfrey, Wynne 52–3
Goldberg, A. 102, 105
Gordon, P. 19, 57
Gordon, R. 130
Greek philosophy 15
'Group Psychology and the Analysis of the Ego' 33
Guggenbuhl-Craig, A. 46
Guyomard, P. 84

Hale, Robert 149
Hayman, P. 61
Hegel, G.W.F. 172
'higher nature' 37
Hinshelwood, R.D. 17, 28, 57, 170
Hippocratic Oath 8, 18, 124, 177
Holder, A. 33
Holmes, J. 55–6, 61
Homer 52
Hubback, J. 107
Human Rights Act 140, 149, 153
human rights legislation 45

Hunter, Margaret 162

Ideal Self 36
individuation process 43
information technology 149
informed consent 56
International Association for Analytical Psychology 21
International Committee of Medical Journal Editors 102
International Psychoanalytic Association 21
Interpretation of Dreams, The 34
Islam and ethics 16

Jacobs, Theodore 113
Jaffe v. Redmond 128
Judaeo-Christian tradition 16
Judaism and ethics 16
Jung, C.G. 22, 27, 28, 39–41, 43, 52, 53, 74, 84, 85, 93, 99, 112–13, 114, 124, 125, 129, 168, 171, 172

Kairos 93, 95
Kalshed, D. 174
Kant, I. 24, 93
Kelly, J. 69
Kermode, F. 93
Kernberg, O.F. 62
King, Michael 152
Klein, Melanie 23, 33, 76, 109–11, 115, 168, 169
play about 94
Klumpner, G.H. 100, 102
Kriss, E. 34
Kubie, L. 111

Lacan, Jacques 83, 87, 89
Lambert, K. 27, 62
Lang, R. 27
legislation, human rights 45
legislation, professional 45
Lester, E. 26
Levinas, Emmanuel 19
Lévy-Bruhl 52

Lindley, R. 55–6, 61
Lipton, E. 106, 108
Little, Margaret 52
Lustman, S. 111

Maillard, C. 85
matrimonial disputes 157
Meers, D. 33
Meltzer, D. 33–4, 36
Mental Health Act 142, 148–9, 153
Menzies Lyth, I. 45
'Moral Agendas for Psychoanalytic
    Practice with Children and
    Families' 162
mores 15
Mosher, P.W. 128
mourning 83
Mrs Klein 94
Murdin, Lesley 87
Murdoch, Iris 17
Narrative of a Child Analysis 109
'narrative truth' 116
Nicomachean Ethics 16
Nussbaum, M.C. 131

Odysseus 65
Oedipus complex 38, 41, 173
'Of Counsel' 20
Ogden, T.H. 130
'On Narcissism' 33

paedophiles, confidentiality 140–1
parents' consent for unwilling child
    158
Parfit, Derek 16, 18
participation mystique 51–3
'Patient as Therapist to his Analyst,
    The' (Searles) 60
patients' records 148
peer supervision 167
personal analysis 34
personal ethical position 41
Phenomenology of the Spirit, The 172
Piaget 41
Plato 17, 92
Poole, Roger 130

Post-Modern Ethics 19
postnatal depression 66
primary caregiver 5
'primary object' 6
prison sentence and psychotherapy
    148
privacy 125
private practice 161
privilege for psychotherapists 146
privileged communication 137, 146
progressive triangulation 174
projected third, intrusion of 53–4
projective identification 51
Proner, B. 108
protective privilege 61
Psychoanalytic Inquiry 113
psychoanalytic model 31
psychoanalytic psychotherapy 62
psychoanalytic research, meaning of
    99
Psychology of Transference, The 85
psychoneurobiology 24
psychotherapist privilege 146
psychotherapy and court order 148
psychotherapy and prison sentence
    148
public peril 61
publication and confidentiality 101
publication of research 145–6
publication, consent to 58

records, access to 147
Redfearn, J. 42
regressive transference neurosis 62
Renik, O. 118–19
reporting 127
research
    and confidentiality 160
    descriptive 146
    empirical 146
    publication of 145–6
retired therapist 90
revealing 126
Richard 110
Ricoeur, P. 85, 115, 116, 118
Rieff, Philip 18

Roman philosophy 15
Rose, J. 174

'safe' environment 140
Sampson, H. 111–12, 115, 117
Samuels, A. 25, 170
Samuels, Robert 87
Sanctum 128
Sandler, J. 33
Sargent, H.D. 115–16
'Saving Masud Khan' 52–3
'saying-true' 116
Schachter, J. 89–91
Schore, Allan 74–6
Second Thoughts 58–9
secrecy 125
'Seeking Patients' Consent' 152
'Seven Sermons to the Dead' 172
Shakespeare in Love 58
Sinason, Valerie 103
Singer, Peter 15
Solomon, H.M. 42, 66, 68, 73, 76,
    85, 88, 123, 167, 174
Souk 129
Sovereignty of Good, The 17
Spence, Donald 110, 111, 113–14,
    115, 117
'Spiritual Problem of Modern Man,
    The' 41
statutory disclosure 142
statutory organisations 144
Stein, L. 115
Stein, Murray 23
Steiner, George 95
Stern, D.N. 24, 32, 42, 66
Stoller, R. 107
Studies on Hysteria 18, 58, 109
suicide 148
Sundelson, D. 61, 100, 126, 127, 128,
    146
superego 22, 33, 36, 41
supervision 142–3, 167–77
Symington, N. 58, 59, 131

Tarasoff Case 61
therapeutic match 42

therapeutic relationship 31, 74
Therapy of Coercion? 17
'time, place and person' 141
'Transcendant Function, The' 172
transfer of authorship 103
triangular psychic space 131–2
triangular space 174
triangulation 170, 172
    progressive 174
    struggle to maintain 9
tripartite schema 172
Tuckett, D. 99, 102, 112, 117, 118,
    120, 132

UN Convention on the Rights of the
    Child 152
unconscious identity 51
University College London, Research
    Training 100

Verney, T. 69

Wallerstein, R. 111–12, 115, 117
Ward, I. 119
Warnock, Mary 123, 124–5, 127
Warwick, S. 125
Wharton, B. 126
Widlöcher, D. 112
Wiener, J. 27, 128, 129
Wiener, Y. 93, 95
Williams, P. 126
Williams, S. 87
Winnicott, D.W. 25, 37, 42, 116, 131
Wittgenstein, Ludwig 95
Wolf Man 87
Word Association Test 173
words, thaumaturgic use of 32
work settings 128–9
Wright, K. 68
Wright, Nicholas 94

Yariv, G. 91–2
Young, William 103

Zentralblatt 113
Zinkin, L. 87, 95